高中英语阅读素养提升课例实践

刘中楷·主编

西安出版社

图书在版编目（CIP）数据

高中英语阅读素养提升课例实践 / 刘中楷主编. —西安：西安出版社，2023.11

ISBN 978-7-5541-7185-1

Ⅰ. ①高… Ⅱ. ①刘… Ⅲ. ①英语课—高中—教学参考资料 Ⅳ. ①G634.413

中国国家版本馆CIP数据核字（2023）第206086号

高中英语阅读素养提升课例实践

GAOZHONG YINGYU YUEDU SUYANG TISHENG KELI SHIJIAN

出版发行：西安出版社
社　　址：西安市曲江新区雁南五路 1868 号影视演艺大厦 11 层
电　　话：（029）85264440
邮政编码：710061
印　　刷：北京政采印刷服务有限公司
开　　本：787mm × 1092mm　1 / 16
印　　张：19
字　　数：310千字
版　　次：2023 年 11 月第 1 版
印　　次：2024 年 1 月第 1 次
书　　号：ISBN 978-7-5541-7185-1
定　　价：58.00 元

编 委 会

目录 CONTENTS

Unit 1

Major Revolutionary Films from 2021

Lesson 1 Major Revolutionary Films from 2021

Task 1: Step into the "reading forest".

Directions: Try to fill in the following blanks according to your imagination.

The Battle at Lake Changjin

Set in the War to Resist US Aggression and Aid Korea（抗美援朝）（1950–1953）, the film centers on __1__ heroic company of the Chinese People's Volunteers Army (CPVA), __2__ CPVA soldiers' iron will and great spirit to safeguard the then __3__ founded People's Republic of China.

The 176-minute film, which cost 1.3 billion *yuan* (202.7 million), became __4__ of its kind in China. By Nov. 24, its overall box office surpassed 5.69 billion *yuan* (891.1 million).

Cliff Walkers

Set in the 1930s in Northeastern China's Harbin during the Japanese invasion, the film follows the Communist Party special agents __5__ they show their wits against their enemies to complete a secret mission.

The film was the first foray of director Zhang Yimou into the spy genre. It __6__ seven nominations, including one for best film, at the 34th edition of Golden Rooster, China's top film awards.

1921

As the biggest tribute film to mark the centenary of the Communist Party of China（中国共产党）, *1921* was put on nationwide on July 1.

The film is narrated over a shorter and more compact course in the title year, when the Communist Party of China held __7__ first National Congress in Shanghai and Jiaxing, Zhejiang Province, in the summer of 1921, laying the __8__ for its rise.

The Pioneer

As the first such biographical film to trace the revolutionary（革命的）footprints of Li Dazhao, one of the key founders of the Communist Party of China, *The Pioneer* __9__ in over 710 IMAX theaters on July 1.

Set amid the turbulent period between 1912 and 1927, the film __10__ on Li Dazhao's memories throughout his life, showing the selfless spirit of struggle in the Chinese communists.

Questions:

1. Which film is the one that is set in the War to Resist US Aggression and Aid Korea (1950–1953)?

____

2. Which film was put on in over 710 IMAX theaters on July 1?

____

3. What do the four films have in common?

____

Task 2: Appreciate "trees" in the "reading forest".

Directions: Fill in each blank with the word or phrase that best fits the context.

The Battle at Lake Changjin

Set in the War to Resist US Aggression and Aid Korea（1950–1953）, the film centers on __1__ heroic company of the Chinese People's Volunteers Army (CPVA) , __2__ (reflect) CPVA soldiers' iron will and great spirit to safeguard the then __3__ (new) founded People's Republic of China.

The 176-minute film, which cost 1.3 billion *yuan* (202.7 million), became __4__ (expense) of its kind in China. By Nov. 24, its overall box office surpassed 5.69 billion *yuan* (891.1 million).

Cliff Walkers

Set in the 1930s in Northeastern China's Harbin during the Japanese invasion, the film follows the Communist Party special agents __5__ they show their wits against their enemies to complete a secret mission.

The film was the first foray of director Zhang Yimou into the spy genre. It __6__ (receive) seven nominations, including one for best film, at the 34th edition of Golden Rooster, China's top film awards.

1921

As the biggest tribute film to mark the centenary of the Communist Party of China, *1921* was put on nationwide on July 1.

The film is narrated over a shorter and more compact course in the title year, when the Communist Party of China held __7__ (it) first National Congress in Shanghai and Jiaxing, Zhejiang Province, in the summer of 1921, laying the __8__ (found) for its rise.

The Pioneer

As the first such biographical film to trace the revolutionary footprints of Li Dazhao, one of the key founders of the Communist Party of China, *The Pioneer* __9__ (put on) in over 710 IMAX theaters on July 1.

Set amid the turbulent period between 1912 and 1927, the film __10__ (focus) on Li Dazhao's memories throughout his life, showing the selfless spirit of struggle in the Chinese communists.

Task 3: Have an overview of the "reading forest".

The Battle at Lake Changjin

Set in the War to Resist US Aggression and Aid Korea (1950–1953), the film centers on a heroic company of the Chinese People's Volunteers Army (CPVA), reflecting CPVA soldiers' iron will and great spirit to safeguard the then newly founded People's Republic of China.

The 176-minute film, which cost 1.3 billion *yuan* (202.7 million), became the most expensive of its kind in China. By Nov. 24, its overall box office surpassed 5.69 billion *yuan* (891.1 million).

Cliff Walkers

Set in the 1930s in Northeastern China's Harbin during the Japanese invasion, the film follows the Communist Party special agents as they show their wits against their enemies to complete a secret mission.

The film was the first foray of director Zhang Yimou into the spy genre. It has received seven nominations, including one for best film, at the 34th edition of Golden Rooster, China's top film awards.

1921

As the biggest tribute film to mark the centenary of the Communist Party of China, *1921* was put on nationwide on July 1.

The film is narrated over a shorter and more compact course in the title year, when the Communist Party of China held its first National Congress in Shanghai and Jiaxing, Zhejiang Province, in the summer of 1921, laying the foundation for its rise.

The Pioneer

As the first such biographical film to trace the revolutionary footprints of Li Dazhao, one of the key founders of Communist Party of China, *The Pioneer* was put on in over 710 IMAX theaters on July 1.

Set amid the turbulent period between 1912 and 1927, the film focuses on Li Dazhao's memories throughout his life, showing the selfless spirit of struggle in the Chinese communists.

Words, phrases and difficult sentences to understand (Translate them into Chinese).

1. set in ______________________________

2. enter on ______________________________

3. War to Resist US Aggression and Aid Korea ______________

4. iron will and great spirit ______________________

5. As they show their wits against their enemies to complete a secret mission.

____

6. put on ______________________________

7. laying the foundation for its rise ______________

8. focus on ______________________________

9. throughout his life ______________________________

10. showing the selfless spirit of struggle in the Chinese communists

____

Task 4: Cultivate your cultural awareness.

War to Resist US Aggression and Aid Korea

In June 1950, the Korean War broke out after the Korean Peninsula was split into the north and south. The United States sent troops, while dispatching ships and aircraft to meddle with Taiwan and the Sino-Korean border. On October 19, 1950, the newly founded People's Republic of China decided to participate in the war to defend its national security and help its neighbor. The Chinese people called it the War to Resist US Aggression and Aid Korea.

Facing American threats, China had several options, sending its army or volunteer soldiers to Korea, or surrendering to the US invasion. In the end, the Chinese government decided to send volunteer soldiers to aid Korea, protecting China's national security and paving the way for future diplomatic mediation.

On the frontlines, thousands of soldiers shed their blood; meanwhile, the Chinese government accused the US of invasion at the United Nations, while preparing for possible negotiations. The prolonged warfare and heavy losses forced the US to the talking table. On July 10, 1951, truce talks began in Kaesong.

Both Korean and Chinese delegations proposed stopping military confrontations, defining the 38th parallel as the dividing boundary, setting up a demilitarized zone, and returning prisoners of war. But the US rejected the proposal, while launching new attacks on the battlefield. But its advanced weapons failed to give Washington an upper hand. Eventually, after talks stalled and resumed for several rounds, the parties signed the Korean Armistice Agreement on July 27, 1953, ending three years of fighting.

The Chinese people safeguarded their national security and won international recognition. The war was also very important for Chinese diplomacy. The government tried to solve the conflict through negotiations, and gained experience while doing so.

But the war was also a painful experience for China. More than 180,000 soldiers were killed, with many more injured or missing. The war also escalated the confrontations between China and the US, and dented China's economic and social development.

Lesson 2　A Special Wedding

Task 1: Step into the "reading forest".

Directions: Try to fill in the following blanks according to your imagination.

On Thursday, Sahar Fares's fiancé and family gave her the wedding party she will never have.

A zaffe band __1__ for her, the flute striking a __2__ tune while drums kept the __3__, as family and friends __4__ rice and flower petals. The musicians, in festive, gold-embroidered white gowns, played while __5__ firefighters carried her white coffin to a waiting hearse.

Ms Fares, a 24-year-old paramedic, was one of at least 145 people __6__ on Tuesday by the massive explosion that leveled most of the Port of Beirut, __7__ entire neighborhoods, injured more than 5,000 people and left hundreds of thousands __8__.

Each death is a unique, unfathomable __9__, but the story of Ms Fares, the young bride-to-be, has rippled across social media, capturing the attention and heartache of many Lebanese. The determined daughter of a family of modest means, she __10__ to break into the nearly all-male world of the Beirut Fire Brigade, __11__ herself to public service and making plans to __12__ a family of her own.

"Our history is one of martyrs and martyrdom," said al-Qaa's mayor, Bachir Mattar, "Sahar is a __13__ to our youth that there are people who __14__ to the nation and lose everything. I wish there was a nation that __15__ such sacrifice and commitment, though. I wish we had a proper state."

Questions:

1. What does the passage mainly talk about?

____

2. What's the structure or clue of the passage?

____

Task 2: Appreciate "trees" in the "reading forest".

Directions: For each blank in the following passage there are four words or phrases marked A, B, C and D. Fill in each blank with the word or phrase that best fits the context.

On Thursday, Sahar Fares's fiancé and family gave her the wedding party she will never have.

A zaffe band __1__ for her, the flute striking a __2__ tune while drums kept the __3__ , as family and friends __4__ rice and flower petals. The musicians, in festive, gold-embroidered white gowns, played while __5__ firefighters carried her white __6__ to a waiting hearse.

Ms Fares, a 24-year-old paramedic, was one of at least 145 people __7__ on Tuesday by the massive explosion that __8__ most of the Port of Beirut, __9__ entire neighborhoods, injured more than 5,000 people and left hundreds of thousands __10__ .

Each death is a unique, unfathomable __11__ , but the story of Ms Fares, the young bride-to-be, has rippled across social media, __12__ the attention and heartache of many Lebanese. The determined daughter of a family of modest means, she __13__ to break into the nearly all-male world of the Beirut Fire Brigade, __14__ public service and making plans to __15__ a family of her own.

"Our __16__ is one of martyrs and martyrdom," said al-Qaa's mayor, Bachir Mattar, "Sahar is a __17__ to our youth that there are people who __18__ the nation and lose everything. I wish there was a nation that was worth such __19__ and commitment, __20__ . I wish we had a proper state."

1. A. blew	B. boasted	C. played	D. performed
2. A. mercy	B. sorrowful	C. exciting	D. joyful
3. A. beat	B. hit	C strike	D.tone
4. A. pulled	B. threw	C. picked	D. dragged
5. A. brave	B. uniformed	C. inspired	D. moved
6. A. coffin	B. dress	C. sculpture	D. status
7. A. dead	B. shot	C. killed	D. swept
8. A. leveled	B. called	C. marked	D. named
9. A. exposed	B. devastaetd	C. struck	D. fired
10. A. hurt	B. lost	C missing	D. homeless
11. A. comedy	B. tragedy	C. tale	D. fiction
12. A. paying	B. drawing	C. attracting	D. capturing
13. A. had failed	B. had managed	C. had attempted	D. had tried
14. A. devoting herself to		B. adapted herself to	
C. absorbing herself in		D. losing herself in	
15. A. build	B. support	C. assist	D. abandon
16. A. nation	B. history	C. state	D. community
17. A. note	B. virtue	C. message	D. belief
18. A. contribute to		B. lead to	
C. look forward to		D. commit to	
19. A. story	B. sacrifice	C. description	D. statement
20. A. though	B. therefore	C. too	D. nevertheless

Task 3: Have an overview of the "reading forest".

On Thursday, Sahar Fares's fiancé and family gave her the wedding party she will never have.

A zaffe band played for her, the flute striking a joyful tune while drums kept the beat, as family and friends threw rice and flower petals. The musicians, in festive, gold-embroidered white gowns, played while uniformed firefighters carried her white coffin to a waiting hearse.

Ms Fares, a 24-year-old paramedic, was one of at least 145 people killed on Tuesday by the massive explosion that leveled most of the Port of Beirut, devastated entire neighborhoods, injured more than 5,000 people and left hundreds of thousands homeless.

Each death is a unique, unfathomable tragedy, but the story of Ms Fares, the young bride-to-be, has rippled across social media, capturing the attention and heartache of many Lebanese. The determined daughter of a family of modest means, she had managed to break into the nearly all-male world of the Beirut Fire Brigade, devoting herself to public service and making plans to build a family of her own.

"Our history is one of martyrs and martyrdom," said al-Qaa's mayor, Bachir Mattar, "Sahar is a message to our youth that there are people who commit to the nation and lose everything. I wish there was a nation that was worth such sacrifice and commitment, though. I wish we had a proper state."

Words, phrases and difficult sentences to understand (Translate them into Chinese).

1. wedding party ________ 2. band ________
3. beat ________ 4. massive explosion ________
5. leave sb. homeless ________ 6. unique ________
7. tragedy ________ 8. ripple ________
9. bride-to-be ________ 10. capture ________
11. determined ________ 12. modest ________
13. manage to do ________ 14. devote oneself to doing ________
15. commit to sth. ________ 16. sacrifice ________

Task 4: Cultivate your cultural awareness.

Disasters are inevitable. Faced with different disasters, so many people devoted themselves to assisting and even lost her life. In the massive explosion, a 24-year-old paramedic, Ms. Fares. who was a bride-to-be, captured our attention. She lost her chance of wedding dressing. Her sacrifice gave youth, people, even nation a message. What can we do to face the disaster as a citizen? How about our nation?

Lesson 3 The Former Kingdom of Bicycles

Task 1: Step into the "reading forest".

Directions: Try to fill in the following blanks according to your imagination.

In the late 1980s and early 1990s, __1__ Foreigners who came to the country for the first time were amazed at the rivers of cyclists who snaked their way through the streets. At the time, cities were smaller, cars were not affordable to the masses, and options for public transportation were limited.

__2__ It allowed its roads to accommodate motor vehicles that grew increasingly popular with the public. In only 25 years, the use of bicycles as transport in Beijing had dropped from 60 percent to only 15 percent. __3__ Perhaps it can be proved by the phrase "I'd rather cry in a BMW than smile on a bicycle", which was a response that had been given by a dating show contestant.

Bicycles, as we all know, are convenient, eco-friendly, and beneficial for the health as a form of exercise. Based on these advantages, some companies have attempted to bring back the popularity of bicycles by introducing the idea of bike-sharing systems throughout China. __4__

However, with lockdowns coming to an end and public transportation still limited, we are once again looking at an opportunity to bring back the bicycles. Is it only a passing fad or is it here to stay? It all depends. But I believe that the popularity of bicycles has very much to do with the availability of bicycle lanes and road. __5__ Nobody intentionally wants to hurt you, but all it takes is a little mistake to fall prey to these fraught waters.

Questions:

1. What does the passage mainly talk about?

____

2. What are the key words that help you understand the passage better?

____

3. What's the structure or clue of the passage?

____

4. What's the author's attitude towards the popularity of bicycles?

____

Task 2: Appreciate "trees" in the "reading forest".

Directions: Choose the right sentences to complete the passage.

In the late 1980s and early 1990s, __1__ Foreigners who came to the country for the first time were amazed at the rivers of cyclists who snaked their way through the streets. At the time, cities were smaller, cars were not affordable to the masses, and options for public transportation were limited.

__2__ It allowed its roads to accommodate motor vehicles that grew increasingly popular with the public. In only 25 years, the use of bicycles as transport in Beijing had dropped from 60 percent to only 15 percent. __3__ Perhaps it can be proved by the phrase "I'd rather cry in a BMW than smile on a bicycle", which was a response that had been given by a dating show contestant.

Bicycles, as we all know, are convenient, eco-friendly, and beneficial for the health as a form of exercise. Based on these advantages, some companies have attempted to bring back the popularity of bicycles by introducing the idea of bike-sharing systems throughout China. __4__

However, with lockdowns coming to an end and public transportation still limited, we are once again looking at an opportunity to bring back the bicycles. Is it only a passing fad or is it here to stay? It all depends. But I believe that the popularity of bicycles has very much to do with the availability of bicycle lanes and road. __5__ Nobody intentionally wants to hurt you, but all it takes is a little mistake to fall prey to these fraught waters.

A. This programme has achieved great success.

B. To me,riding a bike in Shanghai is like swimming with sharks.

C. China became widely known as the "Kingdom of Bicycles".

D. The humble bicycle has actually not changed much, but cities have changed, and so have we.

E. However, China managed to make significant improvements to its construction over the decades.

F. Because people can afford more expensive cars, such as BMW.

G. To their disappointment, the bicycle failed to make a reappear in our lives.

Task 3: Have an overview of the "reading forest".

In the late 1980s and early 1990s, China became widely known as the "Kingdom of Bicycles". Foreigners who came to the country for the first time were amazed at the rivers of cyclists who snaked their way through the streets. At the time, cities were smaller, cars were not affordable to the masses, and options for public transportation were limited.

However, China managed to make significant improvements to its construction over the decades. It allowed its roads to accommodate motor vehicles that grew increasingly popular with the public. In only 25years, the use of bicycles as transport in Beijing had dropped from 60 percent to only 15 percent. The humble bicycle has actually not changed much, but cities have changed, and so have we. Perhaps it can be proved by the phrase "I'd rather cry in a BMW than smile on a bicycle", which was a response that had been given by a dating show contestant.

Bicycles, as we all know, are convenient, eco-friendly, and beneficial for the health as a form of exercise. Based on these advantages, some companies have attempted to bring back the popularity of bicycles by introducing the idea of bike-sharing systems throughout China. To their disappointment, the bicycle failed to make a reappear in our lives.

However, with lockdowns coming to an end and public transportation still limited, we are once again looking at an opportunity to bring back the bicycles. Is it only a passing fad or is it here to stay? It all depends. But I believe that the popularity of bicycles has very much to do with the availability of bicycle lanes and roads. To me, riding a bike in Shanghai is like swimming with sharks. Nobody intentionally wants to hurt you, but all it takes is a little mistake to fall prey to these unpleasant waters.

Words, phrases and difficult sentences to understand (Translate them into Chinese).

1. snake ______________________ 2. accommodate ______________
3. affordable ____________________ 4. significant ________________
5. humble _______________________ 6. convenient ________________
7. come to an end _______________ 8. availability _______________
9. fall prey to sth. ____
10. All it takes is a little mistake to fall prey to these unpleasant waters.

____

Task 4: Cultivate your cultural awareness.

Bicycle demand expected to grow at decadal high of 20% due to pandemic-induced fitness awareness, says Crisil Overall sales growth this fiscal will support the profitability of bicycle makers, Crisil says.

India's bicycle industry is pedalling to a decadal-high demand growth of 20% this fiscal, with sales likely to touch 1.45 crore units compared with 1.2 crore units last fiscal. The ongoing Covid-19 pandemic has spurred demand for bicycles owing to improving fitness consciousness and leisure requirements, said ratings agency Crisil in a news release. The resultant improvement in cash flows—amid higher capital expenditure—will support the credit profiles of CRISIL-rated bicycle manufacturers, which account for ~60% of industry volume.

India is the second-largest manufacturer of bicycles in the world. The industry is classified into four segments — standard, premium, kids and exports.

Demand for standard bicycles, which is the largest segment (accounting for half of all bicycles sold in 2020) is driven by government purchases. Government departments procure these bicycles through a tender process and distribute under various welfare schemes.

Demand for premium and kids bicycles (nearly 40%) is driven by fitness and leisure needs. Exports and sales of other kinds of bicycles constitute the remaining 10% demand.

In the five fiscals through 2019, bicycle sales volume logged a modest compound annual growth rate of ~5%. In fiscal 2020, it contracted a massive 22% as government purchases plunged and a large bicycle manufacturer downed shutters. However, last fiscal saw a turn for the better.

Says Nitesh Jain, Director, CRISIL Ratings Ltd., "The pandemic-induced constraints on fitness and leisure options increased the demand for bicycles, especially in the premium and kids segments. Strong growth in these limited the overall decline in sales volume to just 5% in fiscal 2021 despite a further reduction in government purchases. The momentum is likely to continue this fiscal, too, given the ongoing second wave of pandemic, and should lead to a 22% growth for the premium and kids segments."

"In the past couple of months, however, orders from government departments have started improving. Consequently, demand for standard bicycles is likely to grow after two dull years. Overall sales growth this fiscal will support the profitability of bicycle makers for two reasons. One, improved product mix as the premium and kids segments have higher profitability and their market share has increased 1,000 bps to over 50% now," the Crisil release said. It added, "Second, demand in the premium and kids segments is relatively price-inelastic. That allows manufacturers to pass on any increase in the prices of raw materials such as primarily steel, which accounts for 60%–65% of the total cost of manufacturing a bicycle. This was also evident last fiscal where profit margins improved despite higher steel prices." Says Rakshit Kachhal, Associate Director, CRISIL Ratings Ltd., "We expect the industry's margins to further improve by 110–130 bps this fiscal. While manufacturers will borrow more to enhance their capacities this fiscal, debt metrics will still improve. We see interest coverage rising to~4.8 times from ~3.6 times last fiscal."

While lockdowns have slammed the brakes on sales, Crisil expects that the pent-up demand can be expected once sales outlets open. This analysis assumes demand would decline by a third in the first quarter of the current fiscal. "Recovery is expected from the second quarter with Covid-19 caseloads and lockdowns likely to peak in June, and as vaccinations pick up pace. Any subsequent resurgence in infections will be a monitorable," said the release .

Lesson 4 Why Loafing Can Be Work?

Task1: Step into the "reading forest".

Directions: Try to fill in the following blanks according to your imagination.

What exactly constitutes work? Being at a desk counts __1__ work, as does looking at a screen above a certain size. Responding to email and being in a meeting are __2__ forms of work. So is any __3__ that might arouse sympathy if performed on the weekend—typing, taking a phone call from the boss, opening any type of electronic __4__ .

But these familiar forms of work can __5__ , for two reasons. The first is that what looks like a Stakhanovite effort may be no such thing. Keyboard-tappers may just be __6__ their LinkedIn profiles. Attendees at a meeting are often __7__ in body but not in spirit. Even when actual work is being done, it may not be the most __8__ use of people's time. The second is that things that look like the opposite of work—loafing about, to use the technical term—can be very useful indeed.

__9__ daydreaming. Letting the mind wander is not simply part of being human; it can also be a __10__ of creativity, a way to unlock solutions to tough problems. Albert Einstein's breakthrough moments __11__ came via thought experiments in which he let his imagination drift. Einstein is admittedly a pretty high bar, __12__ zoning out can help ordinary people, too. *Research* published in 2021 found that __13__ work-related problems sparked more daydreaming among professional employees, and that this daydreaming __14__ boosted creativity.

Similarly, going for a walk is not just a __15__ from work, but can be a form of it. It was __16__ with big increases in creativity. Being outside generally seems to improve lateral thinking（横向思维能力）.

The post-pandemic rethink of __17__ is focused on "when" and "where" questions. Asynchronous working（异步工作）is a way for individuals to cooperate at times that suit them. Lots of thought is going into how to make a success of hybrid work.

The "what is work" question gets much __18__ attention. But if you see a colleague __19__ through the park or examining the ceiling for hours, don't assume that work isn't being done. What looks like __20__ may be the very moment when inspiration strikes.

Questions:

1. How do you understand the word "loafing" in the title? Try to find another word or phrase to replace it.

____

2. Why does the writer mention Albert Einstein in Paragraph 3?

____

3. What's the structure of the passage?

____

Task 2: Appreciate "trees" in the "reading forest".

Directions: For each blank in the following passage there are four words or phrases marked A, B, C and D. Fill in each blank with the word or phrase that best fits the context.

What exactly constitutes work? Being at a desk counts __1__ work, as does looking at a screen above a certain size. Responding to email and being in a meeting are __2__ forms of work. So is any __3__ that might arouse sympathy if performed on the weekend—typing, taking a phone call from the boss, opening any type of electronic __4__.

But these familiar forms of work can __5__, for two reasons. The first is that what looks like a Stakhanovite effort may be no such thing. Keyboard-tappers may just be __6__ their LinkedIn profiles. Attendees at a meeting are often __7__ in body but not in spirit. Even when actual work is being done, it may not be the most __8__ use of people's time. The second is that things that look like the opposite of work—loafing about, to use the technical term—can be very useful indeed.

__9__ daydreaming. Letting the mind wander is not simply part of being human; it can also be a __10__ of creativity, a way to unlock solutions to tough problems. Albert Einstein's breakthrough moments __11__ came via thought experiments in which he let his imagination drift. Einstein is admittedly a pretty high bar, __12__ zoning out can help ordinary people, too. *Research* published in 2021 found that __13__ work-related problems sparked more daydreaming among professional employees, and that this daydreaming __14__ boosted creativity.

Similarly, going for a walk is not just a(n) __15__ from work, but can be a form of it. It was __16__ with big increases in creativity. Being outside generally seems to improve lateral thinking.

The post-pandemic rethink of __17__ is focused on "when" and "where" questions. Asynchronous working is a way for individuals to cooperate at times that __18__ them. Lots of thought is going into how to make a success of hybrid work.

The "what is work" question gets much less attention. But if you see a colleague __19__ through the park or examining the ceiling for hours, don't assume that work isn't being done. What looks like __20__ may be the very moment when inspiration strikes.

1. A. in	B. as	C. for	D. from
2. A. successfully	B. surprisingly	C. undoubtedly	D. interestingly
3. A. activity	B. meeting	C. question	D. form
4. A. devices	B. music	C. data	D. documents
5. A. win	B. do	C. pass	D. cheat
6. A. updating	B. making	C. correcting	D. watching
7. A. healthy	B. absent	C. present	D. upset
8. A. entertaining	B. thrilling	C. powerful	D. productive
9. A. Find	B. Take	C. Check	D. Use
10. A. source	B. killer	C. drive	D. effort

11. A. never	B. often	C. seldom	D. once
12. A. and	B. but	C. so	D. because
13. A. easy	B. funny	C. tricky	D. useful
14. A. in turn	B. in advance	C. in all	D. in case
15. A. pay	B. escape	C. bonus	D. break
16. A. familiar	B. content	C. associated	D. occupied
17. A. work	B. money	C. success	D. time
18. A. benefit	B. need	C. serve	D. suit
19. A. rushing	B. wandering	C. flying	D. driving
20. A. happiness	B. hardness	C. laziness	D. loneliness

Task 3: Have an overview of the "reading forest".

What exactly constitutes work? Being at a desk counts as work, as does looking at a screen above a certain size. Responding to email and being in a meeting are undoubtedly forms of work. So is any activity that might arouse sympathy if performed on the weekend—typing, taking a phone call from the boss, opening any type of electronic documents.

But these familiar forms of work can cheat, for two reasons. The first is that what looks like a Stakhanovite effort may be no such thing. Keyboard-tappers may just be updating their LinkedIn profiles. Attendees at a meeting are often present in body but not in spirit. Even when actual work is being done, it may not be the most productive use of people's time. The second is that things that look like the opposite of work—loafing about, to use the technical term—can be very useful indeed.

Take daydreaming. Letting the mind wander is not simply part of being human; it can also be a source of creativity, a way to unlock solutions to tough problems. Albert Einstein's breakthrough moments often came via thought experiments in which he let his imagination drift. Einstein is admittedly a pretty high bar, but zoning out can help ordinary people, too. *Research* published in 2021 found that tricky work-related problems sparked more daydreaming among professional employees, and that this daydreaming in turn boosted creativity.

Similarly, going for a walk is not just a break from work, but can be a form of it. It was associated with big increases in creativity. Being outside generally seems to improve lateral thinking.

The post-pandemic rethink of work is focused on "when" and "where" questions. Asynchronous working is a way for individuals to cooperate at times that suit them. Lots of thought is going into how to make a success of hybrid work.

The "what is work" question gets much less attention. But if you see a colleague wandering through the park or examining the ceiling for hours, don't assume that work isn't being done. What looks like laziness may be the very moment when inspiration strikes.

Words, phrases and difficult sentences to understand (Translate them into Chinese).

1. loaf ____________________ 2. constitute ____________________

3. count as ____________________ 4. arouse ____________________

5.attendee ____________________ 6. wander ____________________

7. tricky ____________________ 8. in turn ____________________

9. boost ____________________ 10. assume ____________________

11. So is any activity that might arouse sympathy if performed on the weekend—typing, taking a phone call from the boss, opening any type of electronic documents.

____

12. *Research* published in 2021 found that tricky work-related problems sparked more daydreaming among professional employees, and that this daydreaming in turn boosted creativity.

____

Task 4: Cultivate your cultural awareness.

Before the pandemic turned everyone into remote employees, managers worried that working from home would be paradise for slackers. But reality has turned out to be different. Employees are demonstratively visible and work has become more procluctive.

The simple act of logging on is now public. Green dots by your name on messaging channels are the virtual equivalents of jackets left on chairs and monitors turned on.

Calendars are now frequently shared: empty ones look lazy; full ones appear virtuous. Communication is more likely to happen on open messaging channels. Colleagues can leave public comments in shared documents, and in the process notify their authors that something approximation work has been done.

Theatre has always been an important part of the workplace. But the prevalence of performative work is bad news for employees who have to catch up on actual tasks once the show is over. By extension it is also bad for productivity. Why, then, does it persist?

One answer lies in the natural desire of employees to demonstrate how hard they work. Another lies in managers' need to see what everyone is up to.

And a third is hinted at in recent research, from academics at two French business schools, which found that white-collar professionals are drawn to a level of "optimal busyness". Rushing from meeting to meeting, triaging emails and hitting a succession of small deadlines can deliver a buzz, even if nothing much is actually being achieved.

The performance is what counts.

Unit 2

Your Daily Dose of "Must Read"

Lesson 1　Your Daily Dose of "Must Read"

Task 1: Step into the "reading forest".

Too Much Blood A Toni Day Mystery Jane Bennett Munro Paperback | E-book | Audiobook $22.95 | $3.99 | $9.99	An infamous local lawyer is found dead in his Mercedes in the middle of a snowy road. Pathologist（病理学家）Toni Day is on the case once again.
The Early Years A Memoir Rachel G. Carrington Hardback | Paperback | E-book | Audiobook $28.95 | $18.95 | $3.99 | $9.99	In her tender memoir, Rachel G. Carrington remembers having her set path changed upon meeting a newly returned WWII veteran（老兵）. In him, she finds a life filled with passion— bound together through their dedication and love for the Heavenly Father.
Murder under the Microscope Jane Bennett Munro Paperback | E-book | Audiobook $23.95 | $5.99 | $9.99	In this exciting murder mystery, a stubborn pathologist must rely on more than her microscope as she looks into a web of lies. Her freedom and life are in danger.
The Forty Year Con Game Everything You Need To Know About Donald Trump's Threat To Democracy Dr. Michael B. Harrington Hardback | Paperback | E-book $29.99 | $19.99 | $3.99	In anticipation of the 2020 election, this book describes Donald Trump's public life, from his mob connections in the 1980s through his first two troubled years in the White House.

Questions:

1. Where can you find this article?

____

2. What does the passage mainly talk about?

____

3. What are the key words that help you understand the passage better?

____

Task 2: Appreciate "trees" in the "reading forest".

Directions: Choose the best answer from A, B, C or D to the questions.

Too Much Blood A Toni Day Mystery Jane Bennett Munro Paperback | E-book | Audiobook $22.95 | $3.99 | $9.99	An infamous local lawyer is found dead in his Mercedes in the middle of a snowy road. Pathologist Toni Day is on the case once again.
The Early Years A Memoir Rachel G. Carrington Hardback | Paperback | E-book | Audiobook $28.95 | $18.95 | $3.99 | $9.99	In her tender memoir, Rachel G. Carrington remembers having her set path changed upon meeting a newly returned WWII veteran. In him, she finds a life filled with passion—bound together through their dedication and love for the Heavenly Father.
Murder under the Microscope Jane Bennett Munro Paperback | E-book | Audiobook $23.95 | $5.99 | $9.99	In this exciting murder mystery, a stubborn pathologist must rely on more than her microscope as she looks into a web of lies. Her freedom and life are in danger.
The Forty Year Con Game Everything You Need To Know About Donald Trump's Threat To Democracy Dr. Michael B. Harrington Hardback | Paperback | E-book $29.99 | $19.99 | $3.99	In anticipation of the 2020 election, this book describes Donald Trump's public life, from his mob connections in the 1980s through his first two troubled years in the White House.

1. Which books talk about mysterious stories?

A. *Murder under the Microscope* and *Too Much Blood*

B. *Too Much Blood* and *The Early Years Con Game*

C. *The Early Years* and *The Forty Year Con Game*

D. *Murder under the Microscope* and *The Forty Year Con Game*

2. What can we infer about *The Forty Year Con Game?*

A. It records the achievement made by Donald Trump.

B. It anticipates the winner of the 2020 election.

C. Donald Trump suffered in his first two years in the White House.

D. Donald Trump opposes democracy in the US.

3. How much will it cost if you want to buy two books in hardback as presents for your friends?

A. $7.98. B. $19.98.

C. $58.94. D. $13.98.

Task 3: Have an overview of the "reading forest".

Too Much Blood A Toni Day Mystery Jane Bennett Munro Paperback | E-book | Audiobook $22.95 | $3.99 | $9.99	An infamous local lawyer is found dead in his Mercedes in the middle of a snowy road. Pathologist Toni Day is on the case once again.
The Early Years A Memoir Rachel G. Carrington Hardback | Paperback | E-book | Audiobook $28.95 | $18.95 | $3.99 | $9.99	In her tender memoir, Rachel G. Carrington remembers having her set path changed upon meeting a newly returned WWII veteran. In him, she finds a life filled with passion—bound together through their dedication and love for the Heavenly Father.
Murder under the Microscope Jane Bennett Munro Paperback | E-book | Audiobook $23.95 | $5.99 | $9.99	In this exciting murder mystery, a stubborn pathologist must rely on more than her microscope as she looks into a web of lies. Her freedom and life are in danger.
The Forty Year Con Game Everything You Need To Know About Donald Trump's Threat To Democracy Dr. Michael B. Harrington Hardback | Paperback | E-book $29.99 | $19.99 | $3.99	In anticipation of the 2020 election, this book describes Donald Trump's public life, from his mob connections in the 1980s through his first two troubled years in the White House.

Words, phrases and difficult sentences to understand:

1. tender ______________ 2. mystery ______________
3. election ______________ 4. connection ______________
5. troubled ______________ 6. hardback ______________
7. fill with passion ______________ 8. in the middle of ______________
9. in anticipation of ______________ 10. in danger ______________

11. In anticipation of the 2020 election, this book describes Donald Trump's public life, from his mob connections in the 1980s through his first two troubled years in the White House.

____

____

Task 4: Cultivate your cultural awareness.

Too Much Blood

Jane Bennett Munro

Universe

(2012)

ISBN 978-1-4759-2918-8

Too Much Blood was an engrossing read, although it was most definitely written by someone with extensive knowledge of human anatomy and conditions. Author Jane Bennett Munro is a semiretired pathologist with over thirty years in the field, which gives her writing the exceptional realism that only comes from personal hands on experience. Don't be worried though, Munro has written *Too Much Blood* in a very tasteful manner so while it's extremely realistic it's not over the top for those who, like me, squeamish when it comes to reading murder mysteries.

Toni Day, the main character in *Too Much Blood* receives a call in the wee hours of the morning because Jay Braithwaite Burke, the local (and sleazy) attorney has been found deceased. Burke's car was discovered in a small snow bank in the middle of a freeway and you wouldn't know it, when the police opened the car up, there was Jay Braithwaite Burke, dead as a door nail, in the driver's seat. Toni is required to perform an autopsy and the question of the day. Was Burke's death due to natural causes or...was it a homicide?

A man died in his car in the middle of the night during a snow storm? Why wouldn't his death be from natural causes?? Probably because nothing in life is ever quite that simple... I think I used the word "sleazy" when previously making reference to Burke and it's an apt description.

Apparently Mr. Burke was promoting a pretty impressive hedge fund and almost every single doctor who worked at Perrine Memorial Hospital invested in it. Unfortunately, when the economy tanked, so did his hedge fund and it was revealed shortly afterward to be a massive Ponzi scheme. Needless to say, after losing their shirts and then some, most of the town had reason to want Burke dead. Now it's just a question of "Who did it?"

I don't want to give away any more of Munro's tale — suffice it to say it was a great book. Munro writes with captivating flair and her storyline is believable and realistic. *Too Much Blood* reads like front page news and I'm certain that murder mystery fans of all ages will enjoy this title.

The Early Years

Rachel G. Carrington was born in a small southern Kentucky town in 1930. She was first-born of eleven children to loving, but strict, low-income parents who struggled to keep food on the table and could afford little more than that. Attending school and earning a high school diploma was a given but, lack of funds making further education impossible.

Author Rachel G. Carrington lays no claim to lofty jobs, higher education, nor grand accomplishments except for a love-filled, multifaceted, family-oriented, poverty-to-plenty life. In *The Early Years*, the first in a series, she shares her story.

As a young teenager, just entering high school in the small town of Denton, Kentucky, Carrington planned to attend college and become a teacher. With coursework geared toward college attendance, she was offered a lucrative scholarship that would help her to attain her goal. However, it took only a single event to send her down a different path. She met a returned World War II veteran who was attempting to pick up the pieces after finding his marriage in irreparable shambles and his children gone. As he struggled, Carrington was there, and they pulled together to clear the many hurdles before them.

In this memoir, she tells the story of their journey and how their love and dedication for each other kept moving them forward. Filled with the joys, disappointments, and struggles of a couple, *The Early Years* narrates how the love for the heavenly Father was the continuous thread that bound Carrington's life together.

Murder under the Microscope

Jane Bennett Munro

Dr. Antoinette Day—a young, successful pathologist known to her friends and colleagues as Toni—has no idea what awaits her when Dr. Sally Shore arrives at Perrine Memorial Hospital in Twin Falls, Idaho, to fill in for a colleague recovering from a heart attack. Toni's lifc is about to become a living hell.

Dr. Shore is supposed to see patients, perform surgeries, and take turns to cover the emergency room until the regular surgeon recovers from his quadruple bypass. But unfortunately, she uses her temporary opportunity to discredit Toni and tarnish her reputation with her medical colleagues. When the visiting surgeon is conveniently murdered—her lifeless body found in Toni's office—Toni is the obvious suspect. But Toni is not going down without a fight. Forced to solve the murder in order to save her future, Toni's life becomes even more complicated when her ex-boyfriend starts stalking her and threatening her husband.

In this riveting murder mystery, a stubborn pathologist must rely on more than just her microscope as she delves into a complicated web of deception, soon discovering that it is not just her freedom at stake—but her life.

The Forty Year Con Game

Everything You Need To Know About Donald Trump's Threat To Democracy

Dr. Michael B. Harrington

Most voters during the 2016 presidential election were largely unaware of Trump's forty-year history as a skilled con man but an incompetent failure otherwise. In anticipation of the 2020 election, this book describes Trump's public life from his mob connections in the early 1980s through his first two stumbling years in the White House. It documents Trump's inescapable history of ignorance, self-absorption, poor judgment, corruption, impulsive decision-making, bigotry, and strong authoritarian instincts. Taken together, all guaranteed a disastrous presidency. His first two years in the White House fulfilled this guarantee, threatening America's constitutional democracy.

Lesson 2 My Cold Turned Out to Be COVID-19

Task1: Step into the "reading forest".

Directions: Try to fill in the following blanks according to your imagination.

Earlier this year, 20-year-old Jonah Stillman, an author and a public speaker, traveled to Thailand, South Korea, Australia, and England. On the flight home to Minneapolis, he says, "I had a minor sore throat and cough."

News about the spread of COVID-19 was just __1__ then, but at the time it seemed to be affecting mostly __2__ people, so he didn't think that could be what he had. "I don't get sick often, I work out every day and I have a very clean diet," he __3__. Still, because he has family members with underlying conditions that he'd heard could raise the __4__ of complications or death from the virus, he called his doctor the next day. "Once they heard all of the __5__ I had been to," Stillman says, "the doctors __6__ wanted to test me." The entire __7__ took about 15 minutes. That was on a Wednesday.

That Saturday, he __8__ the news that he had tested __9__ for COVID-19. His was one of the first cases __10__ in Minnesota. "It was __11__ because it was still relatively new." he says. By Sunday, his sore throat had __12__ considerably, his violent coughs would not stop, and his fever spiked to 103 degrees. "The body __13__ were unlike anything I've experienced. I could __14__ move." Among the most disturbing symptoms was his __15__ of taste and smell. "I couldn't differentiate between cake and pizza. I had to __16__ myself to eat because my gag reflex was so strong."

His __17__ took two full weeks, and Stillman started to tell his story as a way of __18__ other young people to __19__ the disease and social distancing seriously.

"Even if you don't have symptoms, this ___20___ others." he says now.

Questions:

1. What does the passage mainly talk about?

____

2. What are the key words that help you understand the passage better?

____

3. In what order does this article develop?

____

Task 2: Appreciate "trees" in the "reading forest".

Directions: For each blank in the following passage there are four words or phrases marked A, B, C and D. Fill in each blank with the word or phrase that best fits the context.

Earlier this year, 20-year-old Jonah Stillman, an author and a public speaker, traveled to Thailand, South Korea, Australia, and England. On the flight home to Minneapolis, he says, "I had a minor sore throat and cough."

News about the spread of COVID-19 was just ___1___ then, but at the time it seemed to be affecting mostly ___2___ people, so he didn't think that could be what he had. "I don't get sick often, I work out every day and I have a very clean diet," he ___3___. Still, because he has family members with underlying conditions that he'd heard could raise the ___4___ of complications or death from the virus, he called his doctor the next day. "Once they heard all of the ___5___ I had been to," Stillman says, "the doctors ___6___ wanted to test me." The entire ___7___ took about 15 minutes. That was on a Wednesday.

That Saturday, he ___8___ the news that he had tested ___9___ for COVID-19. His was one of the first cases ___10___ in Minnesota. "It was ___11___ because it was still relatively new." he says. By Sunday, his sore throat had ___12___ considerably, his violent coughs would not stop, and his fever spiked to 103 degrees. "The body ___13___ were unlike anything I've experienced. I could ___14___ move." Among the most disturbing symptoms was his ___15___ of taste and smell. "I couldn't differentiate between cake and pizza. I had to __16__ myself to eat because my gag reflex was so strong."

His __17__ took two full weeks, and Stillman started to tell his story as a way of __18__ other young people to __19__ the disease and social distancing seriously. "Even if you don't have symptoms, this __20__ others." he says now.

1. A. showing	B. happening	C. leaking	D. breaking
2. A. healthier	B. fatter	C. older	D. tougher
3. A. answers	B. explains	C. replies	D. wonders
4. A. level	B. risk	C. pressure	D. number
5. A. illnesses	B. stories	C. places	D. situations
6. A. definitely	B. highly	C. probably	D. eagerly
7. A. process	B. operation	C. activity	D. meeting
8. A. heard	B. noticed	C. received	D. admitted
9. A. positive	B. negative	C. pessimistic	D. optimistic
10. A. treated	B. tested	C. observed	D. identified
11. A. dangerous	B. shocking	C. normal	D. surprising
12. A. developed	B. cleared	C. changed	D. worsened
13. A. damages	B. wounds	C. aches	D. injuries
14. A. barely	B. nearly	C. just	D. slightly
15. A. absence	B. desire	C. lack	D. shortage
16. A. force	B. argue	C. encourage	D. persuade
17. A. journey	B. suffering	C. preparation	D. recovery
18. A. protecting	B. preventing	C. urging	D. offering
19.A. take	B. view	C. put	D. regard
20. A. satisfies	B. disturbs	C. impacts	D. separates

Task 3: Have an overview of the "reading forest".

Earlier this year, 20-year-old Jonah Stillman, an author and a public speaker, traveled to Thailand, South Korea, Australia, and England. On the flight home to Minneapolis, he says, "I had a minor sore throat and cough."

News about the spread of COVID-19 was just breaking then, but at the time it seemed to be affecting mostly older people, so he didn't think that could be what he had. "I don't get sick often, I work out every day and I have a very clean diet," he explains. Still, because he has family members with underlying conditions that he'd heard could raise the risk of complications or death from the virus, he called his doctor the next day. "Once they heard all of the places I had been to," Stillman says, "the doctors definitely wanted to test me." The entire process took about 15 minutes. That was on a Wednesday.

That Saturday, he received the news that he had tested positive for COVID-19. His was one of the first cases identified in Minnesota. "It was shocking because it was still relatively new." he says. By Sunday, his sore throat had worsened considerably, his violent coughs would not stop, and his fever spiked to 39.5 degrees Celsius. "The body aches were unlikc anything I've experienced. I could barely move." Among the most disturbing symptoms was his lack of taste and smell. "I couldn't differentiate between cake and pizza. I had to force myself to eat because my gag reflex was so strong."

His recovery took two full weeks, and Stillman started to tell his story as a way of urging other young people to take the disease and social distancing seriously. "Even if you don't have symptoms, this impacts others." he says now.

Words, phrases and difficult sentences to understand (Translate them into Chinese).

1. spread ________________ 2. complication ________________

3. process ________________ 4. identify ________________

5. considerably ____________ 6. violent ________________

7. spike to ________________ 8. lack of taste and smell ____________

9. a very clean diet __________ 10. raise the risk of ____________

11. By Sunday, his sore throat had worsened considerably, his violent coughs would not stop, and his fever spiked to 39.5 degrees Celsius.

____

12. Because he has family members with underlying conditions that he'd heard could raise the risk of complications or death from the virus, he called his doctor the next day.

____

Task 4: Cultivate your cultural awareness.

The COVID-19 pandemic has led to a dramatic loss of human life worldwide and presents an unprecedented challenge to public health, food systems and the world of work. The economic and social disruption caused by the pandemic is devastating: tens of millions of people are at risk of falling into extreme poverty.

Millions of enterprises face an existential threat. Nearly half of the world's 3.3 billion global workforce are at risk of losing their livelihoods. Informal economy workers are particularly vulnerable because the majority lack social protection and access to quality health care and have lost access to productive assets. Without the means to earn an income during lockdowns, many are unable to feed themselves and their families. For most, no income means no food, or, at best, less food and less nutritious food.

The pandemic has been affecting the entire food system and has laid bare its fragility. Border closures, trade restrictions and confinement measures have been preventing farmers from accessing markets, including for buying inputs and selling their produce, and agricultural workers from harvesting crops, thus disrupting domestic and international food supply chains and reducing access to healthy, safe and diverse diets. The pandemic has decimated jobs and placed millions of livelihoods at risk. As breadwinners lose jobs, fall ill and die, the food security and nutrition of millions of women and men are under threat, with those in low-income countries, particularly the most marginalized populations, which include small-scale farmers and indigenous peoples, being hardest hit.

Millions of agricultural workers — waged and self-employed — while feeding the world, regularly face high levels of working poverty, malnutrition and poor health, and suffer from a lack of safety and labour protection as well as other types of abuse. With low and irregular incomes and a lack of social support, many of them are spurred to continue working, often in unsafe conditions, thus exposing themselves and their families to additional risks. Further, when experiencing income losses, they may resort to negative coping strategies, such as distress sale of assets, predatory loans or child labour. Migrant agricultural workers are particularly vulnerable, because they face risks in their transport, working and living conditions and struggle to access support measures put in place by governments. Guaranteeing the safety and health of all agri-food workers — from primary producers to those involved in food processing, transport and retail, including street food vendors — as well as better incomes and protection, will be critical to saving lives and protecting public health, people's livelihoods and food security.

Lesson 3 How to Be a Good Friend?

Task 1: Step into the "reading forest".

Directions: Try to fill in the following blanks according to your imagination.

A good friend listens. Most of our communication consists of a few people waiting for their turn to talk—to tell their better, faster, stronger story. We don't listen to each other. Even if you hear the words someone says, information transmission doesn't equal communication.

You see, when we're truly heard and deeply known, we feel it reverberate throughout our bodies. It's how we relax, settle in, and recognize safety. In order to be a friend—and have a friend—you have to listen. __1__

Be genuinely curious. Put your phone away. Yes, literally out of sight. Invest yourself in the conversation. __2__

__3__ Honesty time: Are you usually waiting for the other person to stop talking so you can start? Or do you ever go on and on, story after story, without stopping? Pay attention to your habits in conversation and be intentional about leaving space for your friends to speak.

Don't give advice unless asked. How often do we take someone else's challenges and turn it into a chance for us to sound smart or give our opinions? Often, when a friend is sharing something hard, we race to dump out advice or condolences to fix it. Resist the urge to make someone else's challenges all about you. __4__ Remember: People aren't problems to solve.

Don't listen as an out from sharing. If this is you, you know who you are. Some of you would give others all the room in every conversation to avoid any kind of spotlight. You let others run their mouths and deflect any attention that shines your way. Don't do that. That's not being a good listener—it's just using listening to hide.

Ask for feedback. __5__ So, get outside your head and get some data. Ask those close to you: "How well do I listen? Do you feel heard when we talk? Do I share enough or too much?" Or the next time you're with a group of friends, be intentional about listening and not talking. Notice if those around you are missing your connection or if they're relishing the ability to be heard.

Questions:

1. What does the passage mainly talk about?

____

2. What are the key words that help you understand the passage better?

____

3. How to be a good friend according to your mind?

____

Task 2: Appreciate "trees" in the "reading forest".

Directions: Fill in each blank with the sentence that best fits the context.

A good friend listens. Most of our communication consists of a few people waiting for their turn to talk—to tell their better, faster, stronger story. We don't listen to each other. Even if you hear the words someone says, information transmission doesn't equal communication.

You see, when we're truly heard and deeply known, we feel it reverberate throughout our bodies. It's how we relax, settle in, and recognize safety. In order to be a friend—and have a friend—you have to listen. __1__

Be genuinely curious. Put your phone away. Yes, literally out of sight. Invest yourself in the conversation. __2__

__3__ Honesty time: Are you usually waiting for the other person to stop talking so you can start? Or do you ever go on and on, story after story, without stopping? Pay attention to your habits in conversation and be intentional about leaving space for your friends to speak.

Don't give advice unless asked. How often do we take someone else's challenges and turn it into a chance for us to sound smart or give our opinions? Often, when a friend is sharing something hard, we race to dump out advice or condolences to fix it. Resist the urge to make someone else's challenges all about you. __4__ Remember: People aren't problems to solve.

Don't listen as an out from sharing. If this is you, you know who you are. Some of you would give others all the room in every conversation to avoid any kind of spotlight. You let others run their mouths and deflect any attention that shines your way. Don't do that. That's not being a good listener—it's just using listening to hide.

Ask for feedback. __5__ So, get outside your head and get some data. Ask those close to you: "How well do I listen? Do you feel heard when we talk? Do I share enough or too much?" Or the next time you're with a group of friends, be intentional about listening and not talking. Noticc if thosc around you are missing your connection or if they're relishing the ability to be heard.

A. Listen more than you talk.

B. Don't talk when others are talking.

C. A good friend isn't your personal cheerleader.

D. Here are some tips for how to be a good friend through listening well.

E. We often have a biased view of how good or bad we are at something.

F. A good friend listens first, leads with empathy, and waits to be invited in.

G. Be curious about what your friend is saying, not saying, and where the conversation might lead.

Task 3: Have an overview of the "reading forest".

A good friend listens. Most of our communication consists of a few people waiting for their turn to talk—to tell their better, faster, stronger story. We don't listen to each other. Even if you hear the words someone says, information transmission doesn't equal communication.

You see, when we're truly heard and deeply known, we feel it reverberate throughout our bodies. It's how we relax, settle in, and recognize safety. In order to be a friend—and have a friend—you have to listen. Here are some tips for how to be a good friend through listening well.

Be genuinely curious. Put your phone away. Yes, literally out of sight. Invest yourself in the conversation. Be curious about what your friend is saying, not saying, and where the conversation might lead.

Listen more than you talk. Honesty time: Are you usually waiting for the other person to stop talking so you can start? Or do you ever go on and on, story after story, without stopping? Pay attention to your habits in conversation and be intentional about leaving space for your friends to speak.

Don't give advice unless asked. How often do we take someone else's challenges and turn it into a chance for us to sound smart or give our opinions? Often, when a friend is sharing something hard, we race to dump out advice or condolences to fix it. Resist the urge to make someone else's challenges all about you. A good friend listens first, leads with empathy, and waits to be invited in. Remember: People aren't problems to solve.

Don't listen as an out from sharing. If this is you, you know who you are. Some of you would give others all the room in every conversation to avoid any kind of spotlight. You let others run their mouths and deflect any attention that shines your way. Don't do that. That's not being a good listener—it's just using listening to hide.

Ask for feedback. We often have a biased view of how good or bad we are at something. So, get outside your head and get some data. Ask those close to you: "How well do I listen? Do you feel heard when we talk? Do I share enough or too much?" Or the next time you're with a group of friends, be intentional about listening and not talking. Notice if those around you are missing your connection or if they're relishing the ability to be heard.

Words, phrases and difficult sentences to understand (Translate them into Chinese).

1. genuinely ____________ 2. challenge ____________

3. connection ____________ 4. spotlight ____________

5. resist ____________ 6. empathy ____________

7. pay attention to ______________ 8. have a biased view of ______________

9. get outside your head ________ 10. leave space for ________________

11. Notice if those around you are missing your connection or if they're relishing the ability to be heard.

____

Task 4: Cultivate your cultural awareness.

What are the qualities of a Good Friend?

A good friend is someone who knows you through and through. When you're with them, your shoulders drop, your body relaxes, your breathing slows, and something inside you says, "I'm safe." A good friend has your back and your front. And they hold you up when times get hard. Of course, there are a million small and big things added together to make a good friend, but I've found that good friends have to have these six key traits:

1. A good friend shows up.

A good friend is there for you. They're with you for the big stuff—like your mom's surgery or a shocking breakup—and for the small stuff. When it's time to celebrate or give support, a good friend wants to be there. That means they don't just show up when it's convenient or when they get something out of it.

Who could you call at 2 a.m. when your spouse is sick and you desperately need someone to watch the kids? Who would check in with you around the holidays because they know being with your family is hard? Who would mow your yard when you're in the ICU? Who would give their thoughts on your new business plan? Who would sacrifice their precious Saturday morning to help you move? Those are good, good friends—especially the moving guy.

You've probably heard my friend Dave Ramsey talk about having an emergency fund for when stuff hits the fan. Well, consider friends your emergency fund for life. It's not a matter of if hard things will happen—it's a matter of when. Your parents will get sick, your kid will get into trouble, and your marriage will have tough seasons. But a good friend shows up and supports you.

2. A good friend listens.

Let's be honest. Most of our communication consists of a few people waiting for their turn to talk—to tell them better, faster, stronger stories. We can't listen to each other. Even if you hear the words someone says, information transmission doesn't equal communication.

You see, when we're truly heard and deeply known, we feel it reverberates throughout our bodies. It's how we relax, settle in, and recognize safety. In order to be a friend—and have a friend—you have to listen.

Here are some tips for how to be a good friend through listening well:

Be genuinely curious. Put your phone away. Yes, literally out of sight. Invest yourself in the conversation. Be curious about what your friend is saying, not saying, and where the conversation might lead.

Listen more than you talk. Honesty time: Are you usually waiting for the other person to stop talking so you can start? Or do you ever go on and on, story after story, without stopping? Pay attention to your habits in conversation and be intentional about leaving space for your friends to speak.

Don't give advice unless asked. How often do we take someone else's challenges and turn them into a chance for us to sound smart or give our opinions? Often, when a friend is sharing something hard, we race to dump out advice or condolences to fix it. Resist the urge to make someone else's challenges all about you. A good friend listens first, leads with empathy, and waits to be invited in. Remember: People aren't problems to solve.

Don't listen as an out from sharing. If this is you, you know who you are. Some of you would give others all the room in every conversation to avoid any kind of spotlight. You let others run their mouths and deflect any attention that shines your way. Don't do that. That's not being a good listener—it's just using listening to hide.

Ask for feedback. We often have a biased view of how good or bad we are at something. So, get outside your head and get some data. Ask those close to you: "How well do I listen? Do you feel heard when we talk? should I share enough or too much?" Or the next time you're with a group of friends, be intentional about listening and not talking. Notice if those around you are missing your connection or if they're relishing the ability to be heard.

And let me give you one final tip that's going to rock your friendship world: The next time your friend is telling a story, and it reminds you of a similar story, and you just so happen to think your story is better, keep it to yourself.

Seriously. Don't say anything. Just listen. Let the conversation be about someone else this time.

3. A good friend holds you accountable.

A good friend isn't your personal cheerleader. Sometimes, they have hard conversations with you because you've given them permission to speak into your life—especially when it stings. When you're acting like a jerk, a good friend calls you out. Friends are people who challenge you, who you can challenge, and who you can argue with without fearing losing them.

Likewise, when someone says or does something hurtful, a good friend speaks up. They give the other person a chance to apologize and show they can be trusted. Good friends don't just cut someone out when times get tough or weird. And they know they screw up, make mistakes, and need to say "I'm sorry" and forgive.

A good friend also doesn't have important conversations like these over text messages or social media. They always, always call or visit in person as much as humanly possible.

4. A good friend has earned your trust.

If you've been hurt by someone you considered a good friend, it's probably because they broke your trust. A good friend should always be honest. They should take responsibility for their actions, leave the past in the past, keep their word, be open, and not talk behind your back.

Some signs of a lack of trust in a friendship include:

Gossiping

Anger and blaming Controlling behavior

Expecting the worst in someone Withholding

One of our core desires as people is to be fully known and still loved. It's not smart or safe to trust everyone with that kind of access to our lives. But you can—and should—be real with a good friend. You should tell them the good, the bad and the painful things from your past.

This is trust. It's how to be a good friend.

And men, practice trusting your friends more. You have feelings whether you want to admit it or not. And your friends do too. Research shows half of women and less than one-third of men have shared personal feelings with a friend in the past week. If you want to have and be a good friend—not an anxious, spun-out, walking zombie all the time—you've got to find people you trust enough to share what's really going on in your life.

5. A good friend is committed to your well-being.

A little while back, one of my best—and most stable—friends called to tell me the bank he worked at had been sold out of the blue. He'd lost his job, and it was hard. We walked through the sale, his financial situation, how his family was doing, and what he was going to do next. Later in the call, when the conversation had gone a different direction, I piped up, "Speaking of getting fired, I just found out I made the bestseller list!"

My friend's immediate reaction was to make some jokes about how Redefining Anxiety, the little "pamphlet" I wrote, actually made *The Wall Street Journal* bestseller list. But he was also genuinely happy and said, "You've been working so hard on all of this for so long. That's really great." What I loved about that conversation is that even though our careers and lives looked painfully different in that moment, we didn't skip over the good stuff or the bad stuff. We brought our full selves to the conversation and embraced each other's reality.

A good friend is by your side. Your success doesn't threaten them, and they celebrate it with you. Some people have no interest in your listening to your good news, coming to your housewarming party, or hearing that your kid finally reached grade-level reading. In the madness of our modern era, your success or good news might even offend other people.

These people aren't friends. If you want to know how to be a good friend, make sure you celebrate the good stuff.

And because your success doesn't threaten them, a good friend pushes you toward wellness. You shouldn't catch them saying anything like:

"Come out with us! You can finish your paper when you get home!"

"It's not a big deal, dude. Just don't tell your wife."

"If you go back and get your MBA, you won't have time for the band, and we need you."

6. A good friend is someone you like being around.

We all want friends who show up and listen well, and who are accountable, trustworthy and committed—these are super important traits, no doubt. But having and being a good friend really comes down to one simple question: Do you enjoy being around each other?

When you think about the good friends you enjoy, you probably noticc a combination of these three things are present in your relationship:

You have shared experiences together. You do things together. You don't just send each other memes on social media or like the messages in your old fraternity's group text. You go to a concert, invite their family over, or ask them to help you paint your living room. And if they live far away, you make an intentional effort to see one another. (But yes, hilarious memes are still important.)

You've done hard things together. Ever wondered why the people you made it through middle school with or started a job with end up being your best friends? Or why military veterans stay connected to their troop long after deployment? Because you did hard things together and came out on the other side. Doing hard things with others can help us evolve and grow, because when someone has walked with us through that change, they know us in a way other people don't.

You genuinely have fun. People become our good friends because we have fun with them. We laugh until our guts hurt, have inside jokes, play sports together, and act bonkers. And what makes having fun with a good friend so much better than with anyone else is that we know we don't always have to be fun in order for them to still care about us.

How to Make Good Friends

When we were kids, we made friends by going up to another kid and saying something brilliant like, "Hey, want to have a sword fight with these sticks and toilet paper rolls?" And BAM, you were best friends. But it doesn't work like that when we're adults. To make good friends, you have to be intentional. Make time. Ask someone to coffee. Go on the hunting trip you don't have time for. Walk up to someone at church and ask what their name is.

And yes, introverts, you can initiate conversations and adventures too. Starting a conversation gets easier the more you do it. It involves the risk of rejection, but here's the truth: All relationships are a risk. Every single one of them. It's what turns random people into your people. Because even though they might not show up, and they don't have to, they still do.

That's what makes friendships scary—and it's what makes them worthwhile.

Human connection and knowing how to be a good friend is a cornerstone of being well—but it's not all there is to it. Wellness comes with understanding the stories that have shaped you and taking ownership for what comes next. In my new book, *Own Your Past, Change Your Future*, we'll unpack the stories that have been weighing you down, how you can change toxic thoughts and actions, and the reason for cultivating real relationships.

Lesson 4 Water Wand

Task 1: Step into the "reading forest".

Direction: Read the passage and answer the questions.

City water can be contaminated（污染）by electronic waste and other sources of heavy metals—but collecting, chemically preserving and transporting samples to laboratories for testing is challenging for remote communities.

To improve the process, Emily Hanhauser, a mechanical engineer at the Massachusetts Institute of Technology, and her colleagues created a low-tech sample-collection device that costs less than two dollars to make. It consists of a plastic handle tipped by mechanic attachments made from polymer mesh（聚合物网）, which contain small packets of absorbent materials that attract heavy metal ions（离子）. Users stir the device in water and then dry it.

Putting the attachments in an acid solution releases the absorbed ions, which can then be measured. Unlike possibly contaminated water samples, which are considered hazardous, the device can be safely mailed to testing facilities. It can also yield results after two years of storage, its creators say. In experiments, the tool accurately reflected the amounts of copper, nickel, lead and cadmium added to a variety of water samples, the researchers reported in March in *Environmental Science and Technology*.

A detailed analysis of water quality ideally would be performed near the source, removing the need for sample shipping entirely, Hanhauser notes. But existing tools designed for that purpose cannot measure small enough amounts of contaminants, and they often have too much variation in measurement to be useful, she says. Her group's device might be able to provide remote communities with a feasible alternative to transporting high-volume liquid samples over long distances. A more advanced version of the device could potentially measure large groups of contaminating metals as well, the researchers add.

"I think this could be a good diagnostic tool because of the low-cost, good metal-recovery numbers and superiority over heavy metal tests," says Siddhartha Roy, an environmental engineer at Virginia Tech. "I can see superior versions of the device being used following contamination events for specific metals."

Questions:

1. What is the genre of this article?

____

2. What does the passage mainly talk about?

____

3. What are the key words that help you understand the passage better?

____

Task 2: Appreciate "trees" in the "reading forest".

Directions: Choose the best answer from A, B, C or D to the questions.

City water can be contaminated by electronic waste and other sources of heavy metals—but collecting, chemically preserving and transporting samples to laboratories for testing is challenging for remote communities.

To improve the process, Emily Hanhauser, a mechanical engineer at the Massachusetts Institute of Technology, and her colleagues created a low-tech sample-collection device that costs less than two dollars to make. It consists of a plastic handle tipped by mechanic attachments made from polymer mesh, which contain small packets of absorbent materials that attract heavy metal ions. Users stir the device in water and then dry it.

Putting the attachments in an acid solution releases the absorbed ions, which can then be measured. Unlike possibly contaminated water samples, which are considered hazardous, the device can be safely mailed to testing facilities. It can also yield results after two years of storage, its creators say. In experiments, the tool accurately reflected the amounts of copper, nickel, lead and cadmium added to a variety of water samples, the researchers reported in March in *Environmental Science and Technology*.

A detailed analysis of water quality ideally would be performed near the source, removing the need for sample shipping entirely, Hanhauser notes. But existing tools designed for that purpose cannot measure small enough amounts of contaminants, and they often have too much variation in measurement to be useful, she says. Her group's device might be able to provide remote communities with a feasible alternative to transporting high-volume liquid samples over long distances. A more advanced version of the device could potentially measure large groups of contaminating metals as well, the researchers add.

"I think this could be a good diagnostic tool because of the low-cost, good metal-recovery numbers and superiority over heavy metal tests," says Siddhartha Roy, an environmental engineer at Virginia Tech. "I can see superior versions of the device being used following contamination events for specific metals."

1. What words can best describe the new device?

A. Cheap but inconvenient.

B. Useful but costly.

C. Eco-friendly and high-tech.

D. Low-cost and safe.

2. What does the underlined word "hazardous" in Paragraph 3 probably mean?

A. Safe. B. Harmful.

C. Wasteful. D. Heavy.

3. What can we infer about the device?

A. The device can test heavy metals in the water near the source.

B. It can provide a new method for transporting samples in downtown area.

C. The samples collected by the device can be used after a long time.

D. The device can measure large groups of contaminating metals.

4. What is the purpose of the author?

A. To explain how to use the new device to measure contaminants in water.

B. To illustrate the process of testing water quality in remote areas.

C. To provide a possible way to transport samples over long distances.

D. To introduce a cheap simple device that detects heavy metals in water.

Task 3: Have an overview of the "reading forest".

City water can be contaminated by electronic waste and other sources of heavy metals—but collecting, chemically preserving and transporting samples to laboratories for testing is challenging for remote communities.

To improve the process, Emily Hanhauser, a mechanical engineer at the Massachusetts Institute of Technology, and her colleagues created a low-tech sample-collection device that costs less than two dollars to make. It consists of a plastic handle tipped by mechanic attachments made from polymer mesh, which contain small packets of absorbent materials that attract heavy metal ions. Users stir the device in water and then dry it.

Putting the attachments in an acid solution releases the absorbed ions, which can then be measured. Unlike possibly contaminated water samples, which are considered hazardous, the device can be safely mailed to testing facilities. It can also yield results after two years of storage, its creators say. In experiments, the tool accurately reflected the amounts of copper, nickel, lead and cadmium added to a variety of water samples, the researchers reported in March in *Environmental Science and Technology*.

A detailed analysis of water quality ideally would be performed near the source, removing the need for sample shipping entirely, Hanhauser notes. But existing tools designed for that purpose cannot measure small enough amounts of contaminants, and they often have too much variation in measurement to be useful, she says. Her group's device might be able to provide remote communities with a feasible alternative to transporting high-volume liquid samples over long distances. A more advanced version of the device could potentially measure large groups of contaminating metals as well, the researchers add.

"I think this could be a good diagnostic tool because of the low-cost, good metal-recovery numbers and superiority over heavy metal tests," says Siddhartha Roy, an environmental engineer at Virginia Tech. "I can see superior versions of the device being used following contamination events for specific metals."

Words, phrases and difficult sentences to understand (Translate them into Chinese).

1. contaminate ________________ 2. remote ________________

3. colleague ________________ 4. mechanic ________________

5. contain ________________ 6. potentially ________________

7. a more advanced version ________ 8. the need for ________________

9. an environmental engineer ________________________________

10. superior versions of ________________________________

11. I think this could be a good diagnostic tool because of the low-cost, good metal-recovery numbers and superiority over heavy metal tests.

____

12. It consists of a plastic handle tipped by mechanic attachments made from polymer mesh, which contain small packets of absorbent materials that attract heavy metal ions.

____

Task 4: Cultivate your cultural awareness.

Urbanization and Water Quality

There's no end to the effects that urbanization (people living together in groups) can have on water bodies: millions of people; landscape manipulation; waste material; dumping of chemicals and fertilizers; withdrawing water for peoples' uses. As you expect, urbanization rarely improves water quality, but in order to prevent problems, one needs to understand how urbanization affects the local water.

To some degree, urbanization has been taking place since ancient times. As populations rose and people mastered techniques to grow food in fixed locations, groups of people became settlements and then towns and cities. In the United States, the speed of this urbanization picked up after World War II, and now many urban areas are growing at a record pace. What are the effects on the local hydrologic system when a rural area is turned into an area full of housing developments, shopping centers, industrial buildings, and roads?

The following shows changes in land and water use when urbanization occurs and the possible effect on the local water system.

Beginning of Urbanization

Change in Land Use:

Remove trees and vegetation. Begin building houses, some with sewers and some with septic tanks. Begin drilling wells.

Effect on Water System:

More storm runoff and erosion because there is less vegetation to slow water as it runs down hills. More sediment is washed into streams. Flooding can occur because water- drainage patterns are changed.

Continuing Urbanization

Change in Land Use:

Urbanization is finished by the addition of more roads, houses, and commercial and industrial buildings. More wastewater is discharged into local streams. New water-supply and distribution systems are built to supply the growing population. Reservoirs may be built to supply water. Some stream channels are changed to accommodate building constructions. Industries might drill some deep, large-capacity wells.

Effect on Water System:

More pavement means less water will soak into the ground, meaning that the underground water table will have less water to recharge it. This will lower the water table. Some existing wells will not be deep enough to get water and might run dry.

The runoff from the increased pavement goes into storm sewers, which then goes into streams. This runoff, which used to soak into the ground, now goes into streams, causing flooding. Changing a stream channel can cause flooding and erosion along the stream banks.

More sewage is discharged into streams that weren't "designed by nature" to handle that much water.

The use of too many large wells can lower the underground water table. This can cause other wells to run dry, can cause saltwater to be drawn into drinking-water wells, and can cause land that was formerly "held up" by underground water to subside, resulting in sinkholes and land subsidence.

Local community takes steps to fix some problems.

Change in Land Use:

Improvements in the storm drainage system are made. Wells are drilled to recharge underground aquifers. Projects to reuse waste water might be started.

Ecological-designed recharge ponds disperse some storm drainage to artificially recharge shallow aquifers.

Effect on Water System:

New storm-drainage systems reduce flooding during storms. Less damage is done to basements, yards, and streets. Water is actually injected into recharge wells to put water back into underground aquifers. Reusing wastewater means less pollution, more water conservation, and additional water for recharging aquifers.

Unit 3

Five Powerful Films about Women

Lesson 1 Five Powerful Films About Women

Task 1: Step into the "reading forest".

Directions: Try to fill in the following blanks according to your imagination.

In the long history of humans, women's stories have often been overlooked. Yet as modern society has allowed women __1__ for themselves, more and more women are standing up to choose how to live their lives. Here __2__ five powerful films that just might inspire you to re-imagine what it means to be a woman.

***Hi, Mom* (2021)**

Directed by Chinese comedian Jia Ling, this heartwarming comedy, about a woman who __3__ meets her mother through time travel, became __4__ hit with audiences this year, leading the mainland box office right after Chinese New Year.

***Leap* (2020)**

This 2020 film about the Chinese __5__ women's volleyball team __6__ their history from 1981, __7__ they won the Women's World Cup, to the year 2016. Actress Gong Li stars as the legendary volleyball player Lang Ping, and Peter Chen from Hong Kong is the director.

***Coco Avant Chanel* (2009)**

The life of Coco Chanel serves as a guide to all women __8__ to establish their own careers. Audrey Tautou, famous for her iconic performance in *Amelie*, stars as the glorious French fashion designer. It is French director Anne Fontaine's most famous film.

***The Joy Luck Club* (1993)**

Based __9__ the novel *The Joy Luck Club*, Chinese director Wang Ying tells the stories of four Chinese women and their daughters who were all born and lived in the

US. Their conflicts also reflect the collision between traditional Chinese culture and American culture.

***The Story of Qiu Ju* (1992)**

Directed by Zhang Yimou, the 1992 film describes a peasant woman Qiu Ju who lives in a rural area of China and fights for justice. It is a screen __10__ of writer Chen Yuanbin's novel *The Wan Family's Lawsuit*.

Questions:

1. What's the purpose of the passage?

____

2. How does Coco Avant Chanel differ from the other 4 movies?

____

3. Which film concerns generation gap?

____

Task 2: Appreciate "trees" in the "reading forest".

Directions: Fill in each blank with the word or phrase that best fits the context.

In the long history of humans, women's stories have often been overlooked. Yet as modern society has allowed women __1__ (speak) for themselves, more and more women are standing up to choose how to live their lives. Here __2__ (be) five powerful films that just might inspire you to re-imagine what it means to be a woman.

***Hi, Mom* (2021)**

Directed by Chinese comedian Jia Ling, this heartwarming comedy, about a woman who __3__ (accidental) meets her mother through time travel, became __4__ hit with audiences this year, leading the mainland box office right after Chinese New Year.

***Leap* (2020)**

This 2020 film about the Chinese __5__ (nation) women's volleyball team __6__ (present) their history from 1981, __7__ they won the Women's World Cup, to the year 2016. Actress Gong Li stars as the legendary volleyball player Lang Ping, and Peter Chen from Hong Kong is the director.

Coco Avant Chanel **(2009)**

The life of Coco Chanel serves as a guide to all women __8__ (wish) to establish their own careers. Audrey Tautou, famous for her iconic performance in *Amelie*, stars as the glorious French fashion designer. It is French director Anne Fontaine's most famous film.

The Joy Luck Club **(1993)**

Based __9__ the novel *The Joy Luck Club*, Chinese director Wang Ying tells the stories of four Chinese women and their daughters who were all born and lived in the US. Their conflicts also reflect the collision between traditional Chinese culture and American culture.

The Story of Qiu Ju **(1992)**

Directed by Zhang Yimou, the 1992 film describes a peasant woman Qiu Ju who lives in a rural area of China and fights for justice. It is a screen __10__ (adapt) of writer Chen Yuanbin's novel *The Wan Family's Lawsuit*.

Task 3: Have an overview of the "reading forest".

In the long history of humans, women's stories have often been overlooked. Yet as modern society has allowed women to speak for themselves, more and more women are standing up to choose how to live their lives. Here are five powerful films that just might inspire you to re-imagine what it means to be a woman.

Hi, Mom **(2021)**

Directed by Chinese comedian Jia Ling, this heartwarming comedy, about a woman who accidentally meets her mother through time travel, became a hit with audiences this year, leading the mainland box office right after Chinese New Year.

Leap **(2020)**

This 2020 film about the Chinese national women's volleyball team presents their history from 1981, when they won the Women's World Cup, to the year 2016. Actress Gong Li stars as the legendary volleyball player Lang Ping, and Peter Chen from Hong Kong is the director.

***Coco Avant Chanel* (2009)**

The life of Coco Chanel serves as a guide to all women wishing to establish their own careers. Audrey Tautou, famous for her iconic performance in *Amelie*, stars as the glorious French fashion designer. It is French director Anne Fontaine's most famous film.

***The Joy Luck Club* (1993)**

Based on the novel *The Joy Luck Club*, Chinese director Wang Ying tells the stories of four Chinese women and their daughters who were all born and lived in the US. Their conflicts also reflect the collision between traditional Chinese culture and American culture.

The Story of Qiu Ju (1992)

Directed by Zhang Yimou, the 1992 film describes a peasant woman Qiu Ju who lives in a rural area of China and fights for justice. It is a screen adaptation of writer Chen Yuanbin's novel *The Wan Family's Lawsuit*.

Words, phrases and difficult sentences to understand (Translate them into Chinese).

1. overlook ________________ 2. modern society ________________
3. powerful ________________ 4. inspire sb. to do ________________
5. accidentally ________________ 6. hit ________________
7. box office ________________ 8. World Cup ________________
9. star ________________ 10. legendary ________________
11. iconic ________________ 12. serve as ________________
13. glorious ________________ 14. based on ________________
15. conflict ________________ 16. collision ________________
17. rural ________________ 18. adaptation ________________

19. Directed by Chinese comedian Jia Ling, this heartwarming comedy, about a woman who accidentally meets her mother through time travel, became a hit with audiences this year, leading the mainland box office right after Chinese New Year.

____

____

Task 4: Cultivate your cultural awareness.

Gone are the days when women were confined to their homes, clinging to the societal clichés of their role in a household. Over the last centuries, women's traditional roles have greatly evolved as they struggle to break the glass ceiling and strive for equal opportunities. Having a work-life balance is especially harder for women, who, besides doing their respective jobs, also have the burden of taking care of her family and children.

In today's society, modern women have their own jobs, hobbies, and income, with a strong self-awareness and self-control. Women who love life, society and family, have extensive interests and hobbies, and a deeper spiritual attainment. Modern women are busy with their own careers without losing the traditional virtues of women. The open external world and the incentive of survival competition have put forward higher requirements for women, and modern women have broken out of the cocoon of thousands of years of old ideas. In the work, they constantly enrich and improve themselves to be wise and thoughtful "professional women".

Acknowledgement:

Some of questions are adapted from the online reading materials, so heartfelt gratitude should go to their examiners.

Lesson 2 I Found Warmth in Greenland

Task 1: Step into the "reading forest".

Directions: Try to fill in the following blanks according to your imagination.

I was about 5 when I first heard the word "Greenland". And my interest __1__ from there. I can't say exactly why, but it was undoubtedly a __2__ of many images that the words conjured up: remoteness, ice, polar bears, and Vikings. __3__ , after decades, I decided to go.

From the plane I could see the east coast of Greenland was nothing but an expanse of ice and snow, with no __4__ of human habitation. But when the plane angled toward the southern part, everything changed. Much of the ice disappeared, __5__ by broad fields of green.

One of my __6__ of going to Greenland was to make contact with some native Greenlanders. I didn't know how I would achieve this, but success came in a(an) __7__ way.

I headed for a hostel, in which I had __8__ a bed. A young couple and their baby were out front, enjoying the sun and unusual warmth. This was my first native contact. Greenlanders speak their own Inuit language and learn Danish in school, and many also speak English well. The young woman' English, however, turned out __9__ . Their eyes __10__ when I identified myself. Another hiker had arrived earlier and, __11__ him for me, they had given him my bed. There was no more space in the hostel. "But don't worry," the young woman said, clearly __12__ for my comfort. Afterwards, she __13__ herself into cleaning a tiny room the family owned. "This is for you," she said. And __14__ that weren't enough, she invited me to eat supper with her __15__ family. We talked __16__ . The themes __17__ from the unusual weather in Greenland, to the concern they felt for the changes as the massive ice sheet __18__ and outside interests cast envious eyes upon the newly discovered mineral wealth.

In Greenland I found myself all but overcome by the emptiness, the vastness, and the silence before I was taken into this Greenlandic home. I can now say that even a cold, empty,and silent landscape __19__ a visit, so long as one has a __20__ and welcoming place to go to.

Questions:

1. What does the warmth probably mean in the title?

____

2. What did the author intend to do in Greenland?

____

3. What made the author's visit to Greenland worthwhile?

____

4. Can you tell the advantages of setting the story in Greenland?

____

Task 2: Appreciate "trees" in the "reading forest".

Directions: Fill in each blank with the word or phrase that best fits the context.

I Found Warmth in Greenland

I was about 5 when I first heard the word "Greenland". And my interest __1__ from there. I can't say exactly why, but it was undoubtedly a __2__ of many images that the words conjured up: remoteness, ice, polar bears, and Vikings. __3__ , after decades, I decided to go.

From the plane I could see the east coast of Greenland was nothing but an expanse of ice and snow, with no __4__ of human habitation. But when the plane angled toward the southern part, everything changed. Much of the ice disappeared, __5__ by broad fields of green.

One of my __6__ of going to Greenland was to make contact with some native Greenlanders. I didn't know how I would achieve this, but success came in a(an) __7__ way.

I headed for a hostel, in which I had __8__ a bed. A young couple and their baby were out front, enjoying the sun and unusual warmth. This was my first native contact. Greenlanders speak their own Inuit language and learn Danish in school, and many also speak English well. The young woman' English, however, turned out __9__. Their eyes __10__ when I identified myself. Another hiker had arrived earlier and, __11__ him for me, they had given him my bed. There was no more space in the hostel. "But don't worry," the young woman said, clearly __12__ for my comfort. Afterwards, she __13__ herself into cleaning a tiny room the family owned. "This is for you," she said. And __14__ that weren't enough, she invited me to eat supper with her __15__ family. We talked __16__. The themes __17__ from the unusual weather in Greenland, to the concern they felt for the changes as the massive ice sheet __18__ and outside interests cast envious eyes upon the newly discovered mineral wealth.

In Greenland I found myself all but overcome by the emptiness, the vastness, and the silence before I was taken into this Greenlandic home. I can now say that even a cold, empty,and silent landscape __19__ a visit, so long as one has a __20__ and welcoming place to go to.

1. A. decreased	B. faded	C. grew	D. appeared
2. A. response	B. combination	C. discovery	D. display
3. A. ctually	B. Gradually	C. Suddenly	D. Finally
4. A. sign	B. signal	C. mark	D. symbol
5. A. replaced	B. distributed	C. wrapped	D. removed
6. A. meanings	B. purposes	C. sights	D. reactions
7. A. exciting	B. disappointing	C.scheduled	D. unexpected
8. A. arranged	B. made	C. reserved	D. purchased
9. A. good	B. common	C. excellent	D. poor
10. A .brightened	B. closed	C. widened	D. beamed
11. A. seeing	B. assuming	C. mistaking	D. believing
12. A. happy	B. concerned	C. sad	D. indifferent

13. A. threw	B. pushed	C. helped	D. urged
14. A. even if	B. as if	C. in that	D. while
15. A. ordinary	B. loving	C. cold	D. happy
16. A. sadly	B. bitterly	C. happily	D. coldly
17. A. ranged	B. differed	C. distinguished	D. transformed
18. A. deepened	B. thickened	C. thinned	D. broadened
19. A. guarantees	B. requires	C. expects	D. deserves
20. A. monotonous	B. cold	C. warm	D. disagreeable

Task 3: Have an overview of the "reading forest".

I Found Warmth in Greenland

I was about 5 when I first heard the word "Greenland", and my interest grew from there. I can't say exactly why, but it was undoubtedly a combination of many images that the words conjured up: remoteness ,ice, polar bears ,and Vikings. Finally, after decades, I decided to go.

From the plane I could see the east coast of Greenland was nothing but an expanse of ice and snow, with no sign of human habitation. But when the plane angled toward the southern part, everything changed. Much of the ice disappeared, replaced by broad fields of green.

One of my purposes of going to Greenland was to make contact with some native Greenlanders. I didn't know how I would achieve this, but success came in an unexpected way.

I headed for a hostel, in which I had reserved a bed. A young couple and their baby were out front, enjoying the sun and unusual warmth. Greenlanders speak their own Inuit language and learn Danish in school, and many also speak English well. The young woman's English, however, turned out poor. Their eyes widened when I identified myself. Another hiker had arrived earlier and, mistaking him for me, they had given him my bed. There was no more space in the hostel. "But don't worry," the young woman said, clearly concerned for my comfort. Afterwards, she threw herself into cleaning a tiny room the family owned. "This is for you," she said. And as if that weren't enough, she invited me to eat supper with her loving family. That evening I sat down to a dinner of fresh fish with them. We talked happily. The themes ranged from the unusual weather in Greenland, to the concern they felt for the changes as the massive ice sheet thinned and outside interests cast envious eyes upon the newly discovered mineral wealth.

In Greenland I found myself all but overcome by the emptiness, the vastness, and the silence before I was taken into this Greenlandic home. I can now say that even a cold, empty, and silent landscape deserves a visit, so long as one has a warm and welcoming place to go to.

Words, phrases and difficult sentences to understand (Translate them into Chinese).

1. undoubtedly ____________________ 2. conjure up ______________

3. angle ____________________ 4. identify myself ______________

5. cast envious eyes ______________ 6. threw... into ______________

7. From the plane I could see the east coast of Greenland was nothing but an expanse of ice and snow, with no sign of human habitation.

____

8. The themes ranged from the unusual weather in Greenland, to the concern they felt for the changes as the massive ice sheet thinned and outside interests cast envious eyes upon the newly discovered mineral wealth.

____

9. In Greenland I found myself all but overcome by the emptiness, the vastness, and the silence before I was taken into this Greenlandic home.

____

Task 4: Cultivate your cultural awareness.

Greenland is the largest island on Earth. It is in the north of Europe. Near Greenland is another island, which is small. Its name is Iceland. Do you think that Greenland is green and warm? Do you think that Iceland is white with ice? If you do, you are wrong. There is a story related to the name. Legend has it that in ancient times, around 982, there was a Norwegian pirate who set out alone in a small boat from Iceland to cross the ocean. His friends thought he was too bold, and they were all worried about his safety. When he returned home, he proudly told his friends, "Not only have I returned safely, but I have found a green continent!" And Greenland became its permanent name.

About threequarters of the island is within the Arctic Circle, creating frigid climate all yearround. The annual average temperature in Greenland is below 0℃. The coldest inland areas in the central part of the island can reach as low as—70℃.

Greenland is white. Most of Greenland is covered with lots of ice. Not many people live on the big island of Greenland.

Since it is extremely cold in Greenland, why did the author feel so warm? The warmth had nothing to do with the temperature. The warmth came form his heart because he was well treated by the local people who had been complete strangers to him before. On reading this simple but moving story, do you have a fascination for the island? Do you have a similar experience like the author?

In addition, people, especially the travellers, need warmth. So every one of us should offer warmth to them selflessly. In this way we can build a harmonious society.

Acknowledgement:

Some of questions are adapted from the online reading materials, so heartfelt gratitude should go to their examiners.

Lesson 3 A Fabric Lights Up the Sky

Task1: Step into the "reading forest".

Directions: Try to fill in the following blanks according to your imagination.

An innovative outdoor fabric stores energy by day and then lights up at night. The sun does all the work, so there are no carbon emissions, __1__ the lighting all-natural and free!

Created by Anai Green, an industrial and product designer based in Tel Aviv, Israel, the shading fabric __2__ organic and solar photovoltaic cells（光伏电池）. It aims to light public space __3__ spreading light pollution—because the light is under a canopy. The cells __4__ sunlight and store the energy in strips with LEDs. When night falls, these __5__ light up.

The fabric, called Lumi Weave, is __6__ as there is no need to set up an infrastructure（基础设施）for it to work. You simply put it __7__ and the sun will do the work. This in itself __8__ 50 percent of the cost of building standard lighting, and it saves 100 percent on the __9__ bills.

This is great news for __10__. For example, the city of Tel Aviv, Green's hometown, is __11__ out Lumi Weave in Atidim Park. The fabric can hang over bike __12__, in children's parks and in walking areas. "Lumi Weave will turn out to be a groundbreaking __13__," the mayor of Tel Aviv, Ron Huldai, said. He added that it is especially important as it __14__ the issue of shading urban areas and uses clean energy.

As there is also use for the fabric in outdoor sitting areas of restaurants and hotels, Green has __15__ a Lumi Weave parasol（遮阳伞）, which can __16__ shade during the day and light at night. As the product stores light, it will __17__ even if there has been no sun for three days. Green is now developing a light motion material. This means that the Lumi Weave parasol can light up when a person __18__ the area and then turn off again when no one is around.

Lumi Weave offers an __19__ solution for urban parks and gardens. People hope that Lumi Weave will soon be lighting up __20__ skies around the world.

Questions:

1. What is the passage talking about?

____

2. How does the Lumi Weave work?

____

3. What are the benefits of using the fabric?

____

Task 2: Appreciate "trees" in the "reading forest".

Directions: read the passage and choose the best answers from A, B, C and D.

An innovative outdoor fabric stores energy by day and then lights up at night. The sun does all the work, so there are no carbon emissions, making the lighting all-natural and free!

Created by Anai Green, an industrial and product designer based in Tel Aviv, Israel, the shading fabric contains organic and solar photovoltaic cells. It aims to light public space without spreading light pollution—because the light is under a canopy. The cells collect sunlight and store the energy in strips with LEDs. When night falls, these strips light up.

The fabric, called Lumi Weace, is cost-effective as there is no need to set up an infrastructure for it to work. You simply put it up and the sun will do the work. This in itself saves 50 percent of the cost of building standard lighting, and it saves 100 percent on the electricity bills.

This is great news for cities. For example, the city of Tel Aviv, Green's hometown, is trying out Lumi Weave in Atidim Park. The fabric can hang over bike paths, in children's parks and in walking areas. "Lumi Weave will turn out to be a groundbreaking project," the mayor of Tel Aviv, Ron Huldai, said. He added that it is especially important as it solves the issue of shading urban areas and uses clean energy.

As there is also use for the fabric in outdoor sitting areas of restaurants and hotels, Green has developed a Lumi Weave parasol, which can provide shade during the day and light at night. As the product stores light, it will work even if there has been no sun for three days. Green is now developing a light motion material. This means that the Lumi Weave parasol can light up when a person approaches the area and then turn off again when no one is around.

Lumi Weave offers an ideal solution for urban parks and gardens. People hope that Lumi Weave will soon be lighting up night skies around the world.

1. What is the purpose of the fabric?

A. To cut down carbon emissions.

B. To beautify the environment.

C. To reduce lighting cost.

D. To light up public areas.

2. What is Paragraph 3 about?

A. How does Lumi Weave works.

B. The benefits of the Lumi Weave.

C. The manufacturing requirment of the Lumi Weave.

D. The application area of the Luni Weave.

3. What does Ron Huldai think of the fabric?

A. It is energy-saving.

B. It is badly needed.

C. It is promising.

D. It is environmental-protection.

4. What can we learn about the light motion material?

A. It can be on the market soon.

B. It can reduce the weight of the Lumi Weave parasol.

C. It can provide electric energy for the Lumi Weave parasol.

D. It can help the Lumi Weave parasol work automatically.

Task 3: Have an overview of the "reading forest".

An innovative outdoor fabric stores energy by day and then lights up at night. The sun does all the work, so there are no carbon emissions, making the lighting all-natural and free!

Created by Anai Green, an industrial and product designer based in Tel Aviv, Israel, the shading fabric contains organic and solar photovoltaic cells. It aims to light public space without spreading light pollution—because the light is under a canopy. The cells collect sunlight and store the energy in strips with LEDs. When night falls, these strips light up.

The fabric, called Lumi Weace, is cost-effective as there is no need to set up an infrastructure for it to work. You simply put it up and the sun will do the work. This in itself saves 50 percent of the cost of building standard lighting, and it saves 100 percent on the electricity bills.

This is great news for cities. For example, the city of Tel Aviv, Green's hometown, is trying out Lumi Weave in Atidim Park. The fabric can hang over bike paths, in children's parks and in walking areas. "Lumi Weave will turn out to be a groundbreaking project," the mayor of Tel Aviv, Ron Huldai, said. He added that it is especially important as it solves the issue of shading urban areas and uses clean energy.

As there is also use for the fabric in outdoor sitting areas of restaurants and hotels, Green has developed a Lumi Weave parasol, which can provide shade during the day and light at night. As the product stores light, it will work even if there has been no sun for three days. Green is now developing a light motion material. This means that the Lumi Weave parasol can light up when a person approaches the area and then turn off again when no one is around.

Lumi Weave offers an ideal solution for urban parks and gardens. People hope that Lumi Weave will soon be lighting up night skies around the world.

Words, phrases and difficult sentences to understand(Translate them into Chinese).

1. innovative ________________ 2. shading ____________________

3. strip ______________________ 4. groundbreaking ________________

5. motion material _____________ 6. approach ___________________

7. As there is also use for the fabric in outdoor sitting areas of restaurants and hotels, Green has developed a Lumi Weave parasol, which can provide shade during the day and light at night.

____

Task 4: Cultivate your cultural awareness.

Green lighting is a concept developed by the US Environmental Protection Agency in 1990s. The green lighting program is an important energy-saving project for the society. The complete green lighting connotation includes energy efficiency, environmental protection, safety and comfort. Efficient lighting equipment is one of the most bases of green lighting; however, humans have realized that lighting equipment is not just a light source though it is the most important aspect. In order to protect the environment, scientists have worked out many ways to generate electricity and have developed some lighting materials, like lighting walls, HPSL. Fabric is a newly found environmental-protection material to generate green electricity, which is cost-effective and energy saving.

Lesson 4 Investing in Good Health

Task 1: Step into the "reading forest".

Directions: Try to fill in the following blanks according to your imagination.

These days, our health and wellness should be a priority. Gone are the days when people take themselves for granted. It is about time that we should start investing in good health. But with all the health and wellness __1__ found on the Internet, which one should you consider doing?

You may already know the __2__ of healthy living. But if you want to boost your efforts, it only makes sense that you use __3__ tested and proven by scientists. Here's what you can consider __4__ in so that you can finally enjoy better health and wellness.

Some people spend a considerable amount of time working while sitting down. You can be working in an office and spending most of your time doing reports on a computer. But if you want to be __5__, get up and walk more often while at work.

This doesn't mean that you should __6__ your role and slack off. Walking more often, even for at least ten minutes at a time, can already help you __7__ better health. You can always do a bit more walking when in a meeting, when going to and from work, and by taking the stairs instead of the __8__.

Making those legs work will help you get more exercise no matter how busy your work __9__ is. Stop thinking that you have no time to go for a walk or run with your friends. By putting your mind on your __10__, you can get more walking even if you already have your hands full at work.

Sitting all day is the new vice of many people. This increases one's risk of diabetes, heart issues and even some cancer. You don't want your mental health to suffer just because you are too lazy to walk while you spend hours at a time working behind a desk.

Questions:

1. Are the excuses for not exercising acceptable or not?

____

2. What exercises can you do during your work?

____

Task 2: Appreciate "trees" in the "reading forest".

Directions: read the passage and choose the best answers from A, B, C and D.

These days, our health and wellness should be a priority. Gone are the days when people take themselves for granted. It is about time that we should start investing in good health. But with all the health and wellness tips found on the Internet, which one should you consider doing?

You may already know the basics of healthy living. But if you want to boost your efforts, it only makes sense that you use strategies tested and proven by scientists. Here's what you can consider investing in so that you can finally enjoy better health and wellness.

Some people spend a considerable amount of time working while sitting down. You can be working in an office and spending most of your time doing reports on a computer. But if you want to be healthier, get up and walk more often while at work.

This doesn't mean that you should ignore your role and slack off. Walking more often, even for at least ten minutes at a time, can already help you achieve better health. You can always do a bit more walking when in a meeting, when going to and from work, and by taking the stairs instead of the elevators.

Making those legs work will help you get more exercise no matter how busy your work schedule is. Stop thinking that you have no time to go for a walk or run with your friends. By putting your mind on your goal, you can get more walking even if you already have your hands full at work.

Sitting all day is the new vice of many people. This increases one's risk of diabetes, heart issues and even some cancer. You don't want your mental health to suffer just because you are too lazy to walk while you spend hours at a time working behind a desk.

1. What kind of exercise should you take when investing in good health?

   A. Heavy load of exercise.

   B. Any exercise you think of.

   C. Methods tested and proven.

   D. All suggested on the Internet.

2. What does the underlined part "slack off" in Paragraph 4 mean?

   A. Put something off.

   B. Not take it seriously.

   C. Treat whole-heartedly.

   D. Be cautious specially.

3. What can be inferred from paragraph 5?

   A. There is no excuse for not going in for walking.

   B. Busy work schedule leaves no time for walking.

   C. You should reduce your work time for walking.

   D. Walking can be done after you finish your work.

4. What might be discussed about in the following part of the text?

   A. How we can walk during work.

   B. What else we can do for exercise.

   C. What effects we will get without walking.

   D. Why walking while working is a priority.

Task 3: Have an overview of the "reading forest".

These days, our health and wellness should be a priority. Gone are the days when people take themselves for granted. It is about time that we should start investing in good health. But with all the health and wellness tips found on the Internet, which one should you consider doing?

You may already know the basics of healthy living. But if you want to boost your efforts, it only makes sense that you use strategies tested and proven by scientists. Here's what you can consider investing in so that you can finally enjoy better health and wellness.

Some people spend a considerable amount of time working while sitting down. You can be working in an office and spending most of your time doing reports on a computer. But if you want to be healthier, get up and walk more often while at work.

This doesn't mean that you should ignore your role and slack off. Walking more often, even for at least ten minutes at a time, can already help you achieve better health. You can always do a bit more walking when in a meeting, when going to and from work, and by taking the stairs instead of the elevators.

Making those legs work will help you get more exercise no matter how busy your work schedule is. Stop thinking that you have no time to go for a walk or run with your friends. By putting your mind on your goal, you can get more walking even if you already have your hands full at work.

Sitting all day is the new vice of many people. This increases one's risk of diabetes, heart issues and even some cancer. You don't want your mental health to suffer just because you were too lazy to walk while you spend hours at a time working behind a desk.

Words, phrases and difficult sentences to understand(Translate them into Chinese).

1. priority ________________________ 2. invest ________________________

3. boost ________________________ 4. strategy ________________________

5. considerable ____________________ 6. ignore ________________________

7. mental ________________________ 8. take... for granted ______________

9. make sense ____

10. But if you want to boost your efforts, it only makes sense that you use strategies tested and proven by scientists.

____

11. You don't want your mental health to suffer just because you were too lazy to walk while you spend hours at a time working behind a desk.

____

Task 4: Cultivate your cultural awareness.

The principle of proper maintenance also applies to your body—and taking excellent care of your physical health has a significant positive impact on your financial health as well.

Investing in good health is not difficult. It means making regular visits to doctors and dentists, and following health advice about any problem you encounter. Many medical issues can be helped—or even prevented—with basic lifestyle changes, such as more exercise and a healthier diet.

Poor health maintenance, on the other hand, has both immediate and long-term negative consequences on your financial goals. Some companies have limited sick days, which means a loss of income once paid days are used up. Obesity and other dietary illnesses make insurance premiums skyrocket, and poor health may force early retirement with lower monthly income for the rest of your life.

Unit 4

The Things That You Can't Miss in Macao

Lesson 1 The Things That You Can't Miss in Macao

Task 1: Step into the "reading forest".

Directions: Try to fill in the following blanks according to your imagination.

Macao Tower AJ Hackett Bungee Jump

The Macao Tower, 338 meters tall,the world's 10th __1__ tower, with a variety of activities, such as gambling, eating and entertainment.

One of the acclaimed __2__ is the bungee jump. Raise your arms and off you go! If you are not daring enough to jump that height, you can try the sky walk on the 57th floor — it's still remarkable . Grab this chance and tick off this item on your bucket list.

Grab a traditional Portuguese dinner

Macao was colonized by Portugal before 1999. As a result, Portuguese culture is deeply immersed __3__ many corners of Macao. Many Portuguese settled and opened Portuguese restaurants in the special administrative region, but the flavor is more adaptable to Chinese people.

Enjoy a Portuguese eggtart

One of the must-try local foods in Macao is the Portuguese egg tart. This iconic dessert is different from the __4__ Cantonese egg tart. Among all bakeries selling Portuguese egg tarts, the most popular is Lord Stow's Bakery in Coloane. Gradually, the bakery has become a __5__ tourist spot in Macao.

Visit a museum

Macao, as a tiny little city with only __6__ area of 30.5 square kilometers, has 23 eye-catching museums.

Due to its unique history, both Eastern and Western historical sites can be found. Many of them are preserved for cultural heritages, tourist spots or museums.

Pop into a casino

Well known as the "Las Vegas of the Orient", Macao has 33 casinos. You can find different themed casinos ___7___ their hotels and resorts around every corner of Macao, especially on Taipa Island, where new casinos are continuously opening.

Selfie at the Ruins of St. Paul

The Ruins of St. Paul is the signature landmark of Macao. The ruins consist of the St. Paul's College and the Church of St. Paul, built in1583. ___8___ , after three intense fires in 1595, 1601 and 1835, the church was seriously damaged.

Grab a meal in a small local restaurant

In Macao, tourists will visit luxury restaurants in hotels for famous Portuguese cuisines. As a rcsult, many tempting small local restaurants, ___9___ as "Cha Chaan Teng", are neglected. Trying those restaurants will bring a tasty surprise.

Watch the Macao Grand Prix

The Macao Grand Prix is a major worldwide car-racing event ___10___ annually, featuring over 300 top drivers every year.

Racing through the small streets and roads over this tiny city, the Macao Grand Prix circuit is the only street circuit racing in the world for car and motorcycle events. Thus, it is also well-known as one of the world's most demanding circuits.

Questions:

1. What does the passage mainly talk about?

____

2. What's genre of this passage?

____

3. Which activity is the most dangerous?

____

Task 2: Appreciate "trees" in the "reading forest".

Directions: Answer questions with the choices given, choose the best one.

Macao Tower AJ Hackett Bungee Jump

The Macao Tower, 338 meters tall, is the world's 10th highest tower, with a variety of activities, such as gambling, eating and entertainment.

One of the acclaimed activities is the bungee jump. Raise your arms and off you go! If you are not daring enough to jump that height, you can try the sky walk on the 57th floor — it's still remarkable. Grab this chance and tick off this item on your bucket list.

Grab a traditional Portuguese dinner

Macao was colonized by Portugal before 1999. As a result, Portuguese culture is deeply immersed into many corners of Macao. Many Portuguese settled and opened Portuguese restaurants in the special administrative region, but the flavor is more adaptable to Chinese people.

Enjoy a Portuguese eggtart

One of the must-try local foods in Macao is the Portuguese egg tart.This iconic dessert is different from the traditional Cantonese egg tart. Among all bakeries selling Portuguese egg tarts, the most popular is Lord Stow's Bakery in Coloane. Gradually, the bakery has become a fixed tourist spot in Macao.

Visit a museum

Macao, as a tiny little city with only an area of 30.5 square kilometers, has 23 eye-catching museums.

Due to its unique history, both Eastern and Western historical sites can be found. Many of them are preserved for cultural heritages, tourist spots or museums.

Pop into a casino

Well known as the "Las Vegas of the Orient", Macao has 33 casinos. You can find different themed casinos with their hotels and resorts around every corner of Macao, especially on Taipa Island, where new casinos are continuously opening.

Selfie at the Ruins of St. Paul

The Ruins of St. Paul is the signature landmark of Macao. The ruins consist of the St. Paul's College and the Church of St. Paul, built in 1583. However, after three intense fires in 1595, 1601 and 1835, the church was seriously damaged.

Grab a meal in a small local restaurant

In Macao, tourists will visit luxury restaurants in hotels for famous Portuguese cuisines. As a result, many tempting small local restaurants, known as "Cha Chaan Teng", are neglected. Trying those restaurants will bring a tasty surprise.

Watch the Macao Grand Prix

The Macao Grand Prix is a major worldwide car-racing event held annually, featuring over 300 top drivers every year.

Racing through the small streets and roads over this tiny city, the Macao Grand Prix circuit is the only street circuit racing in the world for car and motorcycle events. Thus, it is also well-known as one of the world's most demanding circuits.

1. What is remarkable of the Macao Tower AJ Hackett Bungee Jump?

A. The sky walk on the 57th floor. B. The bungee jump.

C. The world's highest tower. D. A variety of activities.

2. How many things can't you miss in Macao?

A. Five. B. Six.

C.Seven. D. Eight.

3. Where can you find this passage?

A. In a travel magazine. B. In a newspaper.

C. In a historic book. D. A poster for travel.

Task 3: Have an overview of the "reading forest".

Macao Tower AJ Hackett Bungee Jump

The Macao Tower, 338 meters tall, is the world's 10th highest tower, with a variety of activities, such as gambling, eating and entertainment.

One of the acclaimed activities is the bungee jump. Raise your arms and off you go! If you are not daring enough to jump that height, you can try the sky walk on the 57th floor —it's still remarkable. Grab this chance and tick off this item on your bucket list.

Grab a traditional Portuguese dinner

Macao was colonized by Portugal before 1999. As a result, Portuguese culture is deeply immersed into many corners of Macao. Many Portuguese settled and opened Portuguese restaurants in the special administrative region, but the flavor is more adaptable to Chinese people.

Enjoy a Portuguese egg tart

One of the must-try local foods in Macao is the Portuguese egg tart.This iconic dessert is different from the traditional Cantonese egg tart. Among all bakeries selling Portuguese eggtarts, the most popular is Lord Stow's Bakery in Coloane. Gradually, the bakery has become a fixed tourist spot in Macao.

Visit a museum

Macao, as a tiny little city with only an area of 30.5 square kilometers, has 23 eye-catching museums.

Due to its unique history, both Eastern and Western historical sites can be found. Many of them are preserved for cultural heritages, tourist spots or museums.

Pop into a casino

Well known as the "Las Vegas of the Orient", Macao has 33 casinos. You can find different themed casinos with their hotels and resorts around every corner of Macao, especially on Taipa Island, where new casinos are continuously opening.

Selfie at the Ruins of St. Paul

The Ruins of St. Paul is the signature landmark of Macao. The ruins consist of the St. Paul's College and the Church of St. Paul, built in 1583. However, after three intense fires in 1595, 1601 and 1835, the church was seriously damaged.

Grab a meal in a small local restaurant

In Macao, tourists will visit luxury restaurants in hotels for famous Portuguese cuisines. As a result, many tempting small local restaurants, known as "Cha Chaan Teng", are neglected. Trying those restaurants will bring a tasty surprise.

Watch the Macao Grand Prix

The Macao Grand Prix is a major worldwide car-racing event held annually, featuring over 300 top drivers every year.

Racing through the small streets and roads over this tiny city, the Macao Grand Prix circuit is the only street circuit racing in the world for car and motorcycle events. Thus, it is also well-known as one of the world's most demanding circuits.

Words, phrases and difficult sentences to understand (Translate them into Chinese).

1. acclaimed ________________ 2. daring ________________

3. immersed ________________ 4. administrative ________________

5. adaptable ________________ 6. spot ________________

7. be preserved for ________________ 8. themed casinos ________________

9. continuously ________________ 10. tick off ________________

11. Many of them are preserved for cultural heritage, tourist spots or museums.

____

12. the Macao Grand Prix circuit is the only street circuit racing in the world for car and motor cycle events.

____

Task 4: Cultivate your cultural awareness.

Small as the sparrow is, it possesses all its internal organs. So, when you visit Macao, you shouldn't miss those things: visiting a museum, a casino, the Ruins of St. Paul, watching the Macao Grand Prix, eating in a small local restaurant, enjoying a Portuguese egg tart... There are so many interesting things you can do in Macao, but do you know Macao? Its origin name is Ao, the Macao Special Administration Region (SAR). Macao is historically Chinese territory and the ancestors of the Chinese people started to live in Macao as early as the New Stone Age. Located in southern China, on the west bank of the Pearl River Delta. Macao is an international free port and a world tourism and leisure center, which has the highest population density in the world. It is also one of the four biggest casinos in the world which implements the capitalist system. The famous light industry, tourism, hotels and casinos make Macao prosperous. All those causations make Macao become one of the most developed and richest regions in the world.

Lesson 2 Making a Difference

Task 1: Step into the "reading forest".

Directions: Try to fill in the following blanks according to your imagination.

A man was __1__ along the beach when he suddenly __2__ from afar what he thought were children __3__. "What on earth are they doing dancing on the beach? " He quickly paced towards them. He was surprised that a boy and a girl were not dancing but picking up the starfish, which were washed ashore by the __4__ ,and throwing them back into the sea. "Excuse me, why are you throwing them back into the sea?" he asked.The children __5__ the remark but they continued picking up the starfish and kept throwing them back into the sea. "Don't you think it is a __6__ of your time as there are hundreds of starfish still lying around? Surely you can't keep this act all day long."

At last the elder boy __7__, "Sir, you see the sun will soon rise and the tide will ebb away.Though my sister and I can't throw all the starfish back into the sea,we are sure it __8__ to the ones we succeed __9__ throwing. Would you like to join us? It would make a __10__." The man smiled and said, "It certainly would," so he also picked up the starfish and threw them into the sea.

Questions:

1. What is the topic of this passage?

____

2. What are the key words that help you understand the passage better?

____

3. Do you think it is a waste of time to help those starfish in this passage?

____

Task 2: Appreciate "trees" in the "reading forest".

Directions: Read the following passage, according to the sentence structure . grammar and context coherence requirements, fill in the blanks with an appropriate word or words used in parentheses in the blanks with the correct form.

A man was strolling along the beach when he suddenly noticed from afar __1__ he thought were children dancing. "What on earth are they doing dancing on the beach?" He quickly paced towards them. He was surprised that a boy and a girl were not dancing but __2__ (pick) up the starfish, __3__ were washed ashore __4__ the tide, and throwing them back into the sea."Excuse me,why are you throwing them back into the sea?"he asked.The children ignored the remark but they continued picking up the starfish and kept throwing them back into the sea. "Don't you think it is a waste of __5__ (you) time as there are hundreds of starfish still __6__ (lie) around? Surely you can't keep this act all day long."

At last the elder boy __7__ (reply),"Sir, you see the sun will soon rise and the tide will ebb away. Though my sister and I can't throw all the starfish back into the sea, we are sure it __8__ (matter) to the ones we succeed __9__ throwing.Would you like to join us? It would make a __10__ (different)."The man smiled and said, "It certainly would," so he too picked up the starfish and threw them into the sea.

Task 3: Have an overview of the "reading forest".

A man was strolling along the beach when he suddenly noticed from afar what he thought were children dancing. "What on earth are they doing dancing on the beach?" He quickly paced towards them. He was surprised that a boy and a girl were not dancing but picking up the starfish, which were washed ashore by the tide, and throwing them back into the sea. "Excuse me, why are you throwing them back into the sea?" he asked. The children ignored the remark, continued picking up the starfish and kept throwing them back into the sea. "Don't you think it is a waste of your time as there are hundreds of starfish still lying around? Surely you can't keep this act all day long."

At last the elder boy replied, "Sir, you see the sun will soon rise and the tide will ebb away. Though my sister and I can't throw all the starfish back into the sea, we are sure it matters to the ones we succeed in throwing. Would you like to join us? It would make a difference." The man smiled and said, "It certainly would," so he too picked up the starfish and threw them into the sea.

Words, phrases and difficult sentences to understand (Translate them into Chinese).

1. stroll ____________ 2. on earth ____________

3. wash ashore ____________ 4. starfish ____________

5. ignore the remark ____________ 6. make a difference ____________

7. Sir, you see the sun will soon rise and the tide will ebb away. Though my sister and I can't throw all the starfishes back into the sea, we are sure it matters to the ones we succeed in throwing.

____

Task 4: Cultivate your cultural awareness.

According to the British "Daily Mail" reported on March 4, British wild life enthusiast Lara Maiklem captured a scene of dead invertebrates on the beach, and tens of thousands of starfish were washed up onto the beach in Lansgate, Kent, a shocking and thought-provoking scene. 47-year-old McLeam and her 5-year-old twins Edie and Beau went to the beach together to see this thrilling scene. She said: "This is simply the end of the world." "It's a natural phenomenon; one day you will find crabs that die, and then it may be starfish or jellyfish and so on."People were surprised by the discovery, but also sadder about this phenomenon. After she uploaded the photos to Facebook, they attracted a lot of attention, and many people commented that this phenomenon could happen elsewhere. So it is urgent that we should take measures to help those marine organisms.

Lesson 3 Seeing the Truth

Task 1: Step into the "reading forest".

Directions: Try to fill in the following blanks according to your imagination.

While the rain was __1__ on the roof, I waited for the train in the station. The __2__ room was full of passengers filled with weariness and boredom.

Suddenly, a short old man with ragged clothes and faded pants appeared in the corner of my view, peering at one person after another in bewilderment, as if __3__ something. The closer I looked at him, the __4__ sympathetic I felt. Besides his ragged clothes, he had nothing, not even a bag for __5__."Poor man. It must be the first time he came to the train station," I guessed.

I couldn't help thinking of my grandpa. If he had been the man, how much I had hoped someone would help him! A feeling of __6__ awoke in my body. Why couldn't I tell him the direction of the __7__ ?

So, I told him. And he repeated the same words, "Thank you, nice guy." The strange thing was, the man didn't move a step, but stood in the same place, glancing at the people around him every now and then. The rainy __8__ became dimmer. Anxiety stormed into my mind. Did I __9__ him? Perhaps he had already got his ticket? Looking at his empty hands, and then at the sandwiches the person beside him was eating, I suddenly got him. "He must be __10__." I said to myself. As soon as possible I fished out a bag of bread from my backpack, __11__ it to the poor man.

At the moment, two policemen suddenly dashed toward the man. __12__ filled my heart just like a blossoming flower. "What did the poor man do wrong?" I asked the police.

"Sir, please don't hinder our job. This man has hung around different __13__ and survived by __14__." I used to believe the phrase" __15__ given, fragrance in hand", and that giving help to others will bring __16__ . But from that day on, I realized that is not always true, and we can never __17__ a book purely by its cover; that's the real __18__ for me.

Questions:

1. What does the passage mainly talk about?

____

2. What are the key words that help you understand the passage better?

____

3. What's the structure of the passage?

____

Task 2: Appreciate "trees" in the "reading forest".

Directions: For each blank in the following passage there are four words or phrases marked A, B, C and D. Fill in each blank with the word or phrase that best fits the context.

While the rain was __1__ on the roof, I waited for the train in the station. The __2__ room was full of passengers filled with weariness and boredom.

Suddenly, a short old man with __3__ clothes and faded pants appeared in the corner of my view, peering at one person after another in bewilderment, as if __4__ something. The closer I looked at him, the __5__ sympathetic I felt. Besides his ragged clothes, he had nothing, not even a bag for __6__. "Poor man. It must be the first time he came to the train station," I guessed.

I couldn't help thinking of my grandpa. If he had been the man, how much I had hoped someone would help him! A feeling of __7__ awoke in my body. Why couldn't I tell him the direction of the __8__ ?

So, I told him. And he repeated the same words, "Thank you, nice guy." The strange thing was, the man didn't move a step, but __9__ in the same place, glancing at the people around him every now and then. The rainy __10__ became dimmer.

Anxiety stormed into my mind. Did I __11__ him? Perhaps he had already got his ticket? Looking at his empty hands, and then at the sandwiches the person beside him was eating, I suddenly got him. "He must be __12__." I said to myself. As soon as possible I fished out a bag of bread from my backpack, __13__ it to the poor man.

At the moment, two policemen suddenly dashed toward the man. __14__ filled my heart just like a blossoming flower. "What did the poor man do wrong?" I asked the police.

"Sir, please don't hinder our job. This man has hung around different __15__ and survived by __16__." I used to believe the phrase" __17__ given, fragrance in hand", and that giving help to others will bring __18__. But from that day on, I realized that is not always true, and we can never __19__ a book purely by its cover; that's the real __20__ for me.

1. A. falling	B. pounding	C. beating	D. hitting
2. A. waiting	B. watching	C. listening	D. feeling
3. A. delicate	B. plain	C. ragged	D. beautiful
4. A. refusing	B. seeking	C. stopping	D. needing
5. A. better	B. less	C. more	D. fewer
6. A. cloth	B. shoes	C. pants	D. necessities
7. A. guilty	B. compassion	C. honor	D. belonging
8. A. reception	B. office	C. bathroom	D. home
9. A. stood	B. si	C. wait	D. look
10. A. sky	B. cloud	C. wind	D. twilight
11. A. interrupt	B. misunderstand	C. miss	D. direct
12. A. homeless	B. unhappy	C. hungry	D. funny
13. A. handing	B. throwing	C. picking	D. speaking
14. A. Sorrow	B. Happiness	C. Curiosity	D. Amazement
15. A. homes	B. restaurants	C. hotels	D. stations
16. A. stealing	B. lying	C. glancing	D. repeating
17. A. Bread	B. Water	C. Milk	D. Roses
18. A. harm	B. satisfaction	C. difference	D. beauty

19. A. see B. read C. buy D. judge

20. A. pleasure B. result C. profoundness D. meaning

Task 3: Have an overview of the "reading forest".

While the rain was pounding on the roof, I waited for the train in the station. The waiting room was full of passengers filled with weariness and boredom.

Suddenly, a short old man with ragged clothes and faded pants appeared in the corner of my view, peering at one person after another in bewilderment, as if seeking something. The closer I looked at him, the more sympathetic I felt. Besides his ragged clothes, he had nothing, not even a bag for necessities. "Poor man. It must be the first time he came to the train station," I guessed.

I couldn't help thinking of my grandpa. If he had been the man, how much I had hoped someone would help him! A feeling of compassion awoke in my body. Why couldn't I tell him the direction of the reception?

So, I told him. And he repeated the same words, "Thank you, nice guy."The strange thing was, the man didn't move a step, but stood in the same place, glancing at the people around him every now and then. The rainy twilight became dimmer. Anxiety stormed into my mind. Did I misunderstand him? Perhaps he had already got his ticket? Looking at his empty hands, and then at the sandwiches the person beside him was eating, I suddenly got him. "He must be hungry." I said to myself. As soon as possible I fished out a bag of bread from my backpack, handing it to the poor man.

At the moment, two policemen suddenly dashed toward the man. Happiness filled my heart just like a blossoming flower. "What did the poor man do wrong?" I asked the police.

"Sir, please don't hinder our job. This man has hung around different stations and survived by stealing." I used to believe the phrase "Roses given, fragrance in hand", and that giving help to others will bring satisfaction. But from that day on, I realized that is not always true, and we can never judge a book purely by its cover; that's the real profoundness for me.

Words, phrases and difficult sentences to understand (Translate them into Chinese).

1. weariness and boredom ______________________
2. faded pants ______________________
3. every now and then ______________________
4. The rainy twilight became dimmer. Anxiety stormed into my mind.

____

5. Roses given, fragrance in hand.

____

Task 4: Cultivate your cultural awareness.

Look deep into nature, and then you will understand everything better. As the old Chinese saying goes, "What you hear about may be false, but what you see is true." We often easily believe in what we see without a shadow of doubt, but as a matter of fact, it is not always so convincing.

Most of you must have the experience that the more distant an object is, the smaller it looks like. The size of it in our eyes seems to be changeable, but nothing really changes. If you put a chopstick into the water, it looks as if it were broken. If you walk in the desert for a long time, you may witness the mirage of the oasis. You can intuitively see these phenomena with the awareness that they are not real. That is to say, you are likely to be taken in by your own eyes and what you see.

What we see at first sight may not be true, since the truth can be covered up. A criminal can arrange the crime scene to make the murder look like suicide. An entrepreneur can create the false prosperity of the market to conceal the potential economic crisis. Even an ordinary person can draw support from the technology of Photoshop to hide his original appearance. Therefore, it is not enough to merely scratch the visible surface and the most crucial step is to expose the essence. For example, the apple falling onto the ground is the surface, and the gravity is the essence. The bubbles shining in the sun is the surface, while the refraction of the sunshine is the essence. And the connection between the surface and the essence is what we should search for from merely seeing.

Lesson 4　Misophonia

Task 1: Step into the "reading forest".

Directions: Answer the following questions according to the passage.

There are some sounds most of us acknowledge are irritating — the crunching of crisps, the humming of the air conditioning or a screaming baby. These noises, for many people, act as a mere inconvenience that can distract us from the task at hand. However, there are some amongst us who have a much more severe response to these noises. The question we ask today is: has a noise ever made you feel so angry that you could explode with rage? If the answer is yes, you may be suffering from misophonia.

The word "misophonia" literally means "a hatred of sound" and is sometimes called Selective Sound Sensitivity Syndrome. There are some experts who doubt the existence of the condition. However, for those who claim to suffer from it, the experience can be traumatic. Certain sounds trigger intense emotional or psychological responses that may seem over the top compared with a non-sufferer's complaints.

So, the next time you see someone fly into a rage because of a sound that is driving them crazy, it may be due to a difficult condition they are trying to manage, and not just because they loathe a certain sound.

Questions:

1. What kind of people may suffer from misophonia?

____

2. What does misophonia mean literally?

____

Task 2: Appreciate "trees" in the "reading forest".

Direction: Fill in the blanks with the right forms of the given words.

There are some sounds most of us acknowledge __1__ (irritate)—the crunching of crisps, the humming of the air conditioning __2__ a screaming baby. These noises, for many people, act __3__ a mere inconvenience __4__ can distract us from the task __5__ hand. However, there are some amongst us who have a much more severe response to these noises. The question we ask today is: has a noise ever made you feel __6__ angry that you could explode with rage? If the answer is yes, you may __7__ (suffer) from misophonia.

The word "misophonia" __8__ (literal) means"a hatred of sound" and is sometimes called Selective Sound Sensitivity Syndrome.There are some experts who doubt the __9__ (exist) of the condition. However, for those who claim to suffer from it, the experience can be traumatic. Certain sounds trigger intense emotional or psychological responses that may seem over the top __10__ (compare) with a non-sufferer's complaints.

Task 3: Have an overview of the "reading forest".

Some difficult sentences to understand.

1. These noises, for many people, act as a mere inconvenience that can distract us from the task at hand.

____

2. However, there are some amongst us who have a much more severe response to these noises.

____

Task 4: Cultivate your cultural awareness.

Although most of us will not feel annoyed with most common sounds, some people are sensitive to some "common" sounds. For these people, some simple sounds can make them go crazy. They are misophonia.

From the passage, we know that certain sounds can trigger their intense emotional or psychological responses. If we can find the kinds of the sounds and avoid them, these people may feel better. On the other side, sometimes, the sounds are not the only causes which drive them crazy. From the passage, we can also know maybe there are some other things making them not feel so good, such as difficult problems, annoying conditions and so on.

So next time you find someone feel so angry due to the sound, you should consider maybe he is dealing with some trouble by himself and give him a hand to help him out. At the same time, if you have this kind of situation, you can find what is annoying you and kill it at the beginning. Having a healthy mind can benefit us a lot.

Unit 5

RV Travel of Friendly Budget

Lesson 1 RV Travel of Friendly Budget

Task 1: Step into the "reading forest".

Directions：Try to fill in the following blanks according to your imagination.

Travel of any kind can be expensive. Experienced RV（房车）travelers already know that there are savings to be found in traveling in an RV as opposed to flying and staying in hotels. __1__. There are a few ways to make these travels even more budget friendly.

Research

Start by spending some time researching RV sites and campgrounds. __2__. You can use the RV park finder and directory here on camping.com. In addition, you can read about the site, learn about the options, and even read guest reviews.

Cook your own food

Another great option you have when RV traveling is having your own kitchen. __3__. Of course you can still enjoy eating out at local restaurants, but you can be much more budget friendly by reserving eating out as a special occasion. Not only do you save money by cooking your own meals you can also take the opportunity to enjoy local flavor by seeking out a farmer's market.

__4__

Try enjoying activities that have little or no cost. Many recreational activities that allow you to explore your destination are also free. Many other activities sometimes do have a minimal cost, but often you can find days when the entrance fees and costs are discounted.

Have fun

With a little research it is easy to find free and low cost activities wherever you go. 5

However, often you will find that you enjoy some fantastic activities that you may not have tried otherwise.

Task 2: Appreciate "trees" in the "reading forest".

Directions: For each blank in the following passage there are sentences marked A, B, C, D, F or G. Fill in each blank with the word or phrase that best fits the context.

Travel of any kind can be expensive. Experienced RV travelers already know that there are savings to be found in traveling in an RV as opposed to flying and staying in hotels. ___1___. There are a few ways to make these travels even more budget friendly.

Research

Start by spending some time researching RV sites and campgrounds. ___2___. You can use the RV park finder and directory here on camping.com. In addition, you can read about the site, learn about the options, and even read guest reviews.

Cook your own food

Another great option you have when RV traveling is having your own kitchen. ___3___. Of course you can still enjoy eating out at local restaurants, but you can be much more budget friendly by reserving eating out as a special occasion. Not only do you save money by cooking your own meals you can also take the opportunity to enjoy local flavor by seeking out a farmer's market.

___4___

Try enjoying actives that have little or no cost. Many recreational activities that allow you to explore your destination are also free. Many other activities sometimes do have a minimal cost, but often you can find days when the entrance fees and costs are discounted.

Have fun

With a little research it is easy to find free and low cost activities wherever you go. ___5___.

However, often you will find that you enjoy some fantastic activities that you may not have tried otherwise.

A. Low cost or free activities

B. Free admission and cheap exploration

C. There are many options for budget camping

D. Budget travel might take a little more effort

E. Few travellers find it convenient to achieve it

F. However, traveling in an RV is still an expensive option

G. One of the biggest expenses is eating out for every meal

Task 3: Have an overview of the “reading forest”.

Travel of any kind can be expensive. Experienced RV travelers already know that there are savings to be found in traveling in an RV as opposed to flying and staying in hotels. However, traveling in an RV is still an expensive option. There are a few ways to make these travels even more budget friendly.

Research

Start by spending some time researching RV sites and campgrounds. There are many options for budget camping. You can use the RV park finder and directory here on camping.com. In addition, you can read about the site, learn about the options, and even read guest reviews.

Cook your own food

Another great option you have when RV traveling is having your own kitchen. One of the biggest expenses is eating out for every meal. Of course you can still enjoy eating out at local restaurants, but you can be much more budget friendly by reserving eating out as a special occasion. Not only do you save money by cooking your own meals you can also take the opportunity to enjoy local flavor by seeking out a farmer’s market.

Low cost or free activities

Try enjoying actives that have little or no cost. Many recreational activities that allow you to explore your destination are also free. Many other activities sometimes do have a minimal cost, but often you can find days when the entrance fees and costs are discounted.

Have fun

With a little research it is easy to find free and low cost activities wherever you go. Budget travel might take a little more effort.

However, often you will find that you enjoy some fantastic activities that you may not have tried otherwise.

Words, phrases and difficult sentences to understand (Translate them into Chinese).

1. experienced ____________ 2. oppose ____________
3. option ____________ 4. budget friendly ____________
5. campground ____________ 6. guest review ____________
7. eat out ____________ 8. local flavor ____________
9. seek out ____________ 10. recreational activities ____________
11. explore your destination ____________ 12. discount ____________
13. budget travel ____________ 14. fantastic ____________
15. Not only do you save money by cooking your own meals you can also take the opportunity to enjoy local flavor by seeking out a farmer's market.

____

Lesson 2　A Lady in a Faded Dress

Task 1: Step into the "reading forest".

Directions：Try to fill in the following blanks according to your imagination.

A lady in a faded dress and her husband walked timidly into the president's outer office. The secretary could tell that they had no ___1___ at Harvard .

For hours, the secretary ___2___ them, hoping that the couple would finally become discouraged and go away. They didn't. And the secretary grew frustrated and ___3___ decided to disturb the president. The president ___4___ in annoyance and nodded.

The lady told the president, "We had a son that attended Harvard for one year. But he was accidentally ___5___. And my husband and I would like to build a memorial to him." The president was shocked and said ___6___, "We can't put ___7___ a statue for every person who attended Harvard and died. If we did, this place would look like a cemetery."

"Oh, no," the lady explained quickly, "We'd like to give a ___8___. " The president ___9___ his eyes. He glanced at the couple, then ___10___ ,"A building! Do you have any earthly idea how much a building ___11___ ? We have over seven and a half million dollars in the physical plant at Harvard."

For a moment the lady was ___12___. The president was pleased. He could ___13___ them now. The lady turned to her husband and said ___14___, "Is that all it costs to start a university? Why don't we just start our own?" Her husband nodded. The couple ___15___ and established a university that bears their name, a memorial to a son that Harvard no longer ___16___ !

Task 2: Appreciate "trees" in the "reading forest".

Directions: For each blank in the following passage there are four words or phrases marked A, B, C and D. Fill in each blank with the word or phrase that best fits the context.

A lady in a faded dress and her husband walked timidly into the president's outer office. The secretary could tell that they had no __1__ at Harvard .

For hours, the secretary __2__ them, hoping that the couple would finally become __3__ and go away. They didn't. And the secretary grew frustrated and __4__ decided to disturb the president. The president __5__ in annoyance and nodded.

The lady told the president, "We had a son that attended Harvard for one year. But he was accidentally __6__. And my husband and I would like to build a memorial to him." The president was shocked and said __7__, "We can't put __8__ a statue for every person who attended Harvard and died. If we did, this place would look like a __9__."

"Oh, no," the lady explained quickly, "We'd like to give a __10__." The president __11__ his eyes. He glanced at the couple, then __12__, "A building! Do you have any earthly idea how much a building __13__? We have over seven and a half million dollars in the __14__ plant at Harvard."

For a moment the lady was __15__. The president was pleased. He could __16__ them now. The lady turned to her husband and said __17__, "Is that all it costs to start a university? Why don't we just start our own?" Her husband nodded. The couple __18__ and established a __19__ that bears their name, a memorial to a son that Harvard no longer __20__!

1. A. difficulty	B. relative	C. money	D. business
2. A. admired	B. criticized	C. controlled	D. ignored
3. A. excited	B. discouraged	C. angry	D. sad
4. A. finally	B. gradually	C. slowly	D. suddenly
5. A. shouted	B. smiled	C. sighed	D. quarrelled
6. A. injured	B. killed	C. dismissed	D. employed
7. A. impatiently	B. delightedly	C. surprisingly	D. certainly

8. A. apart	B. down	C. up	D. away
9. A. cemetery	B. square	C. school	D. church
10. A. present	B. figure	C. note	D. building
11. A. closed	B. rolled	C. wiped	D. dropped
12. A. exclaimed	B. announced	C. argued	D. questioned
13. A. weights	B. covers	C. accommodates	D. costs
14. A. mental	B. physical	C. entire	D. significant
15. A. silent	B. happy	C. upset	D. sad
16. A. laugh at	B. catch up with	C. chat with	D. get rid of
17. A. doubtedly	B. quietly	C. nervously	D. rudely
18. A. walked away	B. begged off	C. worked hard	D. paid off
19. A. committee	B. company	C. university	D. family
20. A. looked for	B. heard of	C. cared about	D. admitted to

Task 3: Have an overview of the "reading forest".

A lady in a faded dress and her husband walked timidly into the president's outer office. The secretary could tell that they had no business at Harvard .

For hours, the secretary ignored them, hoping that the couple would finally become discouraged and go away. They didn't. And the secretary grew frustrated and finally decided to disturb the president. The president sighed in annoyance and nodded.

The lady told the president, "We had a son that attended Harvard for one year. But he was accidentally killed. And my husband and I would like to build a memorial to him." The president was shocked and said impatiently, "We can't put up a statue for every person who attended Harvard and died. If we did, this place would look like a cemetery."

"Oh, no," the lady explained quickly, "We'd like to give a building." The president rolled his eyes. He glanced at the couple, then exclaimed, "A building! Do you have any earthly idea how much a building costs? We have over seven and a half million dollars in the physical plant at Harvard."

For a moment the lady was silent. The president was pleased. He could get rid of them now. The lady turned to her husband and said quietly, "Is that all it costs to start a university? Why don't we just start our own?" Her husband nodded. The couple walked away and established a university that bears their name, a memorial to a son that Harvard no longer cared about!

Words, phrases and difficult sentences to understand (Translate them into Chinese).

1. faded ____________________ 2. timidly ____________________

3. ignore ____________________ 4. frustrated ____________________

5. put up a statue ____________ 6. exclaim ____________________

7. earthly ____________________ 8. the physical plant ____________

9. get rid of _________________ 10. establish __________________

11. The couple walked away and established a university that bears their name, a memorial to a son that Harvard no longer cared about!

____

Task 4: Cultivate your cultural awareness.

This passage is to tell us an anecdote about the establishment of Stanford University. The Stanfords wanted to build a memorial to their son who died accidentally but was ignored by the president of Harvard University and his secretary. Having known the cost to start a university, they established the Stanford University themselves. It tells us that we can't evaluate a person on the basis of physical appearance.

Lesson 3 The First Halloween Celebrations

Task 1: Step into the "reading forest".

Directions: Read the passage and draw a mind map.

In America, the first Halloween celebrations were a way to mark the end-of-year harvest season, and the food that was served mainly consisted of homemade seasonal treats like caramel apples and mixed nuts. There were no soul cakes—or candies, for that matter—to be found.

It wasn't until the 1950s that trick-or-treating gained popularity in the US. Following the Great Depression and World War II, the suburbs were booming, and people were looking for excuses to have fun and get to know their neighbors. The old practice of souling was resurrected and made into an excuse for kids to dress up in costumes and roam their neighborhoods. Common trick-or-treat offerings included nuts, coins, and homemade baked goods. That changed when the candy companies got their hands on the holiday. They had already convinced consumers that they needed candy on Christmas and Easter, and they were looking for an equally lucrative opportunity to market candies in the fall. The new practice of trick-or-treating was almost too good to be true. Manufacturers downsized candies into smaller, bite-sized packages and began marketing them as treats for Halloween. Adults were grateful to have a convenient alternative to baking, kids loved the sweet treats, and the candy companies made billions.

Today, it's hard to imagine Halloween without skittles, chocolate bars, and the perennial candy corn debates. But when you're digging through a bag or bowl of Halloween candy this October, remember that you could have been having eating soul cakes instead.

Task 2: Appreciate "trees" in the "reading forest".

Directions: Read the passage and answer the questions below·.

In America, the first Halloween celebrations were a way to mark the end-of-year harvest season, and the food that was served mainly consisted of homemade seasonal treats like caramel apples and mixed nuts. There were no soul cakes—or candies, for that matter—to be found.

It wasn't until the 1950s that trick-or-treating gained popularity in the US. Following the Great Depression and World War II, the suburbs were booming, and people were looking for excuses to have fun and get to know their neighbors. The old practice of souling was resurrected and made into an excuse for kids to dress up in costumes and roam their neighborhoods. Common trick-or-treat offerings included nuts, coins, and homemade baked goods. That changed when the candy companies got their hands on the holiday. They had already convinced consumers that they needed candy on Christmas and Easter, and they were looking for an equally lucrative opportunity to market candies in the fall. The new practice of trick-or-treating was almost too good to be true. Manufacturers downsized candies into smaller, bite-sized packages and began marketing them as treats for Halloween. Adults were grateful to have a convenient alternative to baking, kids loved the sweet treats, and the candy companies made billions.

Today, it's hard to imagine Halloween without skittles, chocolate bars, and the perennial candy corn debates. But when you're digging through a bag or bowl of Halloween candy this October, remember that you could have been having eating soul cakes instead.

1. What were the Halloween food at first in America?

A. Candies.

B. Coins.

C. Soul cakes.

D. Mixed nuts.

2. What does the underlined word mean in Paragraph 2?

A. Start.

B. Survive.

C. Bring back.

D. Give up.

3. Why were the candies made into smaller packages?

A. Because kids loved such kind of sweet.

B. Because companies made a lot of money.

C. Because adults didn't like to bake cakes for kids.

D. Because companies made it for Halloween treats.

4. What is the best title for the passage?

A. Candies in America.

B. Halloween in America.

C. Candies and Halloween.

D. Americans and Halloween.

Task 3: Have an overview of the "reading forest".

In America, the first Halloween celebrations were a way to mark the end-of-year harvest season, and the food that was served mainly consisted of homemade seasonal treats like caramel apples and mixed nuts. There were no soul cakes—or candies, for that matter—to be found.

It wasn't until the 1950s that trick-or-treating gained popularity in the US. Following the Great Depression and World War II, the suburbs were booming, and people were looking for excuses to have fun and get to know their neighbors. The old practice of souling was resurrected and made into an excuse for kids to dress up in costumes and roam their neighborhoods. Common trick-or-treat offerings included nuts, coins, and homemade baked goods. That changed when the candy companies got their hands on the holiday. They had already convinced consumers that they needed candy on Christmas and Easter, and they were looking for an equally lucrative opportunity to market candies in the fall. The new practice of trick-or-treating was almost too good to be true. Manufacturers downsized candies into smaller, bite-sized packages and began marketing them as treats for Halloween. Adults were grateful to have a convenient alternative to baking, kids loved the sweet treats, and the candy companies made billions.

Today, it's hard to imagine Halloween without skittles, chocolate bars, and the perennial candy corn debates. But when you're digging through a bag or bowl of Halloween candy this October, remember that you could have been having eating soul cakes instead.

Words, phrases and difficult sentences to understand (Translate them into Chinese).

1. harvest season ________________ 2. consist of ________________

3. seasonal ________________ 4. the old practice ________________

5. trick-or-treat ________________ 6. manufacturer ________________

7. grateful ________________ 8. alternative ________________

9. It wasn't until the 1950s that trick-or-treating gained popularity in the US.

____

10.Following the Great Depression and World War II, the suburbs were booming, and people were looking for excuses to have fun and get to know their neighbors.

____

11. Manufacturers downsized candies into smaller, bite-sized packages and began marketing them as treats for Halloween.

____

Task 4: Cultivate your cultural awareness.

What have you learned from the passage?

Lesson 4 Is Tree Planting an Effective Means of Curbing Climate Change?

Task 1: Step into the "reading forest".

Directions: Read the passage and draw a mind map.

Tree planting used to be regarded as an effective means of curbing (抑制) climate change. Perhaps it's time for us to rethink this practice. Trees pull carbon dioxide or CO_2 from the air. This effectively removes CO_2 from the atmosphere, making trees an important part of the fight against climate change. But trees only hold onto carbon dioxide as long as they're alive. Once they die, trees decay (腐烂) and release CO_2 back into the atmosphere.

Recent studies have found that trees around the world are growing faster than ever. Rising atmospheric CO_2 is probably driving that rapid growth, said Roel Brienen. High levels of this gas are boosting temperatures, which in turn speeds tree growth in those areas, he added.

The faster trees grow, the faster they store carbon. It seems like good news. However, it is known that fast-growing tree species, in general, live shorter lives than their slow-growing relatives.

In order to see whether the growth-lifespan trade-off is a universal phenomenon, Brienen and his colleagues analyzed over 210,000 individual tree ring records of 110 tree species from more than 70,000 sites worldwide. "By measuring tree rings' widths one can tell how fast trees grew, while counting rings provides information on tree ages and allows making inferences (推断) about trees' maximum lifespan." Brienen explained.

The team also created a computer program that modeled a forest. Early on, it showed that "the forest could hold more carbon as the trees grew faster", Brienen reported. But after 20 years, these trees started dying and losing this extra carbon again. "We must understand that the only solution to bring down CO_2 levels is to stop emitting（排放）it into the atmosphere," said Brienen.

Task 2: Appreciate "trees" in the "reading forest".

Directions: Read the passage and answer the questions below.

Tree planting used to be regarded as an effective means of curbing climate change. Perhaps it's time for us to rethink this practice. Trees pull carbon dioxide or CO_2 from the air. This effectively removes CO_2 from the atmosphere, making trees an important part of the fight against climate change. But trees only hold onto carbon dioxide as long as they're alive. Once they die, trees decay and release CO_2 back into the atmosphere.

Recent studies have found that trees around the world are growing faster than ever. Rising atmospheric CO_2 is probably driving that rapid growth, said Roel Brienen. High levels of this gas are boosting temperatures, which in turn speeds tree growth in those areas, he added.

The faster trees grow, the faster they store carbon. It seems like good news. However, it is known that fast-growing tree species, in general, live shorter lives than their slow-growing relatives.

In order to see whether the growth-lifespan trade-off is a universal phenomenon, Brienen and his colleagues analyzed over 210,000 individual tree ring records of 110 tree species from more than 70,000 sites worldwide. "By measuring tree rings' widths one can tell how fast trees grew, while counting rings provides information on tree ages and allows making inferences about trees' maximum lifespan." Brienen explained.

The team also created a computer program that modeled a forest. Early on, it showed that "the forest could hold more carbon as the trees grew faster", Brienen reported. But after 20 years, these trees started dying and losing this extra carbon again. "We must understand that the only solution to bring down CO_2 levels is to stop emitting it into the atmosphere," said Brienen.

1. What can we learn from the passage?

A. Climate change is affecting trees' lifespan.

B. Trees planting isn't a reliable solution to global warming.

C. Studies found that trees which die sooner release more CO_2.

D. Scientists are working on whether forests can hold more carbon.

2. Why are trees growing faster?

A. The lifespan of certain species.

B. The number of surrounding trees.

C. The increase of atmospheric CO_2.

D. The decrease of environmental temperature.

3. Which of following statement is TRUE?

A. The faster trees grow, the older they are.

B. The faster trees grow, the younger the die.

C. The faster trees grow, the stronger they become.

D. The faster trees grow, the more they store carbon.

4. What can we know by measuring tree rings' widths?

A. The trees' age.

B. The trees' health.

C. The trees' growth speed.

D. The trees' maximum lifespan.

Task 3: Have an overview of the "reading forest".

Tree planting used to be regarded as an effective means of curbing climate change. Perhaps it's time for us to rethink this practice. Trees pull carbon dioxide or CO_2 from the air. This effectively removes CO_2 from the atmosphere, making trees an important part of the fight against climate change. But trees only hold onto carbon dioxide as long as they're alive. Once they die, trees decay and release CO_2 back into the atmosphere.

Recent studies have found that trees around the world are growing faster than ever. Rising atmospheric CO_2 is probably driving that rapid growth, said Roel Brienen. High levels of this gas are boosting temperatures, which in turn speeds tree growth in those areas, he added.

The faster trees grow, the faster they store carbon. It seems like good news. However, it is known that fast-growing tree species, in general, live shorter lives than their slow-growing relatives.

In order to see whether the growth-lifespan trade-off is a universal phenomenon, Brienen and his colleagues analyzed over 210,000 individual tree ring records of 110 tree species from more than 70,000 sites worldwide. "By measuring tree rings' widths one can tell how fast trees grew, while counting rings provides information on tree ages and allows making inferences about trees' maximum lifespan." Brienen explained.

The team also created a computer program that modeled a forest. Early on, it showed that "the forest could hold more carbon as the trees grew faster", Brienen reported. But after 20 years, these trees started dying and losing this extra carbon again. "We must understand that the only solution to bring down CO_2 levels is to stop emitting it into the atmosphere," said Brienen.

Words, phrases and difficult sentences to understand (Translate them into Chinese).

1. be regarded as ________________ 2. climate change ____________

3. remove from __________________ 4. as long as ________________

5. release ______________________ 6. boost ______________________

7. growth-lifespan ______________________ 8. trade-office ______________________

9. analyze ______________________ 10. emit ______________________

11. This effectively removes CO_2 from the atmosphere, making trees an important part of the fight against climate change.

____

12. By measuring tree rings' widths one can tell how fast trees grew, while counting rings provides information on tree ages and allows making inferences（推断）about trees' maximum lifespan.

____

Task 4: Cultivate your cultural awareness.

Tree planting used to be regarded as an effective means of controlling climate change. But now it's time to rethink the saying. According to the study when trees died, it lost this extra carbon back into the atmosphere. So we must understand that the only solution to bring down CO_2 levels is to reduce or even stop emitting it into the atmosphere eting to meeting, triaging emails and hitting a succession of small deadlines can deliver a buzz, even if nothing much is actually being achieved.

The performance is what counts.

Unit 6

Big Events in These Years

Lesson 1 A Q&A Column

Task 1: Step into the "reading forest".

Directions: Try to fill in the following blanks according to your imagination.

I'm Jesse Dunn, your friend from the US. This is a column where I help solve TEENS readers' problems. I hope I can help you with yours.

Dear Jesse,

One of my best friends suffers from moderate depression（中度抑郁）. He always feels unhappy and stressed out. And recently he hasn't been coming to school. I want to get him better as soon as possible. What should I do?

A confused student

Dear A confused student,

Depression is a very serious subject. And __1__, it is more common than most people know or would like to __2__. The first thing you can do is to __3__ out to your friend. Just ask him how he's doing. You don't have to say much. It's more important that he knows you are there to listen and that you __4__.

A lot of times people feel there is a stigma attached to __5__ that they suffer from depression and are __6__ to get help. You can explain to him that depression is a __7__ condition and is in no way a sign of __8__.

If he does in fact see a doctor, __9__ him to keep up with the treatment can help. Depression can make everything seem a bit overwhelming and knowing that someone else is interested in him sticking with his pursuit to get __10__ is important.

Creating an open safe environment where your friend feels __11__ sharing with you can __12__ a difference. Just spend time with him and ask if he needs help with anything.

But remember that you have to take care of yourself as well. And understand that you are not a __13__ health expert. While your concern for your friend and your urge to get him better are admirable, depression requires treatment from a __14__. Keep up the __15__.

Best of luck to you and your friend.

Jesse

Questions:

1. What is concerning the "Confused Student"?

____

2. What is "depression" ?

____

3. What suggestions does Jesse give to the "Confused Student"?

____

Task 2: Appreciate "trees" in the "reading forest".

Directions: For each blank in the following passage there are four words or phrases marked A, B, C and D. Fill in each blank with the word or phrase that best fits the context.

Dear A confused student,

Depression is a very serious subject. And__1__, it is more common than most people know or would like to __2__.The first thing you can do is to __3__ out to your friend. Just ask him how he's doing. You don't have to say much. It's more important that he knows you are there to listen and that you __4__.

A lot of times people feel there is a stigma attached to __5__ that they suffer from depression and are __6__ to get help. You can explain to him that depression is a __7__ condition and is in no way a sign of __8__.

If he does in fact see a doctor,__9__ him to keep up with the treatment can help. Depression can make everything seem a bit overwhelming and knowing that someone else is interested in him sticking with his pursuit to get __10__ is important.

Creating an open safe environment where your friend feels __11__ sharing with you can __12__ a difference. Just spend time with him and ask if he needs help with anything.

But remember that you have to take care of yourself as well. And understand that you are not a __13__ health expert. While your concern for your friend and your urge to get him better are admirable, depression requires treatment from a __14__. Keep up the __15__.

Best of luck to you and your friend.

Jesse

1. A. luckily	B. finally	C. especially	D. sadly
2. A. allow	B. find	C. acknowledge	D. want
3. A. get	B. try	C. find	D. reach
4. A. see	B. take	C. care	D. mean
5. A. admitting	B. suggesting	C. risking	D. missing
6. A. sorry	B. proud	C. guilty	D. ashamed
7. A. medical	B. physical	C. wrong	D. common
8. A. strength	B. bravery	C. courage	D. weakness
9. A. encouraging	B. talking	C. spotting	D. permitting
10. A. worse	B. better	C. more	D. less
11. A. uneasy	B. comfortable	C. unwilling	D. shy
12. A. take	B. make	C. come	D. get
13. A. mental	B. fatal	C. metal	D. fundamental
14. A. amateur	B. dentist	C. surgeon	D. professional
15. A. battle	B. support	C. discouragement	D. inspiration

Task 3: Have an overview of the "reading forest".

I'm Jesse Dunn, your friend from the US. This is a column where I help solve TEENS readers' problems. I hope I can help you with yours.

Dear Jesse,

One of my best friends suffers from moderate depression. He always feels unhappy and stressed out. And recently he hasn't been coming to school. I want to get him better as soon as possible. What should I do?

A confused student

Dear A confused student,

Depression is a very serious subject. And sadly, it is more common than most people know or would like to acknowledge. The first thing you can do is to reach out to your friend. Just ask him how he's doing. You don't have to say much. It's more important that he knows you are there to listen and that you care.

A lot of times people feel there is a stigma attached to admitting that they suffer from depression and are ashamed to get help. You can explain to him that depression is a medical condition and is in no way a sign of weakness.

If he does in fact see a doctor, encouraging him to keep up with the treatment can help. Depression can make everything seem a bit overwhelming and knowing that someone else is interested in him sticking with his pursuit to get better is important.

Creating an open safe environment where your friend feels comfortable sharing with you can make a difference. Just spend time with him and ask if he needs help with anything.

But remember that you have to take care of yourself as well. And understand that you are not a mental health expert. While your concern for your friend and your urge to get him better are admirable, depression requires treatment from a professional. Keep up the support.

Best of luck to you and your friend.

Jesse

Words, phrases and difficult sentences to understand (Translate them into Chinese).

1. acknoweldge ________________ 2. reach out to sb. ________________
3. be attached to ________________ 4. be ashamed to do ________________
5. medical condition ________________ 6. a sign of weakness ________________
7. overwhelming ________________ 8. pursuit ________________
9. urge to do sth. ________________ 10. keep up the support ________________

11. A lot of times people feel there is a stigma attached to admitting that they suffer from depression and are ashamed to get help.

____

12. While your concern for your friend and your urge to get him better are admirable, depression requires treatment from a professional.

____

Task 4: Cultivate your cultural awareness.

Depression is becoming increasingly common with people around us. But, still a lot of people, including the people who are undergoing depression, don't have a right understanding of the mental condition. It makes the situation even harder for those sufferers. For people who care about thcm and want to help must first know that while being around and supportive and understanding is of great significance, to seek medical treatment from professional psychologists is essential to make the situation better, which is nothing to be ashamed of. To have a clear understanding of this mental situation and avoid stigmatize, it may be the most that we can do for those who are depressed. So, let's join our hands and create a comfortable environment for this community.

Lesson 2 The Baby Who Was Meant to Be Ours

Task 1: Step into the "reading forest".

Directions: Try to fill in the following blanks according to your imagination.

When my best friend, Colleen, was 38 weeks pregnant, she asked me to go with her to Babies "R" Us. She found out she was pregnant around the time I found out I would never __1__.

Focusing on Colleen's good __2__ helped distract me from my own __3__. Now the only thing she needed was a changing __4__, which was what we had come to buy.

As we __5__ to the furniture section, a gray-and-white striped onesie（连体衣）__6__ my eye. The red crab sewed on the backside smiled with bright eyes, __7__ it had a secret. Maybe it __8__ memories from my childhood. If things were different, that crab onesie would have made me laugh. __9__ I said, "If I __10__ have a son, I'd want him to have that."

That night, I told John about the __11__. The next Sunday, John and I went to church for the second time in more than a decade. As we walked in, I noticed a tiny baby nestled __12__ the arms of a woman with white hair tied back in a bun. His head __13__ on her shoulder, and on his backside was the same red crab I'd seen. My breath caught. I turned to John and __14__, "That's the outfit I was telling you about." At the end of the service, the priest stood to make __15__. The white-haired woman walked up beside him, holding the __16__. "This baby needs a home, and he needs it by Thursday." he said. I was __17__ to make a sound. I looked at John. He had __18__ in his eyes too.

Now, our six-year-old son __19__ to be the best unexpected thing that will ever happen to me. And that crab onesie remains __20__ folded in one of my dresser drawers, where I plan to hold on to it—forever.

Questions:

1. What does the passage mainly talk about?

____

2. What are the key words that help you understand the passage better?

____

3. What's the structure or clue of the passage?

____

Task 2: Appreciate "trees" in the "reading forest".

Directions: For each blank in the following passage there are four words or phrases marked A, B, C and D. Fill in each blank with the word or phrase that best fits the context.

When my best friend, Colleen, was 38 weeks pregnant, she asked me to go with her to Babies "R" Us. She found out she was pregnant around the time I found out I would never __1__.

Focusing on Colleen's good __2__ helped distract me from my own __3__. Now the only thing she needed was a changing __4__, which was what we had come to buy.

As we __5__ to the furniture section, a gray-and-white striped onesie（连体衣）__6__ my eye. The red crab sewed on the backside smiled with bright eyes, __7__ it had a secret. Maybe it __8__ memories from my childhood. If things were different, that crab onesie would have made me laugh. __9__ I said, "If I __10__ have a son, I'd want him to have that."

That night, I told John about the __11__. The next Sunday, John and I went to church for the second time in more than a decade. As we walked in, I noticed a tiny baby nestled __12__ the arms of a woman with white hair tied back in a bun. His head __13__ on her shoulder, and on his backside was the same red crab I'd seen. My breath caught.

I turned to John and __14__, "That's the outfit I was telling you about." At the end of the service, the priest stood to make __15__. The white-haired woman walked up beside him, holding the __16__. "This baby needs a home, and he needs it by Thursday." he said. I was __17__ to make a sound. I looked at John. He had __18__ in his eyes too.

Now, our six-year-old son __19__ to be the best unexpected thing that will ever happen to me. And that crab onesie remains __20__ folded in one of my dresser drawers, where I plan to hold on to it—forever.

1. A. give birth B. give up C. give away D. give out
2. A. health B. time C. fortune D. life
3. A. surprise B. excitement C. grief D. fright
4. A. table B. clothes C. book D. bag
5. A. ran B. headed C. moved D. passed
6. A. cast B. caught C. shut D. kept
7. A. waiting B. beginning C. pretending D. suggesting
8. A. reflected B. created C. introduced D. triggered
9. A. Instead B. Rather C. Besides D. However
10. A. even B. never C. ever D. yet
11. A. baby B. outfit C. furniture D. memory
12. A. in B. under C. among D. over
13. A. circled B. put C. stood D. rested
14. A. told B. shouted C. informed D. whispered
15. A. agreements B. comments C. announcements D. differences
16. A. hand B. infant C. onesie D. line
17. A.eager B. afraid C. thirsty D. surprised
18. A. tears B. horror C.astonishment D. embarrassment
19. A.pretends B. insists C. continues D. happens
20. A. temporarily B. casually C. informally D. neatly

Task 3: Have an overview of the "reading forest".

When my best friend, Colleen, was 38 weeks pregnant, she asked me to go with her to Babies "R" Us, one of the only children's shops in Anchorage, Alaska. She found out she was expecting around the time I found out I would never give birth. I was only 29, but doctors said that I had too many medical challenges to conceive, let alone carry a child to term.

Focusing on Colleen's good fortune helped distract me from my own grief. I hosted her baby shower and sewed bedding and curtains for her son's nursery. Now the only thing she needed was a changing table, which was what we had come to buy.

As we headed to the furniture section, a gray-and-white striped onesie caught my eye. The red crab sewn on the backside smiled with bright eyes, suggesting it had a secret. Maybe it triggered memories from my childhood: digging for crabs in the Gulf of Mexico's sands, eating them on the docks in Baltimore with my family, pretending I was Ariel from The Little Mermaid. If things were different, that crab onesie would have made me laugh. Instead I said, "If I ever have a son, I'd want him to have that."

Colleen stopped, grasping my wrist so I would stop too. "Sarah, you have to get it," she said. I shook my head no. I didn't want a reminder of what I couldn't have. Of course, my husband, John, and I had talked about adoption. But I worried that the process would only lead to more rejection.

That night, I told John about the outfit. "Maybe you should've gotten it," he said, pulling me close. I told him no. The next Sunday, John and I went to church for the second time in more than a decade. In a city where people tend to come and go, we ached for connection and figured that this church, which had a reputation for being accepting, might offer that. As we walked in, I noticed a tiny baby nestled in the arms of a woman with white hair tied back in a bun. His head rested on her shoulder, and on his backside was the same red crab I'd seen just eight days before. My breath caught. I turned to John and whispered, "That's the outfit I was telling you about."

He cocked his eyebrows. Throughout the service, I was transfixed by the infant with fine blond hair sticking straight up from his head. I longed to hold him. I tried to distract myself by looking at the bright horizon over the snowy mountains.

At the end of the service, the priest stood to make announcements. The white-haired woman walked up beside him, holding the infant. "Most of you know this woman, and many of you know her daughter's situation," he said. "But what you may not know is that this baby needs a home, and he needs it by Thursday."

I was afraid to make a sound.

The reverend continued, "If you or anyone you know is thinking about adoption, please see us after the service."

I felt a hand on my lap and looked at John. He had tears in his eyes too.

"Are you thinking what I'm thinking?" he whispered.

We picked up our coats and, with our fingers interlaced, walked to the area where a group of people had congregated around the woman and the baby.

The grandmother beckoned us forward, and I saw the child's face for the first time—round with almond-shaped eyes and full lips. John was brave enough to hold him, but I was not. She took our phone numbers, saying the family would follow up.

That evening, they came to our home. The grandmother entered with an air of confident grace, but the young mother, carrying her baby, struggled to look us in our eyes. I didn't know her, but I wanted to hug her. We sat in our living room with a plate of cookies and cups of coffee.

Before we sat down, the mother asked whether I would like to hold her baby. This time I said yes. He fitted perfectly in my arms.

Over the next hour, we learned that he was four weeks old and that twelve families had volunteered to adopt him. The mother shared that she had many challenges that prevented her from parenting. Rather than letting her son become a ward of the state, she was choosing to relinquish her parental rights to the best family. If she picked us, all she asked was that we let her be involved in his life in some way. We agreed wholeheartedly.

I never mentioned the crab onesie. I wanted her to make her decision without being influenced by that coincidence.

When they stood to leave, I passed her baby back to her, and John and I waved goodbye as they walked to their car. Then we turned toward each other, embracing silently.

The next morning as I brushed my teeth, my phone rang. "We picked you" was all I heard.

Two days later, the baby moved into our home. After six months, our adoption was finalized. Our six-year-old son continues to be the best unexpected thing that will ever happen to me. And that crab onesie remains neatly folded in one of my dresser drawers, where I plan to hold on to it—forever.

Words, phrases and difficult sentences to understand (Translate them into Chinese).

1. pregnant ________
2. medical challenges ________
3. let alone carry a baby to term ________
4. distract sb. from sth. ________
5. ache for connection ________
6. nestle ________
7. cock his eyebrows ________
8. reverend ________
9. beckon ________

Task 4: Cultivate your cultural awareness.

When you feel life is hopeless, never mind, there may be a miracle. When you feel you are trapped in some kind of trouble that can't be solved, you should walk out. Maybe there is something amazing waiting for you outside. For a woman who couldn't give birth, she met an onesie that she loved very much. She wished if she could have a son, she would wear that for her son. She and her husband seldom went to church, but they went and met their destined child. So, always remember if a problem can't be solved, walk out and maybe there is a miracle out there.

Lesson 3 How to Properly Deal with Online Bullies

Task 1: Step into the "reading forest".

Directions: Try to get the main idea of the passage.

Emily Temple-Wood was 12 years old the first time she was bullied online. They left ugly comments on her Wikipedia and Facebook pages about her looks "that would make my mother's hair curl," says Temple-Wood, now 22 and in medical school. The reason? "I was a woman on the Internet, "she said.

Over the years, she considered how she might take revenge. Then, as a freshman in college, it hit her: "What do misogynists (men who hate women) hate most? "she asked herself. "Women who are productive!" Her solution. For every offensive comment she received, Temple-Wood would post a biography of a female scientist, and thus, in 2012, Wiki Project Women Scientists was born. She wrote about her heroes, like Barbara McClintock, who was awarded the 1983 Nobel Prize in Physiology or Medicine, and Caroline Still Anderson, one of the first African American women to become a physician in the United States, in the late 1800s. With help from other women, many of the scientists who have also been victimized online, Temple-Wood has published hundreds of these brief biographies and women of all ages have taken notice.

"When I was a kid, I could count the number of women scientists I was aware of on one hand," wrote Siko Bouterse, formerly of the Wikimedia Foundation, "But our daughters are going to have access to much more knowledge about scientists who are like them, thanks to Emily."

"The ugly comments still come," says Temple-Wood. Being a strong woman online is not easy. “We all have days when we break down and need to have a glass of wine,” she says.“I tell people who are being bullied that it’s OK to be upset. But now you need to find a productive way to take revenge. ”

Questions:

1. What does the passage mainly talk about?

____

2. What are the key words that help you understand the passage better?

____

3. What’s the structure or clue of the passage?

____

Task 2: Appreciate “trees” in the “reading forest”.

Directions: Read the passage and choose the right answers.

Emily Temple-Wood was 12 years old when the first time she was bullied online. They left ugly comments on her Wikipedia and Facebook pages about her looks “that would make my mother’s hair curl,” says Temple-Wood, now 22 and in medical school. The reason? “I was a woman on the Internet, ”she said.

Over the years, she considered how she might take revenge. Then, as a freshman in college, it hit her: “What do misogynists (men who hate women) hate most? ”she asked herself. “Women who are productive!” Her solution: For every offensive comment she received, Temple-Wood would post a biography of a female scientist, and thus, in 2012, Wiki Project Women Scientists was born. She wrote about her heroes, like Barbara McClintock, who was awarded the 1983 Nobel Prize in Physiology or Medicine, and Caroline Still Anderson, one of the first African American women to become a physician in the United States, in the lat 1800s. With help from other women, many of them scientists who have also been victimized online, Temple-Wood has published hundreds of these brief biographies and women of all ages have taken notice.

“When I was a kid, I could count the number of women scientists I was aware of on one hand,” wrote Siko Bouterse, formerly of the Wikimedia Foundation, “But our daughters are going to have access to much more knowledge about scientists who are like them, thanks toEmily. ”

“The ugly comments still come,” says Temple-Wood. Being a strong woman online is not easy. “We all have days when we break down and need to have a glass of wine, ” she says, “I tell people who are being bullied that it’s OK to be upset. But now you need to find a productive way to take revenge. ”

1. How did Emily feel when she was first bullied online?

A. Shocked.

B. Disappointed.

C. Excited.

D. Confident.

2. How did Emily react to the ugly comments about her?

A. She paid no attention to them.

B. She posted about great women.

C. She became a talkative woman.

D. She learned from women scientists.

3. What does Siko Bouterse think of Emily’s efforts?

A. They are helpful.

B. They are fruitless.

C. They are creative.

D. They are surprising.

4. What does Emily Temple-Wood advise people to do?

A. Sit down and have a glass of wine.

B. Try hard to be a productive person,

C. Never feel upset about ugly comments.

D. Fight ugly comments in a positive way.

Task 3: Have an overview of the “reading forest”.

Emily Temple-Wood was 12 years old the first time she was bullied online. They left ugly comments on her Wikipedia and Facebook pages about her looks “that would make my mother's hair curl, "says Temple-Wood, now 22 and in medical school. The reason? "I was a woman on the Internet. "she said.

Over the years, she considered how she might take revenge. Then, as a freshman in college, it hit her: "What do misogynists (men who hate women) hate most?" she asked herself. "Women who are productive!"Her solution: For every offensive comment she received, Temple-Wood would post a biography of a female scientist, and thus, in 2012, Wiki Project Women Scientists was born. She wrote about her heroes, like Barbara McClintock, who was awarded the 1983 Nobel Prize in Physiology or Medicine, and Caroline Still Anderson, one of the first African American women to become a physician in the United States, in the lat 1800s. With help from other women, many of them scientists who have also been victimized online, Temple-Wood has published hundreds of these brief biographies and women of all ages have taken notice.

"When I was a kid, I could count the number of women scientists I was aware of on one hand," wrote Siko Bouterse, formerly of the Wikimedia Foundation. "But our daughters are going to have access to much more knowledge about scientists who are like them, thanks to Emily. "

"The ugly comments still come, "says Temple-Wood. Being a strong woman online is not easy. "We all have days when we break down and need to have a glass of wine, " she says. "I tell people who are being bullied that it's OK to be upset. But now you need to find a productive way to take revenge. "

Words, phrases and difficult sentences to understand (Translate them into Chinese).

1. bully ____________________
2. take revenge ____________________
3. rude comment ____________________
4. productive ____________________
5. foundation ____________________

6. Our daughters have the chance to get much more knowledge about scientists who look like them because of Emily.

____

Task 4: Cultivate your cultural awareness.

The increasing reach of the Internet, the rapid spread of mobile information, and the widespread use of social media, have led to the emergence of cyber violence against women and girls (VAWG) as a growing global problem with potentially significant economic and societal consequences.

Research by the World Health Organization shows that one in three women will have experienced a form of violence in her lifetime, and despite the relatively new and growing phenomenon of Internet connectivity, it is estimated that one in ten women has already experienced a form of cyber violence since the age of 15. Access to the Internet is fast becoming a necessity for economic well-being, and is increasingly viewed as a fundamental human right; therefore it is crucial to ensure that this digital public space is a safe and empowering place for everyone, including women and girls. On the Internet, some people spread false information or slander others, which will result in the victim's bad reputation. It is necessary to create a harmonious environment for people who surf the Internet. It is just like an old Chinese saying: "Listen to no evil, see no evil, speak no evil, and do not spread evil."

Lesson 4 The Launch of China's Shenzhou XIV Spaceship

Task 1: Step into the "reading forest".

Directions: Try to fill in the following blanks according to your imagination.

China's Shenzhou XIV spaceship launched into space on Sunday, with the three astronauts aboard tasked with completing construction on the country's first space station.

As people across the country watched the launch __1__, an ink pen drifting in the crew cabin __2__ the attention of many.

In video footage sent back from the spaceship, astronaut Cai Xuzhe was seen letting go of the pen to watch it twirl and float in the cabin.

The pen was produced by Shaoguan Shengyi Stationery Co. Ltd. in Guangdong Province, __3__ is a pioneer in making pens used in outer space.

"The space pen's core, ink and structure are all different from a common pen," said company representative Guo Yi.

"The structure of a common pen can neither withstand the impact and vibration experienced by the spacecraft cabin during rocket launch nor write properly in a zero-gravity environment," Guo said.

The pen has __4__ core made using special alloys and a built-in self-pressurizing device to enable writing in low gravity.

The ink within the pen is also composed of liquid with high viscosity, making writing stick to surfaces tightly instead of flying off as hazardous __5__.

In addition, the head of the pen is less sharp than a normal pen's to avoid __6__ astronauts' space suits or other __7__ equipment.

A space pen developed by the company __8__ into space aboard the Shenzhen X spacecraft in 2013, making China the second country in the world, after the United States, able to independently produce a pen usable in space.

Questions:

1. What does the passage mainly talk about?

____

2. What does the last paragraph imply?

____

3. Please give this passage a suitable title.

____

Task 2: Appreciate "trees" in the "reading forest".

Directions: Fill in the blank space with one appropriate word or the correct form of the word inside the parentheses.

China's Shenzhou XIV spaceship launched into space on Sunday, with the three astronauts aboard tasked with completing __1__ (construct) on the country's first space station.

As people across the country watched the launch __2__ (close), an ink pen drifting in the crew cabin __3__ (catch)the attention of many.

In video footage sent back from the spaceship, astronaut Cai Xuzhe was seen letting go of the pen to watch it twirl and float in the cabin.

The pen was produced by Shaoguan Shengyi Stationery Co. Ltd. in Guangdong Province, __4__ is a pioneer in making pens used in outer space.

"The space pen's core, ink and structure are all different from a common pen," said company representative Guo Yi.

"The structure of a common pen can neither withstand the impact and vibration experienced by the spacecraft cabin during rocket launch __5__ write properly in a zero-gravity environment,"Guo said.

The pen has __6__ core made using special alloy and a built-in self-pressurizing device to enable writing in low gravity.

The ink within the pen is also composed of liquid with high viscosity, making writing stick to surfaces tightly instead of flying off as hazardous __7__ (droplet).

In addition, the head of the pen is less sharp than a normal pen's to avoid __8__ (puncture) astronauts' space suits or other __9__ (value) equipment.

A space pen developed by the company __10__ (sent) into space aboard the Shenzhen X spacecraft in 2013, making China the second country in the world, after the United States, able to independently produce a pen usable in space.

Task 3: Have an overview of the "reading forest".

Pen Catches Internet's Attention

China's Shenzhou XIV spaceship launched into space on Sunday, with the three astronauts aboard tasked with completing construction on the country's first space station.

As people across the country watched the launch closely, an ink pen drifting in the crew cabin caught the attention of many.

In video footage sent back from the spaceship, astronaut Cai Xuzhe was seen letting go of the pen to watch it twirl and float in the cabin.

The pen was produced by Shaoguan Shengyi Stationery Co. Ltd. in Guangdong Province, which is a pioneer in making pens used in outer space.

"The space pen's core, ink and structure are all different from a common pen," said company representative Guo Yi.

"The structure of a common pen can neither withstand the impact and vibration experienced by the spacecraft cabin during rocket launch nor write properly in a zero-gravity environment, "Guo said.

The pen has a core made using special alloys and a built-in self-pressurizing device to enable writing in low gravity.

The ink within the pen is also composed of liquid with high viscosity, making writing stick to surfaces tightly instead of flying off as hazardous droplets.

In addition, the head of the pen is less sharp than a normal pen's to avoid puncturing astronauts' space suits or other valuable equipment.

A space pen developed by the company was sent into space aboard the Shenzhen

X spacecraft in 2013, making China the second country in the world, after the United States, able to independently produce a pen usable in space.

Words, phrases and difficult sentences to understand (Translate them into Chinese).

1. launch ____________________ 2. let go of ____________________
3. pioneer ____________________ 4. withstand ____________________
5. vibration ____________________ 6. zero-gravity ____________________
7. be composed of ____________________ 8. viscosity ____________________
9. hazardous ____________________ 10. puncture ____________________

11. The structure of a common pen can neither withstand the impact and vibration experienced by the spacecraft cabin during rocket launch nor write properly in a zero-gravity environment.

____

12. The ink within the pen is also composed of liquid with high viscosity, making writing stick to surfaces tightly instead of flying off as hazardous droplets.

____

Task 4: Cultivate your cultural awareness.

We all know that one of the most important developing strategies of our country is to build China's strength in science and technology, which accentuates the research and development of aerospace. This passage shows us China's progress in space industry—China became the second country that independently produces a pen usable in space in the world.

Our country is bringing about a great rejuvenation of the Chinese nation step by step.

The development of the country is inseparable from the efforts of each of us Chinese people, and it is closely related to the struggle of every young student. As young people in the new era, the heavy responsibility of the times will soon be shouldered by you. The only thing that you need to do is to study hard, arming yourself with scientific knowledge and resilient spirit.

Please bear in your mind that you are the flowers of the motherland, and the future of the country is created by you.

Unit 7

Trouble Tree

Lesson 1 Trouble Tree

Task 1: Step into the "reading forest".

Directions: Read the passage and answer questions.

I hired a carpenter to help me restore an old farmhouse, and after he had finished a rough day on the job, a __1__ tire made him lose an hour of work, his electric saw __2__ and now his ancient pickup truck __3__ to start. While I drove him home, he sat in stony __4__ . On arriving, he invited me in to meet his family.

As we walked toward the __5__ door, he paused briefly at a small tree, touching tips of the __6__ with his hands.

When opening the door, he underwent an __7__ transformation. His tanned face was wreathed in smiles and he gave his wife a __8__ and hugged his two small children.

After leaving the __9__ family, I passed the tree and my __10__ got a better of me. I asked him, who __11__ me to the car, "Before we went in, why did you stop by the tree __12__ ?" "Oh, that's my __13__ tree." he replied, "I know I can't help having troubles on the __14__ and in my life, but those troubles don't __15__ in the house with my wife and children. I know I can __16__ one thing for sure. I can hang them up on the tree every night when I __17__ home. Then in the morning I pick them up again __18__ I leave for work."

"__19__ thing is," he smiled, "when I come out in the morning to pick them up, there aren't __20__ as many as I remember hanging up the night before."

Questions:

1. What does the passage mainly talk about?

____

2. What are the key words that help you understand the passage better?

____

3. What's the structure or clue of the passage?

____

Task 2: Appreciate "trees" in the "reading forest".

Directions: Fill in each blank with the word or phrase that best fits the context.

I hired a carpenter to help me restore an old farmhouse, and after he had finished a rough day on the job, a __1__ tire made him lose an hour of work, his electric saw __2__ and now his ancient pickup truck __3__ to start. when I drove him home, he sat in stony __4__ . On arriving, he invited me in to meet his family.

As we walked toward the __5__ door, he paused briefly at a small tree, touching tips of the __6__ with his hands.

When opening the door, he underwent an __7__ transformation. His tanned face was wreathed in smiles and he gave his wife a __8__ and hugged his two small children.

After leaving the __9__ family, I passed the tree and my __10__ got the better of me. I asked him, who __11__ me to the car, "Before we went in, why did you stop by the tree __12__ ?" "Oh, that's my __13__ tree." he replied, "I know I can't help having troubles on the __14__ and in my life, but those troubles don't __15__ in the house with my wife and children. I know I can __16__ one thing for sure. I can hang them up on the tree every night when I __17__ home. Then in the morning I pick them up again __18__ I leave for work."

"__19__ thing is," he smiled, "when I come out in the morning to pick them up, there aren't __20__ as many as I remember hanging up the night before."

1. A. broken	B. flat	C. front	D. stuck
2. A. ran over	B. gave out	C. broke down	D. stopped off
3. A. quit	B. tried	C. stopped	D. needed
4. A. satisfaction	B. silence	C. surprise	D. thought
5. A. side	B. back	C. next	D. front
6. A. branches	B. leaves	C. trees	D. shoots

7. A. surprising	B. tiring	C. pleasing	D. amusing
8. A. beat	B. kiss	C. blame	D. surprise
9. A. small	B. poor	C. pitiful	D. happy
10. A. interest	B. exploration	C. anxiety	D. curiosity
11. A. drove	B. walked	C. saw	D. went
12. A. former	B. earlier	C. later	D. ago
13.A. Christmas	B. lucky	C. trouble	D. pine
14. A. study	B. success	C. job	D. way
15. A. belong	B. live	C. move	D. own
16. A. take	B. direct	C. control	D. provide
17. A. leave	B. start	C. come	D. stay
18. A. after	B. when	C. until	D. before
19. A. Funny	B. Doubtful	C. Fearful	D. Comic
20. A. almost	B. roughly	C. hardly	D. nearly

Task 3: Have an overview of the "Reading Forest"

I hired a carpenter to help me restore an old farmhouse, and after he had finished a rough day on the job, a flat tire made him lose an hour of work, his electric saw quit and now his ancient pickup truck refused to start. when I drove him home, he sat in stony silence. On arriving, he invited me in to meet his family.

As we walked toward the front door, he paused briefly at a small tree, touching tips of the branches with his hands.

When opening the door, he underwent an amusing transformation. His tanned face was wreathed in smiles and he hugged his two small children and gave his wife a kiss.

After leaving the happy family, I passed the tree and my curiosity got the better of me. I asked him, who walked me to the car, "Before we went in, why did you stop by the tree earlier?" "Oh, that's my trouble tree." he replied, "I know I can't help having troubles on the job and in my life, but those troubles don't belong in the house with my wife and children. I know I can control one thing for sure. I can hang them up on the tree every night when I come home. Then in the morning I pick them up again before I leave for work."

"Funny thing is," he smiled, "when I come out in the morning to pick them up, there aren't nearly as many as I remember hanging up the night before."

Words, phrases and difficult sentences to understand (Translate them into Chinese).

1. carpenter ______
2. restore ______
3. a rough day ______
4. a flat tire ______
5.quit ______
6. in stony silence ______
7. undergo an amusing transformation ______
8.tanned face ______
9. wreath ______
10. get the better of ______
11. On arriving, he invited me in to meet his family.

______

12. As we walked toward the front door, he paused briefly at a small tree, touching tips of the branches with his hands.

______

Task 4: Cultivate your cultural awareness.

Are you worried? Why not learn from the carpenter's example and plant a "trouble tree"? Don't always entangle in trouble; don't doubt the function of this tree. In fact, when you encounter problems that cannot be solved, what will happen if you don't hang your troubles on the tree? Frown all day and worry that you can't solve your troubles. Troubles do not decrease because of your persistence and anxiety, but accumulate more and more greatly. At this time, your mood will get worse and worse. When you get home, you will ignore the warmth from home. You will feel that the concern of your family will make you more annoyed like superfluous noise;

You will feel that everything around you seems to be against you. You will feel that an unintentional look or action of others has something to do with yourself. You will doubt whether others know your troubles and ridicule you... In short, if you don't hang your troubles on the tree, you can only breed more troubles. In the end, you will be swallowed by your troubles, become a slave of your troubles, and then you can't find a happy self.

Therefore, we all should have a "trouble tree". It can be at your door, in your heart, in your diary, or planted with your friends. When you encounter troubles, you can think for a moment in front of the trouble tree at home and let the trouble hang on the tree. You can take a step back and let the trouble tree in your heart take away your troubles. You can vent in the diary, let the trouble hang on the diary. You can also talk to friends and relatives, so that your troubles can be washed away by whispers... In fact, the trouble tree can be seen everywhere in life, depending on whether you are willing to plant it and often use it to take away your troubles. Plant it, and you will be happier!

Lesson 2 Great Barrier Reef

Task 1: Step into the "Reading Forest".

Directions: Read the passage and answer the questions.

Australia's Great Barrier Reef has been hit by continuous heat. Too hot ocean temperatures, as high as 7 degrees Fahrenheit above average, __1__ (attack) the reef in recent weeks even though autumn normally means cooler conditions. Scientists with Australian government agencies said some __2__ (part) of the reef were turning white as a result.

When temperatures rise, corals lose their important roommates: the symbiotic algae that live inside corals and produce their primary source of food. Those algae give corals their colors __3__ get expelled during periods of heat stress, __4__ (cause) the corals to turn white. "If the water temperature decreases, corals that are affected can recover __5__ this stress," said David Wachenfeld, chief scientist of Australia's Great Barrier Reef Marine Park Authority. "However, weather forecasts show ocean temperatures will likely remain above average in the next few weeks."

The reef has been experiencing warm temperatures. The __6__ (consequent) was severe. After __7__ number of corals turned white in 2016 and 2017, large parts of the Great Barrier Reef lost half of their live corals. Reefs around the world are experiencing similar climate—related damage. A worldwide research found that between 2009 and 2021, 14 percent of the world's corals died. And another similar event raided many places, __8__ worsened the situation in 2022.

Scientists are trying to find ways to give corals a fighting chance, like searching for reefs that can act as shelters because they experience __9__ (natural) cool water.

Others are raising heat-resistant corals. Of course, countries must reduce fossil fuel emissions over the next decade. Even if the world can limit warming to 1.5℃, 70 to 90 percent of coral reefs are likely __10__ (die) off. "We need to really learn from these events," Emily Darling, director of coral reef conservation at the Wildlife Conservation Society, said, "We need to change the current businesses. We need to take action on climate change."

Questions:

1. What does the passage mainly talk about?

____

2. What problems is Great Barrier Reef faced with?

____

3. What solutions are mentioned in the passage?

____

Task 2: Appreciate "trees" in the "reading forest".

Directions: Try to fill in the following blanks according to hints and your imagination.

Australia's Great Barrier Reef has been hit by continuous heat. Too hot ocean temperatures, as high as 7 degrees Fahrenheit above average, __1__ (attack) the reef in recent weeks even though autumn normally means cooler conditions. Scientists with Australian government agencies said some __2__ (part) of the reef were turning white as a result.

When temperatures rise, corals lose their important roommates: the symbiotic algae that live inside corals and produce their primary source of food. Those algae give corals their colors __3__ get expelled during periods of heat stress, __4__ (cause) the corals to turn white. "If the water temperature decreases, corals that are affected can recover __5__ this stress," said David Wachenfeld, chief scientist of Australia's Great Barrier Reef Marine Park Authority. "However, weather forecasts show ocean temperatures will likely remain above average in the next few weeks."

The reef has been experiencing warm temperatures. The __6__ (consequent) was severe. After __7__ number of corals turned white in 2016 and 2017, large parts of the Great Barrier Reef lost half of their live corals. Reefs around the world are experiencing similar climate—related damage. A worldwide research found that between 2009 and 2021, 14 percent of the world's corals died. And another similar event raided many places, __8__ worsened the situation in 2022.

Scientists are trying to find ways to give corals a fighting chance, like searching for reefs that can act as shelters because they experience __9__ (natural) cool water. Others are raising heat-resistant corals. Of course, countries must reduce fossil fuel emissions over the next decade. Even if the world can limit warming to 1.5℃, 70 to 90 percent of coral reefs are likely __10__ (die) off. "We need to really learn from these events," Emily Darling, director of coral reef conservation at the Wildlife Conservation Society, said, "We need to change the current businesses. We need to take action on climate change."

Task 3: Have an overview of the "reading forest"

Australia's Great Barrier Reef has been hit by continuous heat. Too hot ocean temperatures, as high as 7 degrees Fahrenheit above average, have attacked the reef in recent weeks even though autumn normally means cooler conditions. Scientists with Australian government agencies said some parts of the reef were turning white as a result.

When temperatures rise, corals lose their important roommates: the symbiotic algae that live inside corals and produce their primary source of food. Those algae give corals their colors but get expelled during periods of heat stress, causing the corals to turn white. "If the water temperature decreases, corals that are affected can rccover from this stress," said David Wachenfeld, chief scientist of Australia's Great Barrier Reef Marine Park Authority. "However, weather forecasts show ocean temperatures will likely remain above average in the next few weeks."

The reef has been experiencing warm temperatures. The consequence was severe. After a number of corals turned white in 2016 and 2017, large parts of the Great Barrier Reef lost half of their live corals. Reefs around the world are experiencing similar climate—related damage. A worldwide research found that between 2009 and 2021, 14 percent of the world's corals died. And another similar event raided many places, which worsened the situation in 2022.

Scientists are trying to find ways to give corals a fighting chance, like searching for reefs that can act as shelters because they experience naturally cool water. Others are raising heat-resistant corals. Of course, countries must reduce fossil fuel emissions over the next decade. Even if the world can limit warming to 1.5℃, 70 to 90 percent of coral reefs are likely to die off. "We need to really learn from these events," Emily Darling, director of coral reef conservation at the Wildlife Conservation Society, said, "We need to change the current businesses. We need to take action on climate change."

Words, phrases and difficult sentences to understand (Translate them into Chinese).

1. continuous ________________ 2. average ________________
3. expel ________________ 4. decrease ________________
5. forecast ________________ 6. severe ________________
7. as a result ________________ 8. recover from ________________
9. a number of ________________ 10. be likely to do ________________

11. Too hot ocean temperatures, as high as 7 degrees Fahrenheit above average, have attacked the reef in recent weeks even though autumn normally means cooler conditions.

____

Task 4: Cultivate your cultural awareness

The Great Barrier Reef is the only living organic collective visible from Earth's orbit. The Great Barrier Reef, off the east coast of Australia, is one of the wonders of the natural world—it is the world's largest coral reef ecosystem. It was declared a World Heritage area in 1981.

The reef is scattered with beautiful island and idyllic coral cays and covers more than 300,000 square kilometres. The Great Barrier Reef system consists of more than 3000 reefs which range in size from 1 hectare to over 10,000 hectares in area. Dunk Island is one of more than 600 islands of the Great Barrier Reef.

The corals make up the various reefs and cays. These are the basis of the great variety of sea and animal lives in the Reef. Coral consists of individual coral polyps—tiny live creatures which join together to form colonies. Each polyp lives inside a shell of aragonite, a type of calcium carbonate which is the hard shell we recognize as coral. The polyps join together to create forests of colored coral in interesting fan, antler, brain and plate shapes.

The ideal environment for coral is shallow warm water where there is a lot of water movement, plenty of light, where the water is salty and low in nutrients. There are many different types of coral, some are slow growing and live to be hundreds of years old, others are faster growing. The colours of coral are created by algae. Only live coral is coloured. Dead coral is white.

The Great Barrier Reef area abounds with wildlife, including dugong and green turtles, varieties of dolphins and whales, more than 1,500 species of fish, 4,000 types of mollusk and more than 200 species of bird life. However, in 2006 it was reported that over the last 40 years, numbers of nesting loggerhead turtles have declined by between 50 percent and 80 percent; and estimates of dugong populations indicate they are currently only about 3 percent of what they were in the early 1960s. Since 2004, different areas of the Reef were introduced to try and recognize important habitats as well as identify different species of fish as key targets of protection.

Human activities in the Reef area have led to increased pollutants and the reef has suffered damage. Protecting the Reef is the responsibility of the Marine Park Authority. In 2003, the previous Austrian Government and Queensland Government, in partnership with a wide range of industry and community groups, developed the Reef Water Quality Protection Reef Plan as a combined effort to protect the Reef. One of the main aims of the Reef Plan was to maintain biodiversity within the larger ecosystem of the Reef as well as different habitats to help sustain the biodiversity of species and population levels.

Lesson 3 Love and Respect Food

Task 1: Step into the "Reading Forest".

Directions: Read the passage and answer the questions.

Food is part of who we are. We all need it, survive because of it and derive happiness from it. Since food matters so much, why do we let so much of it go rotten in our fridges, or get thrown out in our stores? Sadly, we love food, but we don't take care of it. __1__ . Here are ways to help us love our food better and grow respect for the world behind what we eat.

Reduce your food waste.

Buy only the food you need, store food wisely, donate excess and turn leftover food into the next day's meals. When we waste food, all the resources used for growing, processing, transporting and marketing that food are wasted too. __2__ .

__3__ .

Chefs get awards, stars and recognition for their creations. But what about our farmers? Without them, we wouldn't have the fresh food we need on a daily basis. Shop at your local markets and get to know your farmers. Giving them your business is giving them your recognition and respect.

Adopt a healthier, more sustainable diet.

__4__ . We get energy and maintain health from good food. We normally don't care the power that food and nutrition have over our bodies. Too much of it, or too much of only one kind of it, can lead to obesity, deficiencies or diet-related diseases.

Have a conversation.

By treating each meal with pride, we respect the farmers who produced it, and the resources that went into it. ___5___. Talk to the people around and to the next generation about making informed, healthy and sustainable food choices.

Respecting food means appreciating the back-story of food. When we know the full picture, it is easier to see what our food really stands for and how precious it really is.

Questions:

1. What advice does the passage give?

____

2. Which suggestions are useful in your view? Why?

____

3. What are your suggestions?

____

Task 2: Appreciate "Trees" in the "Reading Forest".

Directions: Choose the best sentence to fill in the blanks with your understanding.

Food is part of who we are. We all need it, survive because of it and derive happiness from it. Since food matters so much, why do we let so much of it go rotten in our fridges, or get thrown out in our stores? Sadly, we love food, but we don't take care of it. ___1___. Here are ways to help us love our food better and grow respect for the world behind what we eat.

Reduce your food waste.

Buy only the food you need, store food wisely, donate excess and turn leftover food into the next day's meals. When we waste food, all the resources used for growing, processing, transporting and marketing that food are wasted too. ___2___.

___3___.

Chefs get awards, stars and recognition for their creations. But what about our farmers? Without them, we wouldn't have the fresh food we need on a daily basis. Shop at your local markets and get to know your farmers. Giving them your business is giving them your recognition and respect.

Adopt a healthier, more sustainable diet.

___4___. We get energy and maintain health from good food. We normally don't care the power that food and nutrition have over our bodies. Too much of it, or too much of only one kind of it, can lead to obesity, deficiencies or diet-related diseases.

Have a conversation.

By treating each meal with pride, we respect the farmers who produced it, and the resources that went into it. __5__ . Talk to the people around and to the next generation about making informed, healthy and sustainable food choices.

Respecting food means appreciating the back-story of food. When we know the full picture, it is easier to see what our food really stands for and how precious it really is.

A. But food is so much more than what is on our plates

B. One third of all food produced globally is lost or wasted

C. Support your local food producers

D. Respcct chef and food

E. Respect can be passed on

F. Our bodies consume calories and nutrients

G. We need more food, less waste

Task 3: Have an overview of the "reading forest".

Food is part of who we are. We all need it, survive because of it and derive happiness from it. Since food matters so much, why do we let so much of it go rotten in our fridges, or get thrown out in our stores? Sadly, we love food, but we don't take care of it. One third of all food produced globally is lost or wasted. Here are ways to help us love our food better and grow respect for the world behind what we eat.

Reduce your food waste.

Buy only the food you need, store food wisely, donate excess and turn leftover food into the next day's meals. When we waste food, all the resources used for growing, processing, transporting and marketing that food are wasted too. But food is so much more than what is on our plates.

Support your local food producers.

Chefs get awards, stars and recognition for their creations. But what about our farmers? Without them, we wouldn't have the fresh food we need on a daily basis.

Shop at your local markets and get to know your farmers. Giving them your business is giving them your recognition and respect.

Adopt a healthier, more sustainable diet.

Our bodies consume calories and nutrients. We get energy and maintain health from good food. We normally don't care the power that food and nutrition have over our bodies. Too much of it, or too much of only one kind of it, can lead to obesity, deficiencies or diet-related diseases.

Have a conversation.

By treating each meal with pride, we respect the farmers who produced it, and the resources that went into it. Respect can be passed on. Talk to the people around and to the next generation about making informed, healthy and sustainable food choices.

Respecting food means appreciating the back-story of food. When we know the full picture, it is easier to see what our food really stands for and how precious it really is.

Words, phrases and difficult sentences to understand (Translate them into Chinese).

1. survive ________________ 2. derive ________________

3. matter ________________ 4. rotten ________________

5. excess ________________ 6. leftover ________________

7. recognition ________________ 8. market ________________

9. be part of ________________ 10. stand for ________________

11. When we know the full picture, it is easier to see what our food really stands for and how precious it really is.

____

Task 4: Cultivate your cultural awareness.

The food we eat every day keeps us alive, but it can also bring big health and environmental costs. A recent study finds that small shifts in the food choices could have great benefits to both health and the planet.

Because many foods with a high health burden, including processed meats or red meats, have high environmental costs, reducing just about 10 percent of a person's daily intake can cut a person's food-based environmental footprint by over 30 percent. Between growing it, packaging it, moving it around, cooking it, and often wasting it, food production makes up about one-fifth to one-third of all annual greenhouse gas emissions globally. For an average household, food makes up about as much of the greenhouse gas footprint as the electricity.

To learn how to reduce negative impacts of food production and consumption on the planet and the body, researchers first assessed damage related to food. Over the past few decades, scientists have developed ways of doing "life cycle analyses" for specific items and assigned them a hard number to show their environmental impact. Meanwhile, public health scientists were doing similar analyses for human bodies. They carefully examined the links between food and health. They concluded that agriculture is a huge piece of the climate puzzle, and agriculture, food, and diet are all linked.

We can't stop eating, so what should we do? For some climate challenges, there are relatively straightforward ways. For example, renewable energy sources can already replace much of the energy needed to power buildings, cars, and more.

There's no substitute for food, but shifting what we eat is possible. If all people on the planet are vegans, greenhouse gas emissions from the food system could be cut by more than half; a planet of vegetarians would trim food emissions by 44 percent.

Lesson 4 Social Media

Task 1: Step into the "Reading Forest".

Directions: Try to fill in the following blanks according to hints and your imagination and answer the questions.

Twenty years ago, the idea of sharing our lives so openly with the world was __1__. However, for young people today it is considered completely normal to share pictures of their __2__ and interact online every day. Fans of social media point out that the world has never been so __3__ as it has allowed people to make friends, learn about the world and celebrate life.

However, many people have __4__ about the effects of this new way of living, particularly about the amount and type of information that is shared so __5__. Spending too much time on social media may have some negative __6__. Researchers __7__ people's attitudes and feelings before and after visiting social media sites. They found that the more time people spent on social media, the __8__ they became.

There are a number of __9__ for this. When browsing social media, people often see photographs and stories __10__ beautiful holidays, fun parties and fashionable clothes. People rarely __11__ negative stories or bad pictures, so it can be misleading. For those looking at these __12__ and comparing them with their own lives, they can __13__ feeling sad and depressed. They might think their lives are worse __14__. Even for those people who post positive stories and pictures, they can also feel __15__ and worried. The number of "likes" and comments on their posts can make them __16__ their popularity. __17__, there is also the problem of "cyber-bullying" where people become victims of being bullied __18__ when others make negative or cruel comments about them.

We don't have to disconnect ___19___ the Internet to live a happy life, but we should realise that the pictures we see and stories we read are ___20___ a part of a bigger picture. If we can do that, we can protect ourselves and enjoy our lives.

Questions:

1. What does the passage mainly talk about?

____

2. What helps you understand the passage better?

____

3. What's your opinion on this topic?

____

Task 2: Appreciate "trees" in the "reading forest".

Directions: Read the passage and answer the questions.

Twenty years ago, the idea of sharing our lives so openly with the world was ___1___. However, for young people today it is considered completely normal to share pictures of their ___2___ and interact online every day. Fans of social media point out that the world has never been so ___3___ as it has allowed people to make friends, learn about the world and celebrate life.

However, many people have ___4___ about the effects of this new way of living, particularly about the amount and type of information that is shared so ___5___. Spending too much time on social media may have some negative ___6___. Researchers ___7___ people's attitudes and feelings before and after visiting social media sites. They found that the more time people spent on social media, the ___8___ they became.

There are a number of ___9___ for this. When browsing social media, people often see photographs and stories ___10___ beautiful holidays, fun parties and fashionable clothes. People rarely ___11___ negative stories or bad pictures, so it can be misleading. For those looking at these ___12___ and comparing them with their own lives, they can ___13___ feeling sad and depressed. They might think their lives are worse ___14___. Even for those people who post positive stories and pictures, they can also feel ___15___ and worried. The number of "likes" and comments on their posts can make them ___16___ their popularity. ___17___, there is also the problem of "cyber-bullying" where people become victims of being bullied ___18___ when others make negative or cruel comments about them.

We don't have to disconnect ___19___ the Internet to live a happy life, but we should realise that the pictures we see and stories we read are ___20___ a part of a bigger picture. If we can do that, we can protect ourselves and enjoy our lives.

1. A. unknown of B. unheard of C. unsure of D. unaware of
2. A. jobs B. family C. lives D. travel
3. A. connected B. touched C. pleasing D. comfortable
4. A. surprise B. support C. opinions D. concerns
5. A. naturally B. loudly C. openly D. differently
6. A. reasons B. effects C. doubts D. purposes
7. A. measured B. considered C. guessed D. changed
8. A. unhealthier B. unhappier C. more interesting D. more boring
9. A. examples B. effects C. reasons D. experiences
10. A. showing B. telling C. remembering D. inviting
11. A. send B. choose C. saw D. post
12. A. parties B. pictures C. holidays D. clothes
13. A. begin B. remain C. go on D. end up
14. A. in return B. in comparison C. in between D. in common
15. A. stressed B. confused C. angry D. hard
16. A. tired of B. surprised at C. proud of D. anxious about
17. A. At first B. For example C. Of course D. At last
18. A. at home B. online C. at school D. at work
19. A. of B. with C. from D. on
20. A. only B. mainly C. hardly D. nearly

Task 3: Have an overview of the "reading forest".

Twenty years ago, the idea of sharing our lives so openly with the world was unheard of. However, for young people today it is considered completely normal to share pictures of their lives and interact online every day. Fans of social media point out that the world has never been so connected as it has allowed people to make friends, learn about the world and celebrate life.

However, many people have concerns about the effects of this new way of living, particularly about the amount and type of information that is shared so openly. Spending too much time on social media may have some negative effects. Researchers measured people's attitudes and feelings before and after visiting social media sites. They found that the more time people spent on social media, the unhappier they became.

There are a number of reasons for this. When browsing social media, people often see photographs and stories showing beautiful holidays, fun parties and fashionable clothes. People rarely post negative stories or bad pictures, so it can be misleading. For those looking at these pictures and comparing them with their own lives, they can end up feeling sad and depressed. They might think their lives are worse in comparison. Even for those people who post positive stories and pictures, they can also feel stressed and worried. The number of "likes" and comments on their posts can make them anxious about their popularity. Of course, there is also the problem of "cyber-bullying" where people become victims of being bullied online when others make negative or cruel comments about them.

We don't have to disconnect from the Internet to live a happy life, but we should realise that the pictures we see and stories we read are only a part of a bigger picture. If we can do that, we can protect ourselves and enjoy our lives.

Words, phrases and difficult sentences to understand (Translate them into Chinese).

1. be unheard of ________________ 2. interact ________________
3. negative ________________ 4. measure ________________
5. misleading ________________ 6. depressed ________________
7. comparison ________________ 8. popularity ________________
9. cyber-bullying ________________ 10. disconnect from ________________

Task 4: Cultivate your cultural awareness.

Many people use social media every day to get in touch with other people and know about news events. Do you think the advantages outweigh the disadvantages?

It is very common to see people, be they youngsters or seniors, browsing social media platforms, such as TikTok and Facebook, to keep contact with others and get themselves well-informed. Personally, I deem this commonplace advantageous.

Modern media provides its users with easier access to both their beloved ones and strangers by overcoming the geographic distance. Those who harbour prejudice toward social media and regard it as the factor of undermining face-to-face interaction are actually old-fashioned and even out of touch, since they pictured the scenes decades ago when friends and family members contacted with each other by merely typing and receiving messages on a cold screen instead of talking face to face. In fact, things have changed with technologies booming unprecedentedly. Social media nowadays has made it possible for users to chat with each other in this virtual world just like the way they communicate in reality. In other words, it is through modern media that people are able to keep in touch by either video-chatting or uploading photos especially during the outbreak of pandemics.

As to news sources, social media also has an edge over traditional forms like newspapers. Admittedly, compared with news shown on social media, which may be fabricated, the stories reported on newspapers are rather authentic, since the strict censorship requires editors to be certain about minute details. Social media users may be misled by some idle gossips, and even worse, accelerate the speed of spreading such fake news via modern platforms. However, this can in effect be prevented as long as readers foster the ability to seek authoritative sources and to distinguish the information they have acquired. Moreover, taking full advantage of news events' travelling fast on social media, readers and viewers can get informed via palm-sized gadgets within a few hours or even minutes rather than wait at least half a day until newspapers are printed.

In a nutshell, the downsides of social media pale into insignificance when set against its upsides. The reality is that social media is part of modern life and it is not going to go away. This research shows us that it is important to find a balance between our online and offline lives.

Unit 8

Immersive Van Gogh

Lesson 1　Immersive Van Gogh

Task 1: Step into the "reading forest".

Directions: Try to read the passage and answer questions below.

From the creators of the blockbuster show in Paris __1__ by over two million visitors and still wowing crowds in Toronto, the west coast premiere of the Immersive Van Gogh Exhibit will bring the art of Vincent to life in Los Angeles.

Immersive art is not just __2__ technical way to represent video and audio in huge spaces. The word immersive indicates a deep commitment of intentions which connect images and sounds in a way that the audience is __3__ to experience a different way of the art.

True to its name, this exhibition transforms the iconic paintings of Vincent van Gogh into moving, wall-filling projections. "Immersive Van Gogh" __4__ half-a-million cubic feet of projections that pull from some of the post-impressionist's __5__ recognizable pieces, including *The Bedroom*, *Sunflowers* and, yes, *The Starry Night*.

You will experience art like never before — lose yourself in entrancing, moving __6__ that highlight brushstrokes, detail, __7__ color — truly illuminating the mind of the genius.

LOCATION

The Immersive Van Gogh Exhibit is located at a secret place situated in the heart of Los Angeles. To be announced before the exhibit opens, existing ticket holders will receive an email with the place name and location once it is made public.

VIP TICKETS—$99.99 Priority access Van Gogh cushion (a gift for you) Limited edition poster	PREMIUM TICKETS—$59.99 Van Gogh cushion (rental) Limited edition poster
BASIC TICKETS—$54.99 Admission only	CHILD TICKETS—$29.99 Aged 6–16 (children 5 and under do not require a ticket) Admission only Child tickets are not subject to change of date fees

Tickets are available online at www.vangoghla.com.

Stop by our Exhibit Gift Shop to take the magic of Van Gogh home __8__ you! From clothing and jewelry to home décor, __9__ books, and so much more, you will find unique and thoughtful souvenirs at the Immersive Van Gogh Exhibit. Also be sure to check out at our online store!

Experience the organic landscapes of Van Gogh's imagination, and journey through his brilliance and madness in a __10__ new and unforgettable way.

Questions:

1. What does the passage mainly talk about?

____

2. What's the main purpose of this passage?

____

3. Where can you probably find this passage?

____

4. Who is the text mainly intended for?

____

Task 2: Appreciate "trees" in the "reading forest".

Directions: Read the following passage and choose the best answer to each question.

From the creators of the blockbuster show in Paris seen by over two million visitors and still wowing crowds in Toronto, the west coast premiere of the Immersive

Van Gogh Exhibit will bring the art of Vincent to life in Los Angeles.

Immersive art is not just a technical way to represent video and audio in huge spaces. The word immersive indicates a deep commitment of intentions which connect images and sounds in a way that the audience is able to experience a different way of the art.

True to its name, this exhibition transforms the iconic paintings of Vincent van Gogh into moving, wall-filling projections. "Immersive Van Gogh" promises half-a-million cubic feet of projections that pull from some of the post-impressionist's most recognizable pieces, including *The Bedroom*, *Sunflowers* and, yes, *The Starry Night*.

You will experience art like never before — lose yourself in entrancing, moving images that highlight brushstrokes, detail, and color — truly illuminating the mind of the genius.

LOCATION

The Immersive Van Gogh Exhibit is located at a secret place situated in the heart of Los Angeles. To be announced before the exhibit opens, existing ticket holders will receive an email with the place name and location once it is made public.

TICKET PRICES

VIP TICKETS—$99.99 Priority access Van Gogh cushion (a gift for you) Limited edition poster	PREMIUM TICKETS—$59.99 Van Gogh cushion (rental) Limited edition poster
BASIC TICKETS—$54.99 Admission only	CHILD TICKETS—$29.99 Aged 6–16 (children 5 and under do not require a ticket) Admission only Child tickets are not subject to change of date fees

Tickets are available online at www.vangoghla.com.

Stop by our Exhibit Gift Shop to take the magic of Van Gogh home with you! From clothing and jewelry to home décor, children's books, and so much more, you will find unique and thoughtful souvenirs at the Immersive Van Gogh Exhibit. Also be sure to check out at our online store!

Experience the organic landscapes of Van Gogh's imagination, and journey through his brilliance and madness in a completely new and unforgettable way.

Questions:

1. According to the passage, the Immersive Van Gogh Exhibit ______.

A. presents Van Gogh's art in a modern way

B. begins a journey to Van Gogh's hometown

C. displays Van Gogh's paintings on moving walls

D. designs projects on Van Gogh's learning experience

2. From where can people find information about the exact location of the exhibit?

A. An email.　　B. A website.

C. The ticket office.　　D. The gift shop.

3. How much should a couple with a 5-year-old child who would like to own a Van Gogh cushion at least pay for the visit?

A. $109.98.　　B. $154.98.

C. $159.98.　　D. $199.98.

Task 3: Have an overview of the "reading forest".

From the creators of the blockbuster show in Paris seen by over two million visitors and still wowing crowds in Toronto, the west coast premiere of the Immersive Van Gogh Exhibit will bring the art of Vincent to life in Los Angeles.

Immersive art is not just a technical way to represent video and audio in huge spaces. The word immersive indicates a deep commitment of intentions which connect images and sounds in a way that the audience is able to experience a different way of the art.

True to its name, this exhibition transforms the iconic paintings of Vincent van Gogh into moving, wall-filling projections. "Immersive Van Gogh" promises half-a-million cubic feet of projections that pull from some of the post-impressionist's most recognizable pieces, including *The Bedroom*, *Sunflowers* and, yes, *The Starry Night*.

You will experience art like never before — lose yourself in entrancing, moving images that highlight brushstrokes, detail, and color — truly illuminating the mind of the genius.

LOCATION

The Immersive Van Gogh Exhibit is located at a secret place situated in the heart of Los Angeles. To be announced before the exhibit opens, existing ticket holders will receive an email with the place name and location once it is made public.

TICKET PRICES

VIP TICKETS—$99.99 Priority access Van Gogh cushion (a gift for you) Limited edition poster	PREMIUM TICKETS—$59.99 Van Gogh cushion (rental) Limited edition poster
BASIC TICKETS—$54.99 Admission only	CHILD TICKETS—$29.99 Aged 6–16 (children 5 and under do not require a ticket) Admission only Child tickets are not subject to change of date fees

Tickets are available online at www.vangoghla.com.

Stop by our Exhibit Gift Shop to take the magic of Van Gogh home with you! From clothing and jewelry to home décor, children's books, and so much more, you will find unique and thoughtful souvenirs at the Immersive Van Gogh Exhibit. Also be sure to check out at our online store!

Experience the organic landscapes of Van Gogh's imagination, and journey through his brilliance and madness in a completely new and unforgettable way.

Words, phrases and difficult sentences to understand (Translate them into Chinese).

1. immersive ____________ 2. technical ____________

3. indicate ____________ 4. projection ____________

5. recognizable pieces ____________ 6. entrancing ____________

7. highlight ____________ 8. unique ____________

9. thoughtful souvenirs ____________ 10. organic landscapes ____________

11. Immersive art is not just a technical way to represent video and audio in huge spaces.

____

12. The word immersive indicates a deep commitment of intentions which connect images and sounds in a way that the audience is able to experience a different way of the art.

____

13. True to its name, this exhibition transforms the iconic paintings of Vincent van Gogh into moving, wall-filling projections.

____

14. You will experience art like never before—lose yourself in entrancing, moving images that highlight brushstrokes, detail, and color—truly illuminating the mind of the genius.

____

Task 4: Cultivate your cultural awareness.

Vincent van Gogh (1853–1890), for whom color was the chief symbol of expression, was born in Groot-Zundert, Holland. The son of a pastor, brought up in a religious and cultured atmosphere, Vincent was highly emotional.

Between 1860 and 1880, when he finally decided to become an artist, van Gogh had had two unsuitable and unhappy romances and had worked unsuccessfully as a clerk in a bookstore, an art salesman, and a preacher in the Borinage (a dreary mining district in Belgium), where he was dismissed for over zealousness. He remained in Belgium to study art, determined to give happiness by creating beauty. The works of his early Dutch period are somber-toned, sharply lit, genre paintings of which the most famous is *The Potato Eaters* (1885). In that year van Gogh went to Antwerp where he discovered the works of Rubens and purchased many Japanese prints.

In 1886 he went to Paris to join his brother Théo, the manager of Goupil's gallery. In Paris, van Gogh studied with Cormon, inevitably met Pissarro, Monet, and Gauguin, and began to lighten his very dark palette and to paint in the short brushstrokes of the Impressionists.

His nervous temperament made him a difficult companion and night-long discussions combined with painting all day undermined his health. He decided to go south to Arles where he hoped his friends would join him and help found a school of art. Gauguin did join him but with disastrous results. In a fit of epilepsy, van Gogh pursued his friend with an open razor, was stopped by Gauguin, but ended up cutting a portion of his ear lobe off. Van Gogh then began to alternate between fits of madness and lucidity and was sent to the asylum in Saint-Remy for treatment.

In May of 1890, he seemed much better and went to live in Auvers-sur-Oise under the watchful eye of Dr. Gachet. Two months later he was dead, having shot himself "for the good of all". During his brief career he had sold one painting. Van Gogh's finest works were produced in less than three years in a technique that grew more and more impassioned in brushstroke, in symbolic and intense color, in surface tension, and in the movement and vibration of form and line. Van Gogh's inimitable fusion of form and content is powerful, dramatic, lyrically rhythmic, imaginative, and emotional, for the artist was completely absorbed in the effort to explain either his struggle against madness or his comprehension of the spiritual essence of man and nature.

Some of his masterpieces: *Roses* (1889), *The Sower* (1888), *Irises, Saint-Remy* (1889), *Wheat Field with Crows* (1890), *Vincent's Chair with His Pipe* (1888), *Sunflowers* (1888), *The Café Terrace on the Place du Forum, Arles, at Night* (1888), *Starry Night* (1889).

Lesson 2 The COVID-19 Epidemic

Task 1: Step into the "reading forest".

Directions: Try to fill in the following blanks according to your imagination.

It was the first day of spring here but it didn't feel like it. The COVID-19 epidemic was __1__ the globe and everywhere there were feelings of fear and loneliness. On the news the numbers of the sick and dead continued to __2__. It felt like there was a weight on the souls of everyone in the world.

My family were __3__ at home as much as possible and as I looked out of my window. I __4__ how long this crisis would last. It was then, however, that I saw something that lifted that weight off my soul, made me smile, and made my heart feel __5__ again. In the street below my house there was an old friend of mine from high school who was a teacher there. With him was my younger son's former aide from the high school as well. They were __6__ the school lunches door to door to the __7__ children who were stuck at home. Watching them made me think of something: "In the __8__ times, always look for the helpers."

I have no doubt that this crisis will __9__ like all the crises before. But it is our __10__ whether it brings out the best in us or the worst in us. Let it bring out the __11__ in you. Use it to strengthen your faith. Use it to free yourself from __12__. Use it to become a kinder, more __13__, and more loving person. Become a __14__ to all those in need and you will be a happy person today and in all the days to __15__.

Questions:

1. What does the passage mainly talk about?

____

2. What are the key words that help you understand the passage better?

____

3. What's the structure or clue of the passage?

____

Task 2: Appreciate "trees" in the "reading forest".

Directions: For each blank in the following passage there are four words or phrases marked A, B, C and D. Fill in each blank with the word or phrase that best fits the context.

It was the first day of spring here but it didn't feel like it. The COVID-19 epidemic was __1__ the globe and everywhere there were feelings of fear and loneliness. On the news the numbers of the sick and dead continued to __2__. It felt like there was a weight on the souls of everyone in the world.

My family were __3__ at home as much as possible and as I looked out of my window. I __4__ how long this crisis would last. It was then, however, that I saw something that lifted that __5__ off my soul, made me smile, and made my heart feel __6__ again. In the street below my house there was an old __7__ of mine from high school who was a teacher there. With him was my younger son's former aide from the high school __8__. They were __9__ the school lunches door to door to the __10__ children who were stuck at home. Watching them made me __11__ something: "In the __12__ times, always look for the helpers."

I have no doubt that this crisis will __13__ like all the crises before. But it is our __14__ whether it brings out the best in us or the worst in us. Let it bring out the __15__ in you. Use it to __16__ your faith. Use it to free yourself from __17__. Use it to become a kinder, more __18__, and more loving person. Become a __19__ to all those in need and you will be a happy person today and in all the days to __20__.

1. A. destroying	B. sweeping	C. connecting	D. defeating
2. A. decline	B. change	C. rise	D. upload
3. A. staying	B. enjoying	C. studying	D. working
4. A. realized	B. wondered	C. believed	D. ignored

5. A. spirit	B. depression	C. burden	D. weight
6. A. lonely	B. happy	C. uninterested	D. calm
7. A. friend	B. customer	C. colleague	D. neighbour
8. A. at last	B. in addition	C. as well	D. by chance
9. A. selling	B. collecting	C. making	D. delivering
10. A. hungry	B. sad	C. angry	D. excited
11. A. talk about	B. look at	C. think of	D. refer to
12. A. modern	B. joyful	C. different	D. bad
13. A. continue	B. pass	C. worsen	D. appear
14. A. doubt	B. hesitation	C. choice	D. belief
15. A. worst	B. strongest	C. funniest	D. best
16. A. restore	B. strengthen	C. defend	D. lose
17. A. fear	B. trouble	C. life	D. worry
18. A. hardworking	B. interesting	C. demanding	D. giving
19. A. winner	B. reminder	C. helper	D. director
20. A. come	B. go	C. live	D. spend

Task 3: Have an overview of the "reading forest".

It was the first day of spring here but it didn't feel like it. The COVID-19 epidemic was sweeping the globe and everywhere there were feelings of fear and loneliness. On the news the numbers of the sick and dead continued to rise. It felt like there was a weight on the souls of everyone in the world.

My family were staying at home as much as possible and as I looked out of my window. I wondered how long this crisis would last. It was then, however, that I saw something that lifted that weight off my soul, made me smile, and made my heart feel happy again. In the street below my house there was an old friend of mine from high school who was a teacher there. With him was my younger son's former aide from the high school as well. They were delivering the school lunches door to door to the hungry children who were stuck at home. Watching them made me think of something: "In the bad times, always look for the helpers."

I have no doubt that this crisis will pass like all the crises before. But it is our choice whether it brings out the best in us or the worst in us. Let it bring out the best in you. Use it to strengthen your faith. Use it to free yourself from fear. Use it to become a kinder, more giving, and more loving person. Become a helper to all those in need and you will be a happy person today and in all the days to come.

Words, phrases and difficult sentences to understand (Translate them into Chinese).

1. sweep ____________________ 2. lift...off ____________________

3. stick ____________________ 4. bring out ____________________

5. strengthen ____________________ 6. free...from ____________________

7. It was then, however, that I saw something that lifted that weight off my soul, made me smile, and made my heart feel happy again.

____

____

Task 4: Cultivate your cultural awareness.

Occasionally, life can be undeniably, impossibly difficult. We are faced with challenges and events that can seem overwhelming, life-destroying to the point where it may be hard to decide whether to keep going. But you always have a choice. And you always have the chance to make a difference to the world and yourself. Just as the author believed, it is your choice to bring out the best in you. It's difficult to define what the best you are like, but it's easy to find a good you in the small choices of your everyday life. As long as you keep choosing to be a good you, you will become the best you, certainly and always. Of course, you can choose to start by doing some small things like the father and the son in the passage.

As long as there are people in need, helping others will remain an important task. Americans are not the only ones who believe in helping others. People in every culture recognize that being helpful is one of the greatest virtues in life, as well as one of the sweetest joys. For Americans, the Christmas season is a great time to renew their commitment to help people in need. But we don't have to choose to be a helper within a certain time. It's not the time that tells us to be helpful but our interior forces that motivate us to be always ready to do someone a favour.

We never know when we ourselves might need a little help. So to help others is to help ourselves, and more importantly, to please ourselves.

Lesson 3 Art Everywhere

Task 1: Step into the "reading forest".

Directions: Try to read the passage and answer questions below.

Art is everywhere. Any public space has been carefully designed by an artistic mind to be both functional and beautiful. Why, then, is art still so widely considered to be "the easy subject" at school, insignificant to wider society, a waste of time and effort?

Art can connect culture with commercial products in a way __1__ not many other things can; art generates money and holds significant emotional and cultural value within communities. When people attend a concert, they are paying for music, sure, maybe even hotel rooms, meals, and transport, but they also gain an incredible experience, __2__ unique atmosphere and a memory that will go through the rest of __3__ lives. People don't just want material things anymore, they want to experience life—the arts are a perfect crossover between culture and commerce.

Furthermore, the arts can bring communities together, __4__ loneliness and making people feel safer. Social bonds are created among __5__ when they share their arts experiences through reflection and discussion, and their expression of common values through artworks in honour __6__ events significant to a nation's experience.

The arts clearly have a pretty positive impact on __7__ and psychological health. It __8__ that people who frequently participate in artistic events are more likely to gain good health __9__ to those who do not; more engagement with the arts is linked to a higher level of people's wellbeing. The Royal Society of Public Health discovered that music and art, when __10__ in hospitals, help to improve the conditions of patients by reducing stress, anxiety and blood pressure.

Children who are involved with the arts make greater achievements in their education; those engaged with drama have greater literary ability while others taking part in musical practice exhibit greater skills in math and languages. Kids with preference for the arts have a greater chance of finding employment in the future. Participating in the arts is essential for child development; encouraging children to express themselves in constructive ways could help to form healthy emotional responses in later life.

Vital to human life, art is celebrated and used by nations across the world for various purposes. Life without art would be boring and dead still, for art is part of what makes us human.

Questions:

1. What is the main idea of the passage?

____

2.What is the structure of the passage? Can you draw a mind-map of it?

____

Task 2: Appreciate "trees" in the "reading forest".

Directions: Read the following passage and fill in the blanks with the correct form of the given word or the word that best fits the context.

Art can connect culture with commercial products in a way that not many other things can; art __1__ (generate) money and holds significant emotional and cultural value within communities. __2__ people attend a concert, they are paying for music, sure, maybe even hotel rooms, meals, and transport, but they also gain an incredible experience, __3__ unique atmosphere and a memory that will go through the rest of __4__ (they) lives. People don't just want material things anymore; they want to experience life—the arts are a perfect crossover between culture and commerce.

Furthermore, the arts can bring communities together, __5__ (reduce) loneliness and making people feel safer. Social bonds are created among __6__ (individual) when they share their arts experiences through reflection and discussion, and their expression of common values through artworks in honour __7__ events significant to a nation's experience.

The arts clearly have a pretty positive impact on __8__ (physics) and psychological health. It __9__ (find) that people who frequently participate in artistic events are more likely to gain good health compared to those who do not; more engagement with the arts is linked to a higher level of people's wellbeing. The Royal Society of Public Health discovered that music and art, when __10__ (use) in hospitals, help to improve the conditions of patients by reducing stress, anxiety and blood pressure.

Task 3: Have an overview of the "reading forest".

Art is everywhere. Any public space has been carefully designed by an artistic mind to be both functional and beautiful. Why, then, is art still so widely considered to be "the easy subject" at school, insignificant to wider society, a waste of time and effort?

Art can connect culture with commercial products in a way that not many other things can; art generates money and holds significant emotional and cultural value within communities. When people attend a concert, they are paying for music, sure, maybe even hotel rooms, meals, and transport, but they also gain an incredible experience, a unique atmosphere and a memory that will go through the rest of their lives. People don't just want material things anymore, they want to experience life—the arts are a perfect crossover between culture and commerce.

Furthermore, the arts can bring communities together, reducing loneliness and making people feel safer. Social bonds are created among individuals when they share their arts experiences through reflection and discussion, and their expression of common values through artworks in honour of events significant to a nation's experience.

The arts clearly have a pretty positive impact on physical and psychological health. It is found that people who frequently participate in artistic events are more likely to gain good health compared to those who do not; more engagement with the arts is linked to a higher level of people's wellbeing. The Royal Society of Public Health discovered that music and art, when used in hospitals, help to improve the conditions of patients by reducing stress, anxiety and blood pressure.

Children who are involved with the arts make greater achievements in their education: those engaged with drama have greater literary ability while others taking part in musical practice exhibit greater skills in math and languages. Kids with preference for the arts have a greater chance of finding employment in the future. Participating in the arts is essential for child development; encouraging children to express themselves in constructive ways could help to form healthy emotional responses in later life.

Vital to human life, art is celebrated and used by nations across the world for various purposes. Life without art would be boring and dead still, for art is part of what makes us human.

Words, phrases and difficult sentences to understand(Translate them into Chinese).

1. insignificant ________________ 2. generate ________________
3. go through ________________ 4. crossover ________________
5. in honour of ________________ 6. frequent ________________
7. more engagement with the arts ________________
8. be involved with ________________
9. with preference for ________________
10. have a greater chance of ________________
11. Those engaged with drama have greater literary ability while others taking part in musical practice exhibit greater skills in math and languages.

____

12. Life without art would be boring and dead still, for art is part of what makes us human.

____

Task 4: Cultivate your cultural awareness.

The values of artistic works, according to cultural relativism, are simply reflections of local social and economic conditions. Such a view, however, fails to explain the ability of some works of art to excite the human mind across cultures and through centuries.

History has witnessed the endless productions of Shakespearean plays in every major language of the world. It is never rare to find that Mozart packs Japanese concert halls, as Japanese painter Hiroshige does Paris galleries. Unique works of this kind are different from today's popular art, even if they began as works of popular art. They have set themselves apart in their timeless appeal and will probably be enjoyed for centuries into the future.

In a 1757 essay, the philosopher David Hume argued that because "the general principles of taste are uniform in human nature", the value of some works of art might be essentially permanent. He observed that Homer was still admired after two thousand years. Works of this type, he believed, spoke to deep and unvarying features of human nature and could continue to exist over centuries.

Now researchers are applying scientific methods to the study of the universality of art. For example, evolutionary psychology is being used by literary scholars to explain the long-lasting themes and plot devices in fiction. The structures of musical pieces are now open to experimental analysis as never before. Research findings seem to indicate that the creation by a great artist is as permanent an achievement as the discovery by a great scientist.

Lesson 4 New Clothes

Task 1: Step into the "reading forest".

Directions: Try to fill in the following blanks according to your imagination.

There's nothing quite like new clothes, is there? The UK certainly loves them. According to a report by the Environmental Audit Committee (EAC), the UK __1__ five times more clothes today than it did in the 1980s. That's more than any other __2__ in Europe and amounts to around 26.7 kgs per person. This results in 235 million garments going to landfill—victims of fast fashion.

Fast fashion is defined as "an accelerated fashion business model" involving "increased numbers of new fashion collections every year", "quick turnarounds" and "lower prices", according to the EAC. Globalisation means that garments are made in countries where labour is __3__. This saving is passed on to consumers, who then consider the fashion items disposable（一次性的）and easily replace them with something more on-trend. And that creates __4__.

First, there's the environmental cost. Manufacturing any kind of clothes costs resources. For example, synthetic fibres（合成纤维）, which are made from plastic, have a larger carbon footprint than __5__ ones. Natural fibres, although more environmentally friendly, still require more water to grow. And further __6__ are used as the cloth is dyed, made into clothing and transported to stores for sale.

Secondly, the fast-fashion industry is under pressure to put the latest trending items on shelves fast, which can lead to workers being exploited and forced to labour in __7__ working conditions. In countries such as Bangladesh, Ethiopia and the Philippines, workers are paid low salaries that are insufficient to live on.

So what can be done in the UK to __8__ clothes waste? The EAC has recommended eighteen improvements to the UK government, from __9__ tax on purchases to fund recycling centres to introducing more sewing lessons in schools, encouraging a make-do-and-mend attitude.

What can we do? Shop "second-hand", recommends Tolly Gregory, a fashion blogger. Kristabel Plummer, a London-based fashion blogger, also __10__ "looking for high quality" and "longevity". So keep an eye out for durable and reusable clothes that resist wear and tear.

Questions:

1. What is the author's attitude towards fast fashion?

____

2. What are the key words that help you understand the passage?

____

3. What's the structure of the passage?

____

Task 2: Appreciate "trees" in the "reading forest".

Directions: Read the following passage and choose the best answer to each question.

There's nothing quite like new clothes, is there? The UK certainly loves them. According to a report by the Environmental Audit Committee (EAC), the UK consumes five times more clothes today than it did in the 1980s. That's more than any other nation in Europe and amounts to around 26.7 kgs per person. This results in 235 million garments going to landfill— victims of fast fashion.

Fast fashion is defined as "an accelerated fashion business model" involving "increased numbers of new fashion collections every year", "quick turnarounds" and "lower prices", according to the EAC. Globalisation means that garments are made in countries where labour is cheaper. This saving is passed on to consumers, who then consider the fashion items disposable— easily replaceable with something more on-trend. And that creates problems.

First, there's the environmental cost. Manufacturing any kind of textile costs resources. For example, synthetic fibres, which are made from plastic, have a larger carbon footprint than natural ones. Natural fibres, although more carbon-efficient, still require more water to grow. And further resources are used as the cloth is dyed, made into clothing and transported to retail for sale.

Secondly, the fast-fashion industry is under pressure to put the latest trending items on shelves fast, which can lead to workers being exploited and forced to labour in poor working conditions. In countries such as Bangladesh, Ethiopia and the Philippines, workers are paid wages that are insufficient to live on.

So what can be done in the UK to reduce clothes waste? The EAC has recommended eighteen improvements to the UK government, from increasing tax on purchases to fund recycling centres to introducing more sewing lessons in schools, encouraging a make-do-and-mend attitude.

What can we do? Shop "second-hand and vintage", recommends Tolly Gregory, an ethical fashion blogger. Kristabel Plummer, a London-based fashion blogger, also recommends "looking for quality" and "longevity". So keep an eye out for durable and reusable clothes that resist wear and tear.

1. Which statement is true about fast fashion in the UK?

A. The UK makes four times as many clothes today as it did in the 1980s.

B. Hundreds of millions of clothes are sent to the landfill in the UK.

C. Each person in the UK consumes about 26.7kgs clothes every year.

D. The government has made eighteen improvements about fast fashion.

2. What can we learn about the effect of fast fashion?

A. Customers pay more noney for new fashion products.

B. Workers get higher salaries for working in poor conditions.

C. Factories pay more tax for producing fashionable items.

D. More resources are costed in the process of manufacturing.

3. What are ordinary people recommended to do in the passage?

A. Fund recycling centres for old clothes.

B. Introduce sewing courses in schools.

C. Purchase well-made and long-lived clothes.

D. Stop buying new fashionable clothes.

4. What's the best title of the text?

A. The Growing Popularity of Fast Fashion in the UK

B. The Negative Effects of Fast Fashion on the Environment

C. The Problems with the Fast Fashion Industry

D. The Recommendations to Reduce Clothes Waste

Task 3: Have an overview of the "reading forest".

There's nothing quite like new clothes, is there? The UK certainly loves them. According to a report by the Environmental Audit Committee (EAC), the UK consumes five times more clothes today than it did in the 1980s. That's more than any other nation in Europe and amounts to around 26.7 kgs per person. This results in 235 million garments going to landfill— victims of fast fashion.

Fast fashion is defined as "an accelerated fashion business model" involving "increased numbers of new fashion collections every year", "quick turnarounds" and "lower prices", according to the EAC. Globalisation means that garments are made in countries where labour is cheaper. This saving is passed on to consumers, who then consider the fashion items disposable— easily replaceable with something more on-trend. And that creates problems.

First, there's the environmental cost. Manufacturing any kind of textile costs resources. For example, synthetic fibres, which are made from plastic, have a larger carbon footprint than natural ones. Natural fibres, although more carbon-efficient, still require more water to grow. And further resources are used as the cloth is dyed, made into clothing and transported to retail for sale.

Secondly, the fast-fashion industry is under pressure to put the latest trending items on shelves fast, which can lead to workers being exploited and forced to labour in poor working conditions. In countries such as Bangladesh, Ethiopia and the Philippines, workers are paid wages that are insufficient to live on.

So what can be done in the UK to reduce clothes waste? The EAC has recommended eighteen improvements to the UK government, from increasing tax on purchases to fund recycling centres to introducing more sewing lessons in schools, encouraging a make-do-and-mend attitude.

What can we do? Shop "second-hand and vintage", recommends Tolly Gregory, an ethical fashion blogger. Kristabel Plummer, a London-based fashion blogger, also recommends "looking for quality" and "longevity". So keep an eye out for durable and reusable clothes that resist wear and tear.

Words, phrases and difficult sentences to understand(Translate them into Chinese).

1. amount to ________________ 2. victim ________________

3. trending ________________ 4. manufacture ________________

5. carbon footprint ____________ 6. insufficient ________________

7. longevity ________________ 8. durable ________________

9. Secondly, the fast-fashion industry is under pressure to put the latest trending items on shelves fast, which can lead to workers being exploited and forced to labour in poor working conditions.

____

10. The EAC has recommended eighteen improvements to the UK government, from increasing tax on purchases to fund recycling centres to introducing more sewing lessons in schools, encouraging a make-do-and-mend attitude.

____

Task 4: Cultivate your cultural awareness.

The fashion industry produces approximately 10% of the world's carbon emissions. This number will increase as "fast fashion" does as well. With climate change becoming more of a threat each day, people are looking into ways to push back against fast fashion.

Fast fashion is a term that refers to the increase in the production of clothing. The industry is at a peak of production that it hasn't seen before. People buy more clothes, get rid of them faster and look for the cheapest options. Meanwhile, companies are putting out more clothing options and collections than ever. Zara, for example, is one of the biggest fashion producers in the world. In 2021, they produced 840 million articles of clothing.

With production that high, the environmental effects increase greatly. Clothing production has approximately doubled since 2000, and it doesn't show signs of slowing down. With the increase come more impacts on the environment than ever before. On top of the industry's CO_2 emissions, it also affects water consumption and air and ocean pollution. It's the second-largest consumer of water. And many of the clothes end up in landfills and oceans.

With fast fashion increasing, so will these effects. But the environment isn't the only area of vulnerability（易受伤害）. The treatment and wages of workers is an area for concern and attention. Many clothing factories all over the globe do not provide healthy working conditions or fair salaries for their employees. And the higher and faster the demand for clothes, the more they will have to work.

You may want to get active to help change your role or involvement with clothing purchases. Luckily, there are small ways that can make a big difference when shopping. Changes on a small scale that come together have the ability to create changes at the industry level.

Unit 9

Graham Moore's Favorite Books

Lesson 1　Graham Moore's Favorite Books

Task 1: Step into the "reading forest".

Directions: Try to fill in the following blanks according to your imagination.

Graham Moore is the best-selling author of *The Sherlockian* and the screenwriter of The Imitation Game. His new book *The Last Days of Night* is out now. He is talking about some of his favorite books.

Murder in Three Acts **By Agatha Christie**

My mother is a crime fiction lover and, when I was having trouble __1__ to read, we'd sit in my bed at home in Chicago and take it in turns to read a paragraph. It was the first book I read cover-to-cover and I later became a writer __2__ that experience. Not only did it give me a love for crime fiction but, more importantly, it __3__ me that reading can be a __4__ experience.

Cryptonomicon **By Neal Stephenson**

This book showed me that historical fiction need not be dry, but can be lively and enjoyable. Stephenson asks readers to take science __5__, but writes the story in a funny way. I'd long known of Alan Turing, but Stephenson's technique（手法）of describing him was __6__. I saw __7__ a writer can bring a real person to life for modern readers.

A Visit from the Goon Squad **By Jennifer Egan**

Egan uses a technique that I drew on when __8__ *The Imitation Game*. She tells stories from different voices and times, and uses many styles that say to readers, " I've done a lot of work, but now you have to join in and work it out for __9__."

With my __10__ book, my greatest hope is that readers will want to get other people discussing the book. I've just started the conversation.

Questions:

1. What helped Moore to be a writer?

____

2. Who was Alan Turing?

____

3. What's the purpose of writing the passage?

____

Task 2: Appreciate "trees" in the "reading forest".

Directions: Fill in each blank with the word or phrase that best fits the context.

Graham Moore is the best-selling author of *The Sherlockian* and the screenwriter of *The Imitation Game*. His new book *The Last Days of Night* is out now. He is talking about some of his favorite books.

Murder in Three Acts **By Agatha Christie**

My mother is a crime fiction lover and, when I was having trouble __1__ (learn) to read, we'd sit in my bed at home in Chicago and take it in turns to read a paragraph. It was the first book I read cover-to-cover and I later became a writer because __2__ that experience. Not only did it give me a love for crime fiction but, more importantly, it __3__ (teach) me that reading can be a __4__ (share) experience.

Cryptonomicon **By Neal Stephenson**

This book showed me that historical fiction need not be dry, but can be lively and enjoyable. Stephenson asks readers to take science __5__ (serious) , but writes the story in a funny way. I'd long known of Alan Turing, but Stephenson's technique of describing him was __6__ (surprise) . I saw __7__ a writer can bring a real person to life for modern readers.

A Visit from the Goon Squad **By Jennifer Egan**

Egan uses a technique that I drew on when writing *The Imitation Game*. She tells stories from different voices and times, and uses many __8__ (style) that say to readers, " I've done a lot of work, but now you have to join in and work it out for __9__ (your) ."

With my___10___ (late) book, my greatest hope is that readers will want to get other people discussing the book. I've just started the conversation.

Task 3: Have an overview of the "reading forest".

Graham Moore is the best-selling author of *The Sherlockian* and the screenwriter of *The Imitation Game*. His new book *The Last Days of Night* is out now. He is talking about some of his favorite books.

Murder in Three Acts **By Agatha Christie**

My mother is a crime fiction lover and, when I was having trouble learning to read, we'd sit in my bed at home in Chicago and take it in turns to read a paragraph. It was the first book I read cover-to-cover and I later became a writer because of that experience. Not only did it give me a love for crime fiction but, more importantly, it taught me that reading can be a shared experience.

Cryptonomicon **By Neal Stephenson**

This book showed me that historical fiction need not be dry, but can be lively and enjoyable. Stephenson asks readers to take science seriously, but writes the story in a funny way. I'd long known of Alan Turing, but Stephenson's technique of describing him was surprising. I saw how a writer can bring a real person to life for modern readers.

A Visit from the Goon Squad **By Jennifer Egan**

Egan uses a technique that I drew on when writing *The Imitation Game*. She tells stories from different voices and times, and uses many styles that say to readers, " I've done a lot of work, but now you have to join in and work it out for yourselves."

With my latest book, my greatest hope is that readers will want to get other people discussing the book. I've just started the conversation.

Words, phrases and difficult sentences to understand (Translate them into Chinese).

1. best-selling ________________________________

2. take it in turns to read ________________________________

3. read cover-to-cover ________________

4. take science seriously ________________

5. draw on ________________

6. get other people discussing the book ________________

7. work it out ________________

8. His new book *The Last Days of Night* is out now

____

9. Not only did it give me a love for crime fiction but, more importantly, it taught me that reading can be a shared experience.

____

10. I saw how a writer can bring a real person to life for modern readers.

____

Task 4: Cultivate your cultural awareness.

The Last Days of Night

From Graham Moore, the Oscar-winning screenwriter of *The Imitation Game* and *New York Times* bestselling author of *The Sherlockian*, comes a thrilling novel—based on actual events—about the nature of genius, the cost of ambition, and the battle to electrify America.

New York, 1888. Gas lamps still flicker in the city streets, but the miracle of electric light is in its infancy. The person who controls the means to turn night into day will make history—and a vast fortune. A young untested lawyer named Paul Cravath, fresh out of Columbia Law School, takes a case that seems impossible to win. Paul's client, George Westinghouse, has been sued by Thomas Edison over a billion-dollar question: Who invented the light bulb and holds the right to power the country?

The case affords Paul entry to the heady world of high society—the glittering parties in Gramercy Park mansions, and the more insidious dealings done behind closed doors. The task facing him is beyond daunting. Edison is a wily, dangerous opponent with vast resources at his disposal—private spies, newspapers in his pocket, and the backing of J. P. Morgan himself. Yet this unknown lawyer shares with his famous adversary a compulsion to win at all costs. How will he do it?

In obsessive pursuit of victory, Paul crosses paths with Nikola Tesla, an eccentric, brilliant inventor who may hold the key to defeating Edison, and with Agnes Huntington, a beautiful opera singer who proves to be a flawless performer on stage and off. As Paul takes greater and greater risks, he'll find that everyone in his path is playing their own game, and no one is quite who they seem.

Graham Moore is a *New York Times* bestselling novelist and Academy Award-winning screenwriter. His screenplay for *THE IMITATION GAME* won the Academy Award and WGA Award for Best Adapted Screenplay in 2015 and was nominated for a BAFTA and a Golden Globe. The film, directed by Morten Tyldum and starring Benedict Cumberbatch and Keira Knightley, received 8 Academy Award nominations, including Best Picture.

Graham's first novel, *THE SHERLOCKIAN* (2010), was published in 16 countries and translated into 13 languages. It was called "sublime" and "clever" and "delightful" by the *New York Times*, "savvy" and "entertaining" by the *Los Angeles Times*, and lots of other nice things as well. Graham's second novel, *THE LAST* DAYS OF NIGHT will be published in fall 2016 by Random House.

Lesson 2 The Return of a Long Lost Friend

Task 1: Step into the "reading forest".

Directions: Try to fill in the following blanks according to your imagination.

When I was seven, my family and I were coming back from a T-ball game. In our driveway, we __1__ two adult geese and a small gosling. The adults were __2__ by our return and flew away, but their baby was still too young to fly and couldn't __3__.

__4__ passed, and night fell. It was clear that the gosling needed __5__,warmth and food to __6__ to the morning. At that point, we had to bring him into our backyard.

We all pretty much slept with one eye open for several days. Each morning, we would try to rush the goose over to his __7__, who kept coming back to our yard. He wouldn't go to them, __8__, and they wouldn't come close enough to __9__ him. The young goose had clearly decided we were his new __10__, and my twin sister Joanna called the little guy Peeper.

Almost a year passed and we settled into a(n) __11__ filled with __12__ hugs and company. One evening, my uncle came over, and my dad threw Peeper up into the air to show he could fly around the house, but this time, Peeper just __13__. Everyone was very sad. Twenty years passed, and Peeper became a fond __14__ for my family.

In 2019, a(n) __15__ adult goose made his way back to my home. At first, I __16__ it was just another Canada goose.After two weeks of the goose coming back __17__, it became clear to me that this wasn't a(n) __18__ goose. He did all of the same things Peeper used to and __19__ to the name Peeper. Much to my __20__, my old best friend had returned, 20 years later.

Questions:

1. What does the passage mainly talk about?

____

2. What's the structure or clue of the passage?

____

Task 2: Appreciate "trees" in the "reading forest".

Directions: For each blank in the following passage there are four words or phrases marked A, B, C and D. Fill in each blank with the word or phrase that best fits the context.

When I was seven, my family and I were coming back from a T-ball game. In our driveway, we __1__ two adult geese and a small gosling. The adults were __2__ by our return and flew away, but their baby was still too young to fly and couldn't __3__ .

__4__ passed, and night fell. It was clear that the gosling needed __5__ ,warmth and food to __6__ to the morning. At that point, we had to bring him into our backyard.

We all pretty much slept with one eye open for several days. Each morning, we would try to rush the goose over to his __7__ , who kept coming back to our yard. He wouldn't go to them, __8__ , and they wouldn't come close enough to __9__ him. The young goose had clearly decided we were his new __10__ , and my twin sister Joanna called the little guy Peeper.

Almost a year passed and we settled into a(n) __11__ filled with __12__ hugs and company. One evening, my uncle came over, and my dad threw Peeper up into the air to show he could fly around the house, but this time, Peeper just __13__ . Everyone was very sad. Twenty years passed, and Peeper became a fond __14__ for my family.

In 2019, a(n) __15__ adult goose made his way back to my home. At first, I __16__ it was just another Canada goose.After two weeks of the goose coming back __17__ , it became clear to me that this wasn't a(n) __18__ goose. He did all of the same things

Peeper used to and ___19___ to the name Peeper. Much to my ___20___, my old best friend had returned, 20 years later.

1. A. looked at	B. spotted	C. caught	D. met
2. A. thrilled	B. confused	C. frightened	D. astonished
3. A. fly	B. leave	C. follow	D. join
4. A. Minutes	B. Days	C. Weeks	D. Hours
5. A. protection	B. safety	C. company	D. shelter
6. A. make it	B. take it	C. carry on	D. go through
7. A. sisters	B. brothers	C. parents	D. friends
8. A. otherwise	B. therefore	C. still	D. though
9. A. forgive	B. challenge	C. annoy	D. claim
10. A. parents	B. family	C. fellows	D. friends
11.A. rule	B. routine	C. order	D. habit
12.A. feathery	B. furry	C. hairy	D. downy
13.A. fell off	B. ran off	C. flew off	D. went off
14. A. memory	B. dream	C. hope	D. desire
15. A. strong	B. weak	C. young	D. aging
16. A. knew	B. assumed	C. realized	D. found
17. A. occasionally	B. repeatedly	C. rarely	D. suddenly
18. A. random	B. deliberate	C. aimless	D. homeless
19. A. answered	B. admitted	C. objected	D. responded
20. A. satisfaction	B. confusion	C. amazement	D. disappointment

Task 3: Have an overview of the "reading forest".

When I was seven, my family and I were coming back from a T-ball game. In our driveway, we spotted two adult geese and a small gosling. The adults were frightened by our return and flew away, but their baby was still too young to fly and couldn't follow.

Hours passed, and night fell. It was clear that the gosling needed protection,warmth and food to make it to the morning. At that point, we had to bring him into our backyard.

We all pretty much slept with one eye open for several days. Each morning,we would try to rush the goose over to his parents, who kept coming back to our yard. He wouldn't go to them,though, and they wouldn't come close enough to claim him. The young goose had clearly decided we were his new family, and my twin sister Joanna called the little guy Peeper.

Almost a year passed and we settled into a routine filled with feathery hugs and company. One evening, my uncle came over, and my dad threw Peeper up into the air to show he could fly around the house, but this time, Peeper just flew off. Everyone was very sad. Twenty years passed, and Peeper became a fond memory for my family.

In 2019, an aging adult goose made his way back to my home. At first, I assumed it was just another Canada goose. After two weeks of the goose coming back repeatedly, it became clear to me that this wasn't a random goose. He did all of the same things Peeper used to and responded to the name Peeper. Much to my amazement, my old best friend had returned, 20 years later.

Words, phrases and difficult sentences to understand (Translate them into Chinese).

1. spot ____________　　2. make it ____________
3. claim ____________　　4. routine ____________
5. feathery ____________　　6. aging ____________
7. assume ____________　　8. repeatedly ____________
9. random ____________　　10. respond ____________

11. Almost a year passed and we settled into a routine filled with feathery hugs and company.

____

12. After two weeks of the goose coming back repeatedly, it became clear to me that this wasn't a random goose.

____

Task 4: Cultivate your cultural awareness.

People have always been desired connection with the animal world since the ancient times. Through Peeper, we have learned so much about ourselves and about the love of animals. Human beings and animals are friends, so we should get along well with each other harmoniously.

Many people like to keep lovely animals as pets and treat them as their family members. By living together with those animals, people have built a strong relationship with their animals , which often moves people deeply. Take the movie *Hachi* for example.

Based on a true story happening in Japan in 1935, the film focuses on a strong bond between a dog and his master. Parker, a university professor, adopted a small Akita dog named Hachi. Every day, Hachi accompanied the professor to the station in the morning and waited for him to come back home in the evening. Unfortunately, the professor died of illness one day, and never returned to the station. Hachi couldn't get his master any longer. However, Hachi still waited at the station for him every day loyally for the next 9 years until he finally died.

Hachi is a moving story about a dog's loyalty that transcends animal-human barrier. Most people who have seen the touching movie are so impressed by the dog's loyalty to his master that they just can't help tearing. Hachi devoted his whole life to waiting for his master Packer. Now people can see a Hachi made in copper, waiting at Segu Station day in and day out...

Therefore, since animals are so important for us human beings, why can't we protect them? If they disappear someday, the balance of the biological system will be broken and there will be a great crisis for human beings to survive.

Lesson 3　Which Is Better: Soap or Hand Sanitizer?

Task 1: Step into the "reading forest".

Directions: Try to fill in the following blanks according to your imagination.

With folds in your hands, there are plenty of hiding places for a virus to stick. If you then touch your face, the virus can infect you. __1__. So which is better?

__2__. A single drop of any brand of soap contains amphiphiles. Their tails compete for space with the lipids that make up the virus's shell to make the whole thing come crashing down. Those amphiphiles then form bubbles. __3__.

Hand sanitizers work like an earthquake. Surround a coronavirus with a high concentration of an alcohol found in most hand-sanitizers. __4__. The overall effect is like removing all of the nails and mortar from a house and then hitting it with an earthquake. The cell's membrane collapses and those spike proteins crumble.

In either method, the actual process of destroying the virus happens in just a second or two. But doctors recommend at least 20 seconds of hand-washing because of the complicated landscape that is your hand. Soap and sanitizer need to get everywhere, including your palms, fingertips, the outsides of your hands, and between your fingers, to protect you properly.

__5__, doctors recommend washing your hands with soap and water whenever possible. It has two benefits: first, it washes away any dirt which could otherwise hide virus particles. But more importantly, it's simply easier to fully cover your hands with soap and water for 20 seconds.

Questions:

1. What does the passage mainly talk about?

____

2. What are the key words that help you understand the passage better?

____

3. What's the structure or clue of the passage?

____

Task 2: Appreciate "trees" in the "reading forest".

Directions: Choose the right sentences to complete the passage.

With folds in your hands, there are plenty of hiding places for a virus to stick. If you then touch your face, the virus can infect you. __1__. So which is better?

__2__. A single drop of any brand of soap contains amphiphiles. Their tails compete for space with the lipids that make up the virus's shell to make the whole thing come crashing down. Those amphiphiles then form bubbles. __3__.

Hand sanitizers work like an earthquake. Surround a coronavirus with a high concentration of an alcohol found in most hand-sanitizers. __4__. The overall effect is like removing all of the nails and mortar from a house and then hitting it with an earthquake. The cell's membrane collapses and those spike proteins crumble.

In either method, the actual process of destroying the virus happens in just a second or two. But doctors recommend at least 20 seconds of hand-washing because of the complicated landscape that is your hand. Soap and sanitizer need to get everywhere, including your palms, fingertips, the outsides of your hands, and between your fingers, to protect you properly.

__5__, doctors recommend washing your hands with soap and water whenever possible. It has two benefits: first, it washes away any dirt which could otherwise hide virus particles. But more importantly, it's simply easier to fully cover your hands with soap and water for 20 seconds.

A. Apply water, and you'll wash that whole bubble away

B. When it comes to a coronavirus outbreak

C. Here is the principle of soap

D. There are two simple ways you can stop that happening: soap and water, and hand sanitizer

E. These sanitizers actually kill viruses

F. This gives the molecules room to move around

G. When you wash your hands

Task 3: Have an overview of the "reading forest".

With folds in your hands, there are plenty of hiding places for a virus to stick. If you then touch your face, the virus can infect you. There are two simple ways you can stop that happening: soap and water, and hand sanitizer. So which is better?

Here is the principle of soap. A single drop of any brand of soap contains amphiphiles. Their tails compete for space with the lipids that make up the virus's shell to make the whole thing come crashing down. Those amphiphiles then form bubbles. Apply water, and you'll wash that whole bubble away.

Hand sanitizers work like an earthquake. Surround a coronavirus with a high concentration of an alcohol found in most hand-sanitizers. This gives the molecules room to move around. The overall effect is like removing all of the nails and mortar from a house and then hitting it with an earthquake. The cell's membrane collapses and those spike proteins crumble.

In either method, the actual process of destroying the virus happens in just a second or two. But doctors recommend at least 20 seconds of hand-washing because of the complicated landscape that is your hand. Soap and sanitizer need to get everywhere, including your palms, fingertips, the outsides of your hands, and between your fingers, to protect you properly.

When it comes to a coronavirus outbreak, doctors recommend washing your hands with soap and water whenever possible. It has two benefits: first, it washes away any dirt which could otherwise hide virus particles. But more importantly, it's simply easier to fully cover your hands with soap and water for 20 seconds.

Words, phrases and difficult sentences to understand (Translate them into Chinese)

1. fold ________________ 2. stick ________________
3. collapse ________________ 4. landscape ________________
5. hand sanitizer ________________ 6. crash down ________________
7. stop doing ________________ 8. fall prey to sth. ________________
9. The overall effect is like removing all of the nails and mortar from a house and then hitting it with an earthquake.

____

Task 4: Cultivate your cultural awareness.

Respiratory viruses like coronavirus disease (COVID-19) spread when mucus or droplets containing the virus get into your body through your eyes, nose or throat. Often, the virus can easily spread from one person to the next via hands.

During a global pandemic, one of the cheapest, easiest, and most important ways to prevent the spread of a virus is to wash your hands frequently with soap and water.

Here's everything you need to know about how to wash your hands the right way:

1. How do I wash my hands properly?

To eliminate all traces of the virus on your hands, a quick scrub and a rinse won't cut it. Below is a step-by-step process for effective handwashing.

Step 1: Wet hands with running water.

Step 2: Apply enough soap to cover wet hands.

Step 3: Scrub all surfaces of the hands — including back of hands, between fingers and under nails — for at least 20 seconds.

Step 4: Rinse thoroughly with running water.

Step 5: Dry hands with a clean cloth or single-use towel.

2. How long should I wash my hands?

You should wash your hands for at least 20–30 seconds. An easy way to time it is by singing the full happy birthday song, twice. The same goes for hand sanitizer: use a sanitizer that contains at least 60% alcohol and rub it into your hands for at least 20 seconds to ensure full coverage.

3. When should I wash my hands?

In the context of COVID-19 prevention, you should make sure to wash your hands at the following times:

After blowing your nose, coughing or sneezing.

After visiting a public space, including public transportation, markets and places of worship.

After touching surfaces outside of the home, including money.

Before, during and after caring for a sick person.

Before and after eating.

In general, you should always wash your hands at the following times:

After using the toilet.

Before and after eating.

After handling garbage.

After touching animals and pets.

After changing babies' diapers or helping children use the toilet.

When your hands are visibly dirty.

4. Do I need to use warm water to wash my hands?

No, you can use any temperature of water to wash your hands. Cold water and warm water are equally effective at killing germs and viruses — as long as you use soap!

5. Do I need to dry my hands with a towel?

Germs spread more easily from wet skin than from dry skin, so drying your hands completely is an important step. Paper towels or clean clothes are the most effective way to remove germs without spreading them to other surfaces.

Lesson 4 Worried by Numbers

Task 1: Step into the "reading forest".

Directions: Try to fill in the following blanks according to your imagination.

Do you get nervous thinking about geometry, equations (方程式) or a coming math test? If yes, you are __1__ alone. Math anxiety has become a common psychological __2__ among students around the world. Students in countries with higher levels of math anxiety __3__ to achieve lower math grades, according to a study published in the *Proceedings of the National Academy of Sciences* on Feb. 15.

Math anxiety—a __4__ emotional reaction to the core subject —causes __5__, physical suffering and behavior problems among young pupils, according to a University of Cambridge study. In ordinary life, many people experience some degree of __6__ when confronted with a math problem, __7__ from mild tension to strong fear.

Some people also __8__ physical symptoms such as sweaty palms or a __9__ heart. They may then try to avoid every situation involving __10__, meaning they are __11__ from pursuing careers __12__ this subject, such as science, technology or engineering, according to *The Guardian*.

Reassurance comes from the fact that those with math anxiety aren't destined to be bad at math. "If a child has math anxiety, don't __13__ that they're not good at __14__. They may have had a really bad experience with math and there are ways to improve math achievement," Daniel Ansari, the senior author of the study told the London Free Press, "Students with math anxiety are not cognitively __15__."

Also, there are ways to __16__ your stress related to math. If you're feeling stressed before a math exam, it may help to spend a few minutes __17__ those feelings before the exam begins. "It's about making sure you're interpreting your feelings correctly, "Sian Beilock, a cognitive scientist in the US told the BBC, "Just because you have a fast heartbeat and sweaty palms, that does not necessarily mean you will __18__."

A little math anxiety could be taken as a positive challenge to __19__. Just like many people get stage fright before delivering a speech, this nervous energy can help to __20__, according to Ian Lyons, a psychologist at Georgetown University in the US.

Questions:

1. What does the passage mainly talk about?

____

2. What are the key words that help you understand the passage better?

____

3. What can you do to overcome math anxiety?

____

Task 2: Appreciate "trees" in the "reading forest".

Directions: For each blank in the following passage there are four words or phrases marked A, B, C and D. Fill in each blank with the word or phrase that best fits the context.

Do you get nervous thinking about geometry, equations or a coming math test? If yes, you are __1__ alone. Math anxiety has become a common psychological __2__ among students around the world. Students in countries with higher levels of math anxiety __3__ to achieve lower math grades, according to a study published in the *Proceedings of the National Academy of Sciences* on Feb. 15.

Math anxiety— a __4__ emotional reaction to the core subject —causes __5__, physical suffering and behavior problems among young pupils, according to a University of Cambridge study. In ordinary life, many people experience some degree of __6__ when confronted with a math problem, __7__ from mild tension to strong fear.

Some people also __8__ physical symptoms such as sweaty palms or a __9__ heart. They may then try to avoid every situation involving __10__, meaning they are

__11__ from pursuing careers __12__ this subject, such as science, technology or engineering, according to *The Guardian*.

Reassurance comes from the fact that those with math anxiety aren't destined to be bad at math. "If a child has math anxiety, don't __13__ that they're not good at __14__. They may have had a really bad experience with math and there are ways to improve math achievement," Daniel Ansari, the senior author of the study told The London Free Press, "Students with math anxiety are not cognitively __15__."

Also, there are ways to __16__ your stress related to math. If you're feeling stressed before a math exam, it may help to spend a few minutes __17__ those feelings before the exam begins. "It's about making sure you're interpreting your feelings correctly, "Sian Beilock, a cognitive scientist in the US told the BBC, "Just because you have a fast heartbeat and sweaty palms, that does not necessarily mean you will __18__."

A little math anxiety could be taken as a positive challenge to __19__. Just like many people get stage fright before delivering a speech, this nervous energy can help to __20__, according to Ian Lyons, a psychologist at Georgetown University in the US.

1. A. behind	B. aside	C. away from	D.far from
2. A. choice	B. doubt	C. condition	D. answer
3. A. hope	B. tend	C. pretend	D. decide
4. A. negative	B. angry	C. positive	D. fierce
5. A. fear	B. excitement	C.regret	D. sorrow
6. A. disagreement	B. distrust	C. discomfort	D.dishonest
7. A. changing	B. ranging	C. fading	D. spreading
8. A. predict	B. experience	C. monitor	D. ignore
9. A. beating	B. breaking	C. worrying	D. racing
10. A. grades	B. numbers	C. results	D. types
11. A. held on	B. held out	C. held up	D. held back
12. A. committed to	B. adjusted to	C. related to	D. compared to
13. A. assume	B. expect	C. promise	D. remind
14. A. Japanese	B. Chinese	C. math	D. English

15. A. disadvantaged	B. shocked	C. thrilled	D. ashamed
16. A. prove	B. maintain	C. manage	D. gain
17. A. promoting	B. exploring	C. tolerating	D. observing
18. A. fail	B. continue	C. choose	D. admit
19. A. face	B. attempt	C. abandon	D. overcome
20. A. participate	B. contribute	C. hesitate	D. motivate

Task 3: Have an overview of the "reading forest".

Do you get nervous thinking about geometry, equations or a coming math test? If yes, you are far from alone. Math anxiety has become a common psychological condition among students around the world. Students in countries with higher levels of math anxiety tend to achieve lower math grades, according to a study published in the *Proceedings of the National Academy of Sciences* on Feb. 15.

Math anxiety — a negative emotional reaction to the core subject — causes fear, physical suffering and behavior problems among young pupils, according to a University of Cambridge study. In ordinary life, many people experience some degree of discomfort when confronted with a math problem, ranging from mild tension to strong fear.

Some people also experience physical symptoms such as sweaty palms or a racing heart. They may then try to avoid every situation involving numbers, meaning they are held back from pursuing careers related to this subject, such as science, technology or engineering, according to *The Guardian*.

Reassurance comes from the fact that those with math anxiety aren't destined to be bad at math. "If a child has math anxiety, don't assume that they're not good at math. They may have had a really bad experience with math and there are ways to improve math achievement," Daniel Ansari, the senior author of the study told the London Free Press, "Students with math anxiety are not cognitively disadvantaged."

Also, there are ways to manage your stress related to math. If you're feeling stressed before a math exam, it may help to spend a few minutes exploring those feelings before the exam begins. "It's about making sure you're interpreting your feelings correctly, "Sian Beilock, a cognitive scientist in the US told the BBC, "Just because you have a fast heartbeat and sweaty palms, that does not necessarily mean you will fail."

A little math anxiety could be taken as a positive challenge to overcome. Just like many people get stage fright before delivering a speech, this nervous energy can help to motivate, according to Ian Lyons, a psychologist at Georgetown University in the US.

Words, phrases and difficult sentences to understand (Translate them into Chinese).

1. far from ____________________ 2. core ____________________

3. race ____________________ 4. hold back ____________________

5. assume ____________________ 6. motivate ____________________

7. In ordinary life, many people experience some degree of discomfort when confronted with a math problem, ranging from mild tension to strong fear.

____

8. They may then try to avoid every situation involving numbers, meaning they are held back from pursuing careers related to this subject, such as science, technology or engineering, according to *The Guardian*.

____

Task 4: Cultivate your cultural awareness.

Seeing Maths as a Code

Math doesn't come easy, no matter how clever you are. Leonardo da Vinci, the famous Italian artist, was a huge fan of mathematics. But his notebooks show that Da Vinci couldn't do fractions（分数）. He could never grasp, for instance, that dividing a number by one-quarter is the same as multiplying by four, resulting in a higher number than the original.

How to Prevent Math Anxiety

If your child struggles with these challenges, you've probably found yourself wondering how to handle math anxiety. It can affect any student, and the best way to prevent it is to build positive study habits.

Check out these math anxiety strategies to find out how to improve your child's performance in the classroom.

Four Math Anxiety Tips:

Positive Reinforcement

Students coping with math anxiety need to feel that they can excel at math.

Review homework with your child and point out all the questions he or she got right. Put an emphasis on correct answers rather than mistakes. If possible, surround the student with positive teachers and students.

Get a Tutor

Teachers can have a great impact on a student's feelings toward math. Even if the teacher is enthusiastic about math, supplement teaching with a qualified tutor. Tutors can provide personal attention that is hard to get at school. They can help students work through their problems in a low-pressure environment. Tutoring can also improve students' self confidence.

Reframe Anxiety

Reframing anxiety can have an improvement in mathematics performance. Have a student write down his or her worries about math before doing it. By having to think critically, students can realize their fears are unfounded.Young children can draw pictures as a substitute for writing. Assist reframing by having students see tests and assignments as challenges instead of threats.

Make Math Fun!

Try to create positive emotions by making math fun. One way to do this is to connect math to the child's interests. For example, if the student likes sports, use sport-related word problems.

Unit 10

University Shotokan Karate Club

Lesson 1 University Shotokan Karate Club

Task 1: Step into the "reading forest".

Directions: Try to fill in the following blanks according to your imagination.

University Shotokan Karate Club

Learn Karate—self-defense and fitness

The university karate club was __1__ in 1962. All grades from beginners to advanced are welcome. The classes are __2__ for both men and women and several women have obtained their black belt.

TUESDAY AND THURSDAY

6.00–8.00 p.m.

WEAVER HOUSE GYM

FIRST LESSON FREE

Hardly any of us have __3__ real violence, but, over the last few years, attacks on innocent people have increased. Each of us has some __4__ to defend ourselves, and by learning a form of self-defence, we are not only increasing that ability, but also doing something to build our own sense of respect. Karate will show you a lot of simple and effective techniques to protect yourself, giving you increase self-confidence.

Far too many people think martial arts（武术）are about __5__. Martial arts training is based on a lot of respect, self-discipline, self-control and non-violence. We learn basic etiquette, courtesy and tolerance. Good manners and consideration for others are expected at all times.

Karate is the practice of blocking and striking techniques for the purpose of self-defence, health and self-development. Karate __6__ the entire body. Techniques are practised on both sides of the body, therefore muscle imbalances do not occur and the strength, coordination, flexibility and agility of both sides of the body are __7__. Regular training in Karate improves the body's physical endurance and flexibility. It also helps concentration and produces the mental calm and assurance that come from knowing we can defend ourselves.

Karate has many __8__ but they do not come easily or overnight. Training requires __9__ commitment and hard work. Some of you will __10__, but a few of you will get your black belt.

Questions:

1. What does the passage mainly talk about?

____

2. What is the Martial arts training based on?

____

3. What's the benefits of Karate?

____

Task 2: Appreciate "trees" in the "reading forest".

Directions: Read the passage again and choose the best answers from the following three questions.

University Shotokan Karate Club

Learn Karate—self-defense and fitness

The university karate club was founded in 1962. All grades from beginners to advanced are welcome. The classes are suitable for both men and women and several women have obtained their black belt.

TUESDAY AND THURSDAY

6.00–8.00 p.m.

WEAVER HOUSE GYM

FIRST LESSON FREE

Hardly any of us have experienced real violence, but, over the last few years, attacks on innocent people have increased. Each of us has some ability to defend ourselves, and by learning a form of self-defence, we are not only increasing that ability, but also doing something to build our own sense of respect. Karate will show you a lot of simple and effective techniques to protect yourself, giving you increase self-confidence.

Far too many people think martial arts are about violence. Martial arts training is based on a lot of respect, self-discipline, self-control and non-violence. We learn basic etiquette, courtesy and tolerance. Good manners and consideration for others are expected at all times.

Karate is the practice of blocking and striking techniques for the purpose of self-defence, health and self-development. Karate exercises the entire body. Techniques are practised on both sides of the body, therefore muscle imbalances do not occur and the strength, coordination, flexibility and agility of both sides of the body are improved. Regular training in Karate improves the body's physical endurance and flexibility. It also helps concentration and produces the mental calm and assurance that come from knowing we can defend ourselves.

Karate has many benefits but they do not come easily or overnight. Training requires ongoing commitment and hard work. Some of you will give up, but a few of you will get your black belt.

1. The purpose of this passage is to ______.

A. introduce the club

B. attract readers to join the club

C. correct people's misunderstanding of Karate

D. tell readers the advantages of Karate

2. According to the passage, which of the following statements is true about University Shotokan Karate Club?

A. Many members have their black belt.

B. It opens every day.

C. Members need to pay for all the lessons.

D. It offers 4 hours of lessons every week.

3. What can be learned about Karate?

   A. It cultivates people's respect for themselves as well as for others.

   B. It only involves people's arm muscles.

   C. It makes people healthy physically more than mentally.

   D. It makes people easily get their black belt.

Task 3: Have an overview of the "reading forest".

University Shotokan Karate Club

Learn Karate—self-defense and fitness

The university karate club was founded in 1962. All grades from beginners to advanced are welcome. The classes are suitable for both men and women and several women have obtained their black belt.

TUESDAY AND THURSDAY

6.00–8.00 p.m.

WEAVER HOUSE GYM

FIRST LESSON FREE

Hardly any of us have experienced real violence, but, over the last few years, attacks on innocent people have increased. Each of us has some ability to defend ourselves, and by learning a form of self-defence, we are not only increasing that ability, but also doing something to build our own sense of respect. Karate will show you a lot of simple and effective techniques to protect yourself, giving you increase self-confidence.

Far too many people think martial arts（武术）are about violence. Martial arts training is based on a lot of respect, self-discipline, self-control and non-violence. We learn basic etiquette, courtesy and tolerance. Good manners and consideration for others are expected at all times.

Karate is the practice of blocking and striking techniques for the purpose of self-defence, health and self-development. Karate exercises the entire body. Techniques are practised on both sides of the body, therefore muscle imbalances do not occur and the strength, coordination, flexibility and agility of both sides of the body are improved.

Regular training in Karate improves the body's physical endurance and flexibility. It also helps concentration and produces the mental calm and assurance that come from knowing we can defend ourselves.

Karate has many benefits but they do not come easily or overnight. Training requires ongoing commitment and hard work. Some of you will give up, but a few of you will get your black belt.

Words, phrases and difficult sentences to understand (Translate them into Chinese).

1. be suitable for ________________ 2. obtain ________________________

3. self-confidence ______________ 4. self-discipline _________________

5. self-control __________________ 6. non-violence __________________

7. etiquette ____________________ 8. courtesy _______________________

9. coordination _________________ 10. agility ________________________

11. We learn basic etiquette, courtesy and tolerance. Good manners and consideration for others are expected at all times.

____

12. Training requires ongoing commitment and hard work.

____

Task 4: Cultivate your cultural awareness.

Martial arts are not about violence, neither is the karate. We can exercise and build our body by learning it. Karate is the practice of blocking and striking techniques for the purpose of self-defence, health and self-development. It can improve our strength, coordination, flexibility and agility of both sides of the body. What's more, it also helps concentration and produces the mental calm and assurance that come from knowing we can defend ourselves. So come to join it, you'll get many benefits!

The black belt is mentioned twice in this passage.The black belt signifies the highest proficiency in karate. The usual colors awarded are, in ascending order, white, green, brown, and black. Besides, karate became the new event of the Tokyo Olympic Games in 2021.

Lesson 2 Animal lovers

Task 1: Step into the "reading forest".

Directions: Try to fill in the following blanks according to your imagination.

You can tell a lot about a man by how he treats his dogs.

For many years, I enjoyed living with my dogs, Tilly and Chance. Their __1__ was nearly enough to keep my loneliness at bay. Last year, I started dating, but with __2__. When I first dated Steve, I __3__ he had a dog, Molly, and a cat, Flora. While I was __4__ that he was an animal lover, I __5__ that three dogs were perhaps too many, and my dogs might attack __6__, the cat.

The next week we __7__ our dogs together. It was a hot day. When we paused to catch our __8__, Steve got down on one knee. Was he proposing（求婚）? I liked him too, but so __9__? He poured water from a bottle into his hand and offered it to my dogs. __10__, I began to fall for him.

We __11__ to date, though neither of us brought up the future. And then in late November, Tilly had an operation on her __12__. I took the dogs out four times a day, and I worried that Tilly __13__ climbing the stairs could reopen the wound. Then Steve __14__ his house. All worked __15__. The three dogs formed a pack that, with coaching, __16__ Flora's space; Steve and I formed a good team __17__ for Tilly. We made good housemates.

A year later, much to my __18__, this man produced a little box with a ring and proposed to me. He did not kneel（跪）down, nor did I __19__ him to. That's only for giving __20__ to the dogs that brought us together.

Questions:

1. What does the passage mainly talk about?

____

2. What are the key words that help you understand the passage better?

____

3. What's the structure or clue of the passage?

____

Task 2: Appreciate "trees" in the "reading forest".

Directions: For each blank in the following passage there are four words or phrases marked A, B, C and D. Fill in each blank with the word or phrase that best fits the context.

You can tell a lot about a man by how he treats his dogs.

For many years, I enjoyed living with my dogs, Tilly and Chance. Their __1__ was nearly enough to keep my loneliness at bay. Last year, I started dating, but with __2__. When I first dated Steve, I __3__ he had a dog, Molly, and a cat, Flora. While I was __4__ that he was an animal lover, I __5__ that three dogs were perhaps too many, and my dogs might attack __6__, the cat.

The next week we __7__ our dogs together. It was a hot day. When we paused to catch our __8__, Steve got down on one knee. Was he proposing? I liked him too, but so __9__? He poured water from a bottle into his hand and offered it to my dogs. __10__, I began to fall for him.

We __11__ to date, though neither of us brought up the future. And then in late November, Tilly had an operation on her __12__. I took the dogs out four times a day, and I worried that Tilly __13__ climbing the stairs could reopen the wound. Then Steve __14__ his house. All worked __15__. The three dogs formed a pack that, with coaching, __16__ Flora's space; Steve and I formed a good team __17__ for Tilly. We made good housemates.

A year later, much to my __18__, this man produced a little box with a ring and proposed to me. He did not kneel down, nor did I __19__ him to. That's only for giving __20__ to the dogs that brought us together.

1.A. ownership	B. membership	C. companionship	D. leadership
2. A. reservation	B. expectation	C. confidence	D. prejudice
3. A. feared	B. doubted	C. hoped	D. learned
4. A. unsatisfied	B. amused	C. terrified	D. thrilled
5. A. predicted	B. worried	C. regretted	D. insisted
6. A. Flora	B. Chance	C. Moll	D. Tilly
7. A. tied	B. walked	C. bathed	D. fed
8. A. breath	B. balance	C. attention	D. imagination
9. A. calm	B. sure	C. soon	D. real
10. A. By the way		B. In that case	
C. By all means		D. In that moment	
11. A. continued	B. decided	C. intended	D. pretended
12. A. eye	B. tail	C. ear	D. leg
13. A. secretly	B. constantly	C. eventually	D. unwillingly
14. A. left	B. sold	C. suggested	D. searched
15. A. late	B. hard	C. fine	D. free
16. A. emptied	B. respected	C. occupied	D. discovered
17. A. looking	B. caring	C. waiting	D. calling
18. A. delight	B. credit	C. interest	D. disadvantage
19. A. beg	B. trust	C. need	D. aid
20. A. toys	B. awards	C. food	D. water

Task 3: Have an overview of the "reading forest".

Animals lovers

You can tell a lot about a man by how he treats his dogs.

For many years, I enjoyed living with my dogs, Tilly and Chance. Their companionship was nearly enough to keep my loneliness at bay. Last year, I started dating, but with reservation. When I first dated Steve, I learned he had a dog, Molly, and a cat, Flora. While I was thrilled that he was an animal lover, I worried that three dogs were perhaps too many, and my dogs might attack Flora , the cat.

The next week we walked our dogs together. It was a hot day. When we paused to catch our breath, Steve got down on one knee. Was he proposing（求婚）? I liked him too, but so soon? He poured water from a bottle into his hand and offered it to my dogs. In that moment, I began to fall for him.

We continued to date, though neither of us brought up the future. And then in late November, Tilly had an operation on her leg. I took the dogs out four times a day, and I worried that Tilly constantly climbing the stairs could reopen the wound. Then Steve suggested his house. All worked fine. The three dogs formed a pack that, with coaching, respected Flora's space; Steve and I formed a good team caring for Tilly. We made good housemates.

A year later, much to my delight, this man produced a little box with a ring and proposed to me. He did not kneel（跪）down, nor did I need him to. That's only for giving water to the dogs that brought us together.

Words, phrases and difficult sentences to understand (Translate them into Chinese).

1. companionship ______________ 2. loneliness ______________
3. reservation ______________ 4. date ______________
5. thrilled ______________ 6. attack ______________
7. catch our breath ______________ 8. got down on one knee ______________
9. propose ______________ 10. fall for ______________
11. brought up the future ______________________________
12. The three dogs formed a pack that, with coaching, respected Flora's space; Steve and I formed a good team caring for Tilly. We made good housemates.

____

Task 4: Cultivate your cultural awareness.

"Watch your thoughts, and they become words.Watch your words,and they become actions.Watch your actions, and they become habits.Watch your habits, and they become character.Watch your character, and it becomes your destiny. So when we have a closer look at these sentences, we can draw a conclusion that: thoughts ≧wo rds≧actions≧habits≧character≧destiny. It's acknowledged that one's character decides one's destiny. Nevertheless, there are so many people who can't understand the sentence fully. If you have a better understanding of the sentences mentioned above, then, I believe you know what I mean. Please look at the following sentence: "Your thoughts decide your destiny."It is a little difficult to know somebody, because most of us are not good at reading others'mind. We can't see clearly what they are thinking. Also, we can't always believe what the others are saying. But the habbits and character can't easily be changed, so we can know more about a person by contacting with the person for a long time. We can observe how the person treats other people and even animals. If a person treats others well, behaves well, is respected by others, then we can at least say the person is worth getting on with.

Lesson 3　The Louvre

Task 1: Step into the "reading forest".

Directions: Try to fill in the following blanks according to your imagination.

The Louvre, one of the world's largest museums, lies on the right bank of the Seine. It is __1__ in the centre of Paris, and is visited by many people __2__ the world every year. On the __3__ hand, all kinds of objects from prehistory to the 21st century, __4__ from sculpture to paintings, are exhibited in the Louvre. However, __5__ with structural problems with the building, the museum was once closed __6__ the history. In __7__ of guidelines, neither cameras nor video recorders __8__ inside. For the sake of __9__, it is necessary __10__ in to the official website of Louvre Museum to buy tickets.

Questions:

1. Where is The Louvre located?

____

2. What caused the closing of it in the history?

____

3. How can visitors can buy tickets for convenience?

____

Task 2: Appreciate "trees" in the "reading forest".

Directions: For each blank in the following passage there are four words or phrases marked A, B, C and D. Fill in each blank with the word or phrase that best fits the context.

The Louvre , one of the world's largest museums , lies on the right bank of the

Seine. It is __1__ in the centre of Paris, and is visited by many people __2__ the world every year. On the __3__ hand, all kinds of objects from prehistory to the 21st century, __4__ from sculpture to paintings, are exhibited in the Louvre. However, __5__ with structural problems with the building, the museum was once closed __6__ the history. In __7__ of guidelines, neither cameras nor video recorders __8__ inside. For the sake of __9__, it is necessary __10__ in to the official website of Louvre Museum to buy tickets.

1. A. situated	B. arranged	C. found	D. promised
2. A. as	B. around	C. by	D. through
3. A. none	B. some	C. other	D. either
4. A. crying	B. driving	C. worrying	D. ranging
5. A. ordered	B. incited	C. allowed	D. faced
6. A. up	B. with	C. in	D. by
7. A. sight	B. terms	C. wake	D. response
8. A. are forbidden	B. are cooked	C. slept	D. waited
9. A. problem	B. convenience	C. environment	D. surprise
10. A.plan	B. change	C.sign	D. write

Task 3: Have an overview of the "reading forest".

The Louvre, one of the world's largest museums, lies on the right bank of the Seine. It is situated in the centre of Paris, and is visited by many people around the world every year. On the other hand, all kinds of objects from prehistory to the 21st century, ranging from sculpture to paintings, are exhibited in the Louvre. However, faced with structural problems with the building, the museum was once closed in the history. In terms of guidelines, neither cameras nor video recorders are forbidden inside. For the sake of convenience, it is necessary to sign in to the official website of Louvre Museum to buy tickets.

Words, phrases and difficult sentences to understand (Translate them into Chinese).

1. be situated in ________________ 2. rang from...to ________________

3. in terms of ________________ 4. are forbidden ________________

5. for the sake of ________________

Task 4: Cultivate your cultural awareness.

The Louvre is one of the largest royal palace buildings in France, located on the south side of the Opera Square in Paris, on the banks of the Seine.

As early as 1546, François I decided to build a new royal palace on the basis of the original castle.

After that, the nine monarchs continued to expand, which lasted more than 300 years, forming a magnificent U-shaped palace complex.

The east facade of the Louvre is a representative work of European classicism.

According to statistics, the Louvre Museum covers an area of 19 hectares including the courtyard. It lies on the right bank of the Seine from east to west. The lengths on both sides are 690 meters.

The hundreds of spacious halls used to showcase the treasures are magnificent, with fine murals and fine reliefs on the walls and top of the hall.

The main façade of the Louvre is about 172m long and 28m high.

It is divided into three parts according to a complete column: the bottom is the pedestal, the middle section is the two-story pillar, and the upper part is the crotch and the parapet wall.

The main body is an empty colonnade formed by double columns. There are protruding parts at the center and at both ends, dividing it into five paragraphs.

The convex portions at both ends are decorated with wall columns, while the central portion has a chair column with mountain flowers, so the main axis is clear.

There was a guard in front of the guard, and a bridge was placed in front of the gate.

The laterally unfolded façade is divided into 5 sections on the left and right, and 3 sections on the upper and lower sides.

The traditional French high-sloping roof was replaced by an Italian-style flat roof, and the east facade of the Louvre opened a small doorway on the high pedestal for people to enter and exit.

There are also a large number of antiques from Greece, Rome, Egypt and the East, and ancient relics from France and Italy, with an exhibition area of 55,000 square meters.

The transparent pyramid building at the entrance to the main entrance of the Louvre is a masterpiece of Chinese-American architect Pei Ming.

Lesson 4　Forgiveness

Task 1:Step into the "reading forest".

Directions: Try to fill in the following blanks according to your imagination.

When we are born,we are unblemished（无缺点的）.__1__ we grow,we develop many complexities because of many influences in our lives.

Our brain __2__ all information from the moment we are born. We have both physiological and psychological memories. We are complex emotional beings in __3__ compared to any other living animal. Physical and psychological memories strongly influence our emotions. Interestingly,we can create, store and release emotions like energy. __4__, if we do not process our emotions properly,they can find a way out violently and unexpectedly.

__5__ ,we carry our guilts throughout our lives. We become heavy with guilt and anger for things we couldn't achieve and we can't have. Both guilt and anger are __6__ for us.They give us no advantage. Actually,we should process and address our emotions in order to __7__ from our system.We cannot just wish them away.

Is there a better way to __8__ our burden? Luckily, we have natural gift to process our feelings and emotions. Forgiveness stands first of all other natural treatment. We should learn to readily forgive others. When we learn to forgive ourselves, we also naturally forgive others.

By forgiving, we can throw away the emotional baggage we __9__ for years, if not decades. Forgive your past mistakes. The moment you start forgiving, you feel a lot __10__ and years of heaviness lifted magically! To your surprise, you start feeling energetic and optimistic in your daily life.

Questions:

1. What is the topic of this passage?

____

2. What are the key words that help you understand the passage better?

____

3. Do you think forgiving is an effective way to solve emotional problems mentioned in this passage?

____

Task 2:Appreciate "trees" in the "reading forest".

Directions: Read the following passage, and choose the best answer from the four choices marked A, B, C and D .

When we are born,we are unblemished. As we grow,we develop many complexities because of many influences in our lives.

Our brain collects all information from the moment we are born. We have both physiological and psychological memories. We are complex emotional beings in nature compared to any other living animal. Physical and psychological memories strongly influence our emotions. Interestingly,we can create, store and release emotions like energy. Moreover, if we do not process our emotions properly,they can find a way out violently and unexpectedly.

Unfortunately,we carry our guilts throughout our lives. We become heavy with guilt and anger for things we couldn't achieve and we can't have. Both guilt and anger are useless for us.They give us no advantage.Actually,we should process and address our emotions in order to remove from our system.We cannot just wish them away.

<u>Is there a better way to unload our burden?</u> Luckily, we have natural gift to process our feelings and emotions. Forgiveness stands first of all other natural treatment. We should learn to readily forgive others. When we learn to forgive ourselves, we also naturally forgive others.

By forgiving, we can throw away the emotional baggage we carry for years, if not decades. Forgive your past mistakes. The moment you start forgiving, you feel a lot lighter and years of heaviness lifted magically! To your surprise, you start feeling energetic and optimistic in your daily life.

1. It can be inferred from the passage that______.

   A. only human beings have complex emotions

   B. our emotions have strong effect on our memories

   C. we can do nothing about guilty and anger

   D. we can find a way to get rid of guilty and anger

2. When we don't deal with emotions properly, they will ______.

   A. affect us greatly　　B. disappear naturally

   C. become better　　D. exist all the time

3. The underlined sentence in Paragraph 4 is to ______.

   A. provide an example　　B. make a comparison

   C. introduce a solution　　D. develop a previous statement

4. According to the passage, what's the author's attitude towards forgiving?

   A. Neutral.　　B. Positive.

   C. Negative.　　D. Doubtful.

Task 3: Have an overview of the "reading forest".

When we are born,we are unblemished（无缺点的）. As we grow,we develop many complexities because of many influences in our lives.

Our brain collects all information from the moment we are born. We have both physiological and psychological memories. We are complex emotional beings in nature compared to any other living animal. Physical and psychological memories strongly influence our emotions. Interestingly,we can create, store and release emotions like energy. Moreover, if we do not process our emotions properly,they can find a way out violently and unexpectedly.

Unfortunately,we carry our guilts throughout our lives. We become heavy with guilt and anger for things we couldn't achieve and we can't have. Both guilt and anger are useless for us.They give us no advantage.Actually,we should process and address our emotions in order to remove from our system.We cannot just wish them away.

Is there a better way to unload our burden? Luckily, we have natural gift to process our feelings and emotions. Forgiveness stands first of all other natural treatment. We should learn to readily forgive others. When we learn to forgive ourselves, we also naturally forgive others.

By forgiving, we can throw away the emotional baggage we carry for years, if not decades. Forgive your past mistakes. The moment you start forgiving, you feel a lot lighter and years of heaviness lifted magically! To your surprise, you start feeling energetic and optimistic in your daily life.

Words, phrases and difficult sentences to understand (Translate them into Chinese).

1. complexity ____________________ 2. in nature ________________

3. process ______________________ 4. find a way out ____________

5. guilt ________________________ 6. address _________________

7. unload our burden ____________ 8. light ___________________

9. Actually,we should process and address our emotions in order to remove from our system.We cannot just wish them away.

____

10. The moment you start forgiving, you feel a lot lighter and years of heaviness lifted magically!

____

Task 4: Cultivate your cultural awareness.

Why are you always emotionally disturbed by surroundings? What will you do when you feel down? What if you do nothing about it? Actually, human beings are more prone to be influenced compared with other living things. We have been collecting various information since we were born, which will be our psychological and physical memories as a result. These memories will influence our emotions. If these emotions are negative , we should find a way to get rid of them. Luckily, human beings are naturally equipped with abilities to create, store and release emotions. For example, few of us can avoid experiencing guilt and anger throughout our lives. But this does not necessarily mean we should allow these negative emotions to affect us all the time. Instead, different from animals, we have a natural gift to deal with them by forgiving. Forgiving can help us relieve from emotional burden, and then life will be much easier for us and we will feel energetic and optimistic every day. Therefore, why not let go of the unhappy past? Remember to forgive and embrace a better life.

Unit 11

Life in Colorful Aspects

Lesson 1　Pace for Coffee and Life

Task 1: Step into the "reading forest".

Directions: Try to fill in the following blanks according to your imagination.

A cup of coffee helps for a quieter life.

Last year my children __1__ me a stainless steel（钢）coffee pot. I couldn't __2__ to use it and looked forward to the following morning's coffee making, knowing that I probably wouldn't break this pot as __3__ as I had done so often in the past.

But as I __4__ my first cup of coffee, the pot spilled（洒）all over the table. __5__ no one was around to see my disappointed face! I kept trying, but each morning would __6__ me spilling the coffee. Then I realized that if I poured very slowly there would be no spilling.

This was at first a very __7__ experience. My normal __8__ was to rush through breakfast so that I could get on with my day.

But in time I learned not only to pour slowly but to enjoy the experience: the smell, the taste, and the __9__ of a new day.

It reminded me to __10__ whether there were other areas of life I was rushing through. __11__ of life, it seemed.

I stared to leave extra time to do even the most __12__ tasks. When shop owners would __13__ for keeping me waiting, I'd say, "Not a problem, I'm not in a hurry." Even listening to the __14__ singing in the trees around me became part of my __15__.

__16__, one of my favorite experiences living in the __17__ for many years was leisurely spending time with strangers. We sat on the steps, each of us with a cup of coffee in our hands, listening to each other's stories. It was one of the __18__ things about living in a busy land. It was as if the world around us slowed to a pace we could both __19__ .

Stillness not only slows the pace of life, but also __20__ the soul, helping us to enjoy the world's small pleasure.

Questions:

1. Why did the author often break the coffee pots in the past?

____

2. What did the author learn when she slowed to pour the coffee?

____

Task 2: Appreciate "trees" in the "reading forest".

Directions: For each blank in the following passage there are four words or phrases marked A, B, C and D. Fill in each blank with the word or phrase that best fits the context.

A cup of coffee helps for a quieter life.

Last year my children __1__ me a stainless steel coffee pot. I couldn't __2__ to use it and looked forward to the following morning's coffee making, knowing that I probably wouldn't break this pot as __3__ as I had done so often in the past.

But as I __4__ my first cup of coffee, the pot spilled all over the table. __5__ no one was around to see my disappointed face! I kept trying, but each morning would __6__ me spilling the coffee. Then I realized that if I poured very slowly there would be no spilling.

This was at first a very __7__ experience. My normal __8__ was to rush through breakfast so that I could get on with my day.

But in time I learned not only to pour slowly but to enjoy the experience: the smell, the taste, and the __9__ of a new day.

It reminded me to __10__ whether there were other areas of life I was rushing through. __11__ of life, it seemed.

I stared to leave extra time to do even the most __12__ tasks. When shop owners would __13__ for keeping me waiting, I'd say, "Not a problem, I'm not in a hurry." Even listening to the __14__ singing in the trees around me became part of my __15__.

__16__, one of my favorite experiences living in the __17__ for many years was leisurely spending time with strangers. We sat on the steps, each of us with a cup of coffee in our hands, listening to each other's stories. It was one of the __18__ things about living in a busy land. It was as if the world around us slowed to a pace we could both __19__.

Stillness not only slows the pace of life, but also __20__ the soul, helping us to enjoy the world's small pleasure.

1. A. awarded　B. gifted　C. lent　D. threw
2. A. stand　B. believe　C. spare　D. wait
3. A. easily　B. rarely　C. hard　D. far
4. A. ordered　B. drank　C. made　D. poured
5. A. Undoubtedly　B. Unfortunately　C. Surprisingly　D. Thankfully
6. A. bring　B. see　C. have　D. worry
7. A. boring　B. interesting　C. painful　D. frightening
8. A. reaction　B. answer　C. practice　D. use
9. A. preference　B. excitement　C. hope　D. quietness
10. A. reflect upon　B. agree on　C. look through　D. leave behind
11. A. Little　B. Most　C. None　D. Any
12. A. unimportant　B. difficult　C. ordinary　D. challenging
13. A. prepare　B. pay　C. look　D. apologize
14. A. children　B. worms　C. birds　D. strangers
15. A. routine　B. influence　C. time　D. task
16. A. Still　B. Besides　C. However　D. Instead
17. A. inner city　B. coastal beach　C. jungle forest　D. ancient island
18. A. most hopeful　B. most adventurous
　C. warmest　D. kindest
19. A. enjoy　B. handle　C. improve　D. continue
20. A. saves　B. ruins　C. feeds　D. shows

Task 3: Have an overview of the "reading forest".

A cup of coffee helps for a quieter life.

Last year my children gifted me a stainless steel coffee pot. I couldn't wait to use it and looked forward to the following morning's coffee making, knowing that I probably wouldn't break this pot as easily as I had done so often in the past.

But as I poured my first cup of coffee, the pot spilled all over the table. Thankfully no one was around to see my disappointed face! I kept trying, but each morning would see me spilling the coffee. Then I realized that if I poured very slowly there would be no spilling.

This was at first a very painful experience. My normal practice was to rush through breakfast so that I could get on with my day.

But in time I learned not only to pour slowly but to enjoy the experience: the smell, the taste, and the quietness of a new day.

It reminded me to reflect upon whether there were other areas of life I was rushing through. Most of life, it seemed.

I stared to leave extra time to do even the most ordinary tasks. When shop owners would apologize for keeping me waiting, I'd say, "Not a problem, I'm not in a hurry." Even listening to the birds singing in the trees around me became part of my routine.

Besides, one of my favorite experiences living in the inner city for many years was leisurely spending time with strangers. We sat on the steps, each of us with a cup of coffee in our hands, listening to each other's stories. It was one of the warmest things about living in a busy land. It was as if the world around us slowed to a pace we could both continue.

Stillness not only slows the pace of life, but also feeds the soul, helping us to enjoy the world's small pleasure.

Words, phrases and difficult sentences to understand (Translate them into Chinese).

1. stainless ____________________ 2. pour ____________________

3. thankfully ____________________ 4. spill ____________________

5. normal practice ____________________ 6. remind sb. of sth. ____________________

7. reflect on / upon ____________________ 8. ordinary ____________________

9. apologize ____________________ 10. routine ____________________

11. the inner city ________________ 12. leisurely ____________________

13. pace ______________________ 14. stillness ____________________

15. I couldn't wait to use it and looked forward to the following morning's coffee making, knowing that I probably wouldn't break this pot as easily as I had done so often in the past.

____

16. It was as if the world around us slowed to a pace we could both continue.

____

Task 4: Cultivate your cultural awareness.

George Prochnik would like the world to put a sock in it. He makes his case in a new book, *Listening for Meaning in a World of Noise*. Here he explains himself (using his indoor voice):

"We've become so accustomed to noise, there's almost a deep prejudice against the idea that silence might be beneficial. If you tell someone to be quiet, you sound like an old man. But it's never been more important to find continuing quiet. Silence focuses us, improves our health, and is a key to lasting peace and satisfaction."

"We need to excite people about the sounds you start to hear if you merely quiet things down a little. During a Japanese tea ceremony, the smallest sounds become a kind of art — the spoons making a light ringing sound on a bowl, the edges of a kimono（和服）brushing against the floor."

"Deaf people are very attentive（专注的）in almost every aspect of life. If two deaf people are walking together, using sign language, they constantly watch out for each other and protect each other by paying steady attention to the other. They are connected yet also fully aware of their surroundings. Even deaf teenagers! We in the hearing world can learn from them. If we remove the powerful blasts（一阵阵）of noise, we become aware of an extraordinarily rich world around us—of little soft sounds and the sound of footsteps, of bird songs and ice cracking（开裂声）. It's astonishing how beautiful things sound when you can really listen. "

Lesson 2 Don't Judge on One's Physical Appearance

Task1: Step into the "reading forest".

Directions: Try to fill in the following blanks according to your imagination.

Sometimes we can't help impressing ourselves on what a person wears. __1__, it was on a sunny Saturday afternoon of 1949 that I learned an important life lesson about judging others on their physical __2__.

As a high-school piano student, I worked part-time as a __3__ in Wall's Music Center in New York, a job that provided me a modest income. My weekly paycheck __4__ a base salary plus extra __5__ earned on the sales. So for __6__, especially on sales of higher-priced items, two other teenage clerks and I used the "up" system, __7__ to greet customers entering the shop.

There were a dozen or so different kinds of radios in fashion, of which the most __8__ — and costly — in the store was Zenith Trans-Oceanic model 8G005Y and __9__ at a high price (at that time) of $125. Thus all of us were in enthusiasm to try to sell one __10__ possible.

On that unforgettable afternoon, the music shop's glass door opened wide and __11__ in a tall, unshaven man wearing a wrinkled hat, dirty clothing and shabby shoes more suitable for __12__ work than for shopping in a music store.

This fellow was my "__13__", but after glancing at his appearance, I quickly concluded my efforts would be more __14__ spent with a "suitable" customer, so I __15__ Norman, my co-worker, a sign that I quit my turn to him. Norman approached __16__ this unseemly（不体面的）looking fellow walked to the radio display, pointed at the Trans-Oceanic and asked whether he had six in stock.

Norman __17__, looked disbelievingly at me, and then rushed into the stock room to check. Within a minute he returned to reply "YES!" Then the buyer opened his checkbook to write a $750 receipt. Adding further __18__ to me, I was asked to help carry the six radio boxes to the buyer's Lincoln Continental convertible（敞篷汽车）__19__ nearby.

Ever since that afternoon, I have avoided judging others __20__ on what they look like at the first sight.

Questions:

1. Why did the clerks use the "up" system?

____

2. Why did the author emphasize the buyer's car?

____

Task 2: Appreciate "trees" in the "reading forest".

Directions: For each blank in the following passage there are four words or phrases marked A, B, C and D. Fill in each blank with the word or phrase that best fits the context.

Sometimes we can't help impressing ourselves on what a person wears. __1__, it was on a sunny Saturday afternoon of 1949 that I learned an important life lesson about judging others on their physical __2__.

As a high-school piano student, I worked part-time as a __3__ in Wall's Music Center in New York, a job that provided me a modest income. My weekly paycheck __4__ a base salary plus extra __5__ earned on the sales. So for __6__, especially on sales of higher-priced items, two other teenage clerks and I used the "up" system, __7__ to greet customers entering the shop.

There were a dozen or so different kinds of radios in fashion, of which the most __8__ — and costly — in the store was Zenith Trans-Oceanic model 8G005Y and __9__ at a high price (at that time) of $125. Thus all of us were in enthusiasm to try to sell one __10__ possible.

On that unforgettable afternoon, the music shop's glass door opened wide and ___11___ in a tall, unshaven man wearing a wrinkled hat, dirty clothing and shabby shoes more suitable for ___12___ work than for shopping in a music store.

This fellow was my "___13___", but after glancing at his appearance, I quickly concluded my efforts would be more ___14___ spent with a "suitable" customer, so I ___15___ Norman, my co-worker, a sign that I quit my turn to him. Norman approached ___16___ this unseemly looking fellow walked to the radio display, pointed at the Trans-Oceanic and asked whether he had six in stock. Norman ___17___, looked disbelievingly at me, and then rushed into the stock room to check. Within a minute he returned to reply "YES!" Then the buyer opened his checkbook to write a $750 receipt. Adding further ___18___ to me, I was asked to help carry the six radio boxes to the buyer's Lincoln Continental convertible ___19___ nearby.

Ever since that afternoon, I have avoided judging others ___20___ on what they look like at the first sight.

1. A. Therefore	B. moreover	C. Otherwise	D. However
2. A. activities	B. condition	C. appearance	D. characteristics
3. A. salesman	B. accountant	C. waiter	D. manager
4. A. included	B. combined	C. earned	D. demanded
5. A. prize	B. award	C. present	D. scholarship
6. A. kindness	B. business	C. fairness	D. wariness
7. A. coming out	B. taking turns	C. making up	D. keeping in mind
8. A. expensive	B. complicated	C. traditional	D. desirable
9. A. affordable	B. acceptable	C. available	D. agreeable
10. A. whenever	B. whoever	C. wherever	D. whatever
11. A. wandered	B. rushed	C. slipped	D. dropped
12. A. musical	B. full-time	C. labor	D. part-time
13. A. in	B. up	C. out	D. down
14. A. costly	B. financially	C. economically	D. profitably
15. A. watched	B. stepped behind	C. gave	D. reached for
16. A. as	B. to	C. until	D. since
17. A. cried	B. laughed	C. nodded	D. blinked

18. A. requirement	B. embarrassment	C. astonishment	D. compliment
19. A. stored	B. rented	C. bought	D. parked
20. A. merely	B. deliberately	C. hardly	D. eventually

Task 3: Have an overview of the "reading forest".

Sometimes we can't help impressing ourselves on what a person wears. However, it was on a sunny Saturday afternoon of 1949 that I learned an important life lesson about judging others on their physical appearance.

As a high-school piano student, I worked part-time as a salesman in Wall's Music Center in New York, a job that provided me a modest income. My weekly paycheck combined a base salary plus extra prize earned on the sales. So for fairness, especially on sales of higher-priced items, two other teenage clerks and I used the "up" system, taking turns to greet customers entering the shop.

There were a dozen or so different kinds of radios in fashion, of which the most desirable — and costly — in the store was Zenith Trans-Oceanic model 8G005Y and available at a high price (at that time) of $125. Thus all of us were in enthusiasm to try to sell one whenever possible.

On that unforgettable afternoon, the music shop's glass door opened wide and wandered in a tall, unshaven man wearing a wrinkled hat, dirty clothing and shabby shoes more suitable for labor work than for shopping in a music store.

This fellow was my "up", but after glancing at his appearance, I quickly concluded my efforts would be more profitably spent with a "suitable" customer, so I gave Norman, my co-worker, a sign that I quitted my turn to him. Norman approached as this unseemly looking fellow walked to the radio display, pointed at the Trans-Oceanic and asked whether he had six in stock. Norman blinked, looked disbelievingly at me, and then rushed into the stock room to check. Within a minute he returned to reply "YES!" Then the buyer opened his checkbook to write a $750 receipt. Adding further embarrassment to me, I was asked to help carry the six radio boxes to the buyer's Lincoln Continental convertible parked nearby.

Ever since that afternoon, I have avoided judging others merely on what they look like at the first sight.

Words, phrases and difficult sentences to understand (Translate them into Chinese).

1. physical appearance ________ 2. a modest income ________
3. weekly paycheck ________ 4. combine ________
5. base salary ________ 6. extra prize ________
7. fairness ________ 8. desirable ________
9. enthusiasm ________ 10. wrinkled ________
11. shabby ________ 12. labor work ________
13. glance ________ 14. profitably ________
15. approach ________ 16. in stock ________
17. blink ________ 18. checkbook ________
19. embarrassment ________

20. On that unforgettable afternoon, the music shop's glass door opened wide and wandered in a tall, unshaven man wearing a wrinkled hat, dirty clothing and shabby shoes more suitable for labor work than for shopping in a music store.

____

Task 4: Cultivate your cultural awareness.

What Was a Dollar's Worth?

In the 1950s, 1 dollar was quite valuable. At that time, 1 ounce (equal to 28 grams) of gold was worth 35 dollars. That revealed 1 dollar could buy 0.8 gram of gold! According to the present gold price (approx. 60 dollars for 1 gram), it is easy to calculate out that 1 dollar in the 1950s was worth 48 dollars in present purchase! So the $125 Zenith Trans-Oceanic model 8G005Y was worth $6,000 now.

Lesson 3 This Way to Dreamland

Task 1: Step into the "reading forest".

Directions: Try to fill in the following blanks according to your imagination.

Daydreaming means people think about something pleasant, especially when this makes them forget what they should be doing. Daydreamers have a bad reputation for being unaware of what's happening around them. They can seem forgetful and clumsy. __1__ They annoy us because they seem to be ignoring us and missing the important things.

But daydreamers are also responsible for some of the greatest ideas and achievements in human history. __2__ Can you imagine what kind of world we would have without such ideas and inventions?

So how can you come up with brilliant daydreams and avoid falling over tree roots or otherwise looking like a fool?

First, understand that some opportunities（机会）for daydreaming are better than others. Feeling safe and relaxed will help you to slip into daydreams. __3__ And if you want to improve your chances of having a creative idea while you're daydreaming, try to do it while you are involved in another task — preferably something simple, like taking a shower or walking, or even making meaningless drawings.

It's also important to know how to avoid daydreams for those times when you really need to concentrate. "Mindfulness", being focused, is a tool that some people use to avoid falling asleep. __4__

Finally, you never know what wonderful idea might strike while your mind has moved slowly away. __5__

Always remember that your best ideas might come when your head is actually in the clouds.

Questions:

1. What does the passage mainly talk about?

____

2. What are the key words that help you understand the passage better?

____

Task 2: Appreciate "trees" in the "reading forest".

Directions: Choose the right sentences to complete the passage.

Daydreaming means people think about something pleasant, especially when this makes them forget what they should be doing. Daydreamers have a bad reputation for being unaware of what's happening around them. They can seem forgetful and clumsy. __1__ They annoy us because they seem to be ignoring us and missing the important things.

But daydreamers are also responsible for some of the greatest ideas and achievements in human history. __2__ Can you imagine what kind of world we would have without such ideas and inventions?

So how can you come up with brilliant daydreams and avoid falling over tree roots or otherwise looking like a fool?

First, understand that some opportunities for daydreaming are better than others. Feeling safe and relaxed will help you to slip into daydreams. __3__ And if you want to improve your chances of having a creative idea while you're daydreaming, try to do it while you are involved in another task — preferably something simple, like taking a shower or walking, or even making meaningless drawings.

It's also important to know how to avoid daydreams for those times when you really need to concentrate. "Mindfulness", being focused, is a tool that some people use to avoid falling asleep. __4__

Finally, you never know what wonderful idea might strike while your mind has moved slowly away. __5__

Always remember that your best ideas might come when your head is actually in the clouds.

A. Having interesting things to think about also helps.

B. They stare off into space and wander by themselves.

C. Without wandering minds, we wouldn't have relatively, Coke or Post-it notes.

D. At one time, daydreaming was thought to be a cause of some mental illnesses.

E. It involves slow, steady breathing for self-control that helps people stay calm and attentive.

F. Daydreams are often very simple and direct, quite unlike sleep dreams, which may be hard to understand.

G. Therefore, it's a good idea to keep a notebook or voice recorder nearby when you're in the daydream zone.

Task 3: Have an overview of the "reading forest".

Daydreaming means people think about something pleasant, especially when this makes them forget what they should be doing. Daydreamers have a bad reputation for being unaware of what's happening around them. They can seem forgetful and clumsy. They stare off into space and wander by themselves. They annoy us because they seem to be ignoring us and missing the important things.

But daydreamers are also responsible for some of the greatest ideas and achievements in human history. Without wandering minds, we wouldn't have relatively, Coke or Post-it notes. Can you imagine what kind of world we would have without such ideas and inventions?

So how can you come up with brilliant daydreams and avoid falling over tree roots or otherwise looking like a fool?

First, understand that some opportunities for daydreaming are better than others. Feeling safe and relaxed will help you to slip into daydreams. Having interesting things to think about also helps. And if you want to improve your chances of having a creative idea while you're daydreaming, try to do it while you are involved in another task — preferably something simple, like taking a shower or walking, or even making meaningless drawings.

It's also important to know how to avoid daydreams for those times when you really need to concentrate. "Mindfulness", being focused, is a tool that some people use to avoid falling asleep. It involves slow, steady breathing for self-control that helps people stay calm and attentive.

Finally, you never know what wonderful idea might strike while your mind has moved slowly away. Therefore, it's a good idea to keep a notebook or voice recorder nearby when you're in the daydream zone.

Always remember that your best ideas might come when your head is actually in the clouds.

Words, phrases and difficult sentences to understand(Translate them into Chinese).

1. reputation ________________ 2. be unaware of ________________
3. clumsy ________________ 4. ignore ________________
5. be responsible for ________________ 6. achievement ________________
7. relatively ________________ 8. invention ________________
9. creative ________________ 10. concentrate ________________
11. mindfulness ________________ 12. steady ________________

13. ...while you're daydreaming, try to do it while you are involved in another task — preferably something simple, like taking a shower or walking, or even making meaningless drawings.

____

Task 4: Cultivate your cultural awareness.

No one can fail to stand in awed admiration of the great discoveries of history — Newton's laws of motion; Kepler's principles of planetary movement; Einstein's general theory of relativity. Equally awe-inspiring are artistic creations in painting, theatre, music and literature, which have also been brought about by discovery through personal efforts. What do these extraordinary achievements of well-known scientists and artists have to do with problem solving?

A great scientific discovery or a great work of art is surely the result of problem-solving activities. The solution to a problem, we are told, often comes to thinkers in a "flash of insight", although they may have been turning the problem over in their minds for some time. As a particular form of problem solving, these creative acts are based on the broad knowledge gained in the past, whether this be of the "public" sort known to science, or of the "private" sort known to the artists.

Many creative thinkers state that they have completely devoted themselves to the subject matter of the problem, often over fairly long periods of time. Indeed, it would be strange if they had not done this. Nothing in such statements supports the idea that there is anything very different about the problem solving that leads to discoveries of the great contributions to the society. The act of discovery, even in the relatively predictable sense that it occurs in everyday learning, involves a "sudden insight" which changes the problem situation into a solution situation. As we see, everyday discoveries also requires that the learner has the knowledge of the rules gaining in the past, which is involved in the solution.

Lesson 4 Forgiveness Is a Virtue

Task 1: Step into the "reading forest".

Directions: Try to fill in the following blanks according to your imagination.

To forgive is a virtue, but no one has ever said it is easy. When someone has deeply hurt you, it can be extremely difficult to let go of your hate. However, forgiveness is possible, and it can be surprisingly beneficial to your physical and mental health. People who forgive show less sadness, anger and stress and more hopefulness, according to a recent research.

__1__ Try the following steps:

Calm yourself. __2__ You can take a couple of breaths and think of something that gives you pleasure: a beautiful scene in nature or someone you love.

Don't wait for an apology. Many times the persons who hurt you does not intend to apologize. They may have wanted to hurt you or they just don't see things the same way. __3__ Keep in mind that forgiveness does not necessarily mean becoming friends again with the person who upset you.

Take the control away from your offender（冒犯者）. Rethinking about your hurt gives power to the person who caused you pain. Instead of focusing on your wounded feelings, learn to look for the love, beauty and kindness around you.

__4__ If you understand your offender ,you may realize that he or she was acting out of unawareness, fear, and even love. You may want to write a letter to yourself from your offender's point of view.

Don't forget to forgive yourself. __5__ But it can rob you of your self-confidence if you don't do it.

Questions:

1. Why is forgiveness important?

____

2. How many ways are introduced to help you start to forgive? List them please.

____

Task 2: Appreciate "trees" in the "reading forest".

Directions: For each blank in the following passage there are four words or phrases marked A, B, C and D. Fill in each blank with the word or phrase that best fits the context.

To forgive is a virtue, but no one has ever said it is easy. When someone has deeply hurt you, it can be extremely difficult to let go of your hate. However, forgiveness is possible, and it can be surprisingly beneficial to your physical and mental health. People who forgive show less sadness, anger and stress and more hopefulness, according to a recent research.

__1__ Try the following steps:

Calm yourself. __2__ You can take a couple of breaths and think of something that gives you pleasure: a beautiful scene in nature or someone you love.

Don't wait for an apology. Many times the persons who hurt you does not intend to apologize. They may have wanted to hurt you or they just don't see things the same way. __3__ Keep in mind that forgiveness does not necessarily mean becoming friends again with the person who upset you.

Take the control away from your offender. Rethinking about your hurt gives power to the person who caused you pain. Instead of focusing on your wounded feelings, learn to look for the love, beauty and kindness around you.

__4__ If you understand your offender ,you may realize that he or she was acting out of unawareness, fear, and even love. You may want to write a letter to yourself from your offender's point of view.

Don't forget to forgive yourself. __5__ But it can rob you of your self-confidence if you don't do it.

A. Why should you forgive?

B. How could you start to forgive?

C. Recognize the benefits of forgiveness.

D. Try to see things from your offender's angle.

E. For some people, forgiving themselves is the biggest challenge.

F. To make your anger die away, try a simple stress-management technique.

G. If you wait for people to apologize, you could be waiting an awfully long time.

Task 3: Have an overview of the "reading forest".

To forgive is a virtue, but no one has ever said it is easy. When someone has deeply hurt you, it can be extremely difficult to let go of your hate. However, forgiveness is possible, and it can be surprisingly beneficial to your physical and mental health. People who forgive show less sadness, anger and stress and more hopefulness, according to a recent research.

How could you start to forgive? Try the following steps:

Calm yourself. To make your anger die away, try a simple stress-management technique. You can take a couple of breaths and think of something that gives you pleasure: a beautiful scene in nature or someone you love.

Don't wait for an apology. Many times the persons who hurt you do not intend to apologize. They may have wanted to hurt you or they just don't see things the same way. If you wait for people to apologize, you could be waiting an awfully long time. Keep in mind that forgiveness does not necessarily mean becoming friends again with the person who upset you.

Take the control away from your offender. Rethinking about your hurt gives power to the person who caused you pain. Instead of focusing on your wounded feelings, learn to look for the love, beauty and kindness around you.

Try to see things from your offender's angle. If you understand your offender, you may realize that he or she was acting out of unawareness, fear, and even love. You may want to write a letter to yourself from your offender's point of view.

Don't forget to forgive yourself. For some people, forgiving themselves is the biggest challenge. But it can rob you of your self-confidence if you don't do it.

Words, phrases and difficult sentences to understand(Translate them into Chinese).

1. virtue ________________ 2. beneficial ________________

3. physical and mental health ________ 4. scene ________________

5. apologize ________________ 6. angle ________________

7. unawareness ________________ 8. challenge ________________

9. rob ________________

10. Keep in mind that forgiveness does not necessarily mean becoming friends again with the person who upset you. ________________

Task 4: Cultivate your cultural awareness.

Forgiving someone who has hurt you or let you down is never an easy thing. Several new studies, however, say that it could have a lot of health benefits. When you think of forgiveness, you probably don't think of it as being a healthy or medical problem. Studies from Stanford University, on the other hand, show that something like anger can change your well-being.

When cartoon book characters like the incredible Hulk get angry, they change colours and often gain special power. In the real world, anger is less obvious and may be more dangerous. That's why Professor Fred Luskin, founder of the Stanford Forgiveness Project and author of Forgive for Good, says holding on to anger and hatred can harm your physical and mental health. Two new studies seem to show the same idea.

The studies find that people who are able to forgive feel less stress, less back pain, and less depression. They also have fewer headaches, lower blood pressure, and fewer problems on sleeping.

So it doesn't matter if your anger is caused by the traffic or other things. Learning to let it go is important. Techniques such as deep breath or thought can help. Or just ask yourself if it's worthy to hurt yourself by staying angry with someone else.

Forgiveness does not mean that you simply accept what happened and say it's OK. Instead, it's a way of making peace with yourself about what happened in the past.

Unit 12

A Special Examination

Lesson 1　A Special Examination

Task 1: Step into the "reading forest".

Directions: Try to fill in the following blanks according to your imagination.

It was the last day of the final examination in a large Eastern university. On the steps of one building, a group of engineering senior students waited for it together, talking about the exam due to begin in a few minutes. On their faces was ___1___. This was their last ___2___ then they would find the jobs. Some talked of jobs they already had; others talked of jobs they would get. With all this learning of four years of college, they felt ___3___ and were able to ___4___ the world. The coming exam, they knew, would be ___5___. The professor had said they could bring any books or notes they wanted. Asking only that they did not talk to each other ___6___ the test.

Happily they ___7___ the classroom. The professor passed out the papers. And smiles became ___8___ as the students found there were only five questions. Three hours passed. Then the professor began to collect the papers. The students ___9___ looked confident. On their faces was a ___10___ expression. No one spoke as papers in hand, the professor faced the class.

He looked the worried faces before him, then asked: "How many completed all five questions?" Not a hand was ___11___.

"How many answered four?" Still no hands.

"Three? Two?" The students moved ___12___ in their seats.

"One, then? Certainly somebody finished one."

But the class kept ___13___. The professor put down the papers. "That is exactly what I ___14___," he said. "I just want to ___15___ upon you that, ___16___ you have completed four years of __17__, there are still many things about the subject you don't know. These questions you could not answer are very __18__ in everyday practice." Then, smiling, he added: "You will all __19__ this course, but remember — even though you are now college graduates, your education has just __20__."

The years have made the name of this professor unclear, but not the lesson he taught.

Questions:

1. What is the main idea of the passage?

____

2. What kind of information can help you understand this passage?

____

Task 2: Appreciate "trees" in the "reading forest".

Directions: For each blank in the following passage there are four words or phrases marked A, B, C and D. Fill in each blank with the word or phrase that best fits the context.

It was the last day of final examination in a large Eastern university. On the steps of one building, a group of engineering seniors students waited for it together, talking about the exam due to begin in a few minutes. On their faces was __1__. This was their last __2__ then they would find the jobs. Some talked of jobs they already had; others of jobs they would get. With all this learning of four years of college, they felt __3__ and able to __4__ the world. The coming exam, they knew, would be __5__. The professor had said they could bring any books or notes they wanted. Asking only that they did not talk to each other __6__ the test.

Happily they __7__ the classroom. The professor passed out the papers. And smiles began __8__ as the students found there were only five questions. Three hours passed. Then the professor began to collect the papers. The students __9__ looked confident. On their faces was a __10__ expression. No one spoke as papers in hand, the professor faced the class.

He looked the worried faces before him, then asked: "How many completed all five questions?" Not a hand was __11__.

"How many answered four?" Still no hands.

"Three? Two?" The students moved __12__ in their seats.

"One, then? Certainly somebody finished one."

But the class kept __13__ . The professor put down the papers. "That is __14__ what I expected," he said. "I just want to __15__ upon you that, __16__ you have completed four years of __17__ , there are still many things about the subject you don't know. These questions you could not answer are very __18__ in everyday practice." Then, smiling, he added: "You will all __19__ this course, but remember—even though you are now college graduates, your education has just __20__ ."

The years have made the name of this professor unclear, but not the lesson he taught.

1. A. anxiety	B. confidence	C.curiosity	D. content
2. A. exam	B. competition	C. trial	D. experience
3. A. happy	B. nervous	C. ready	D. excited
4. A. face	B. abandon	C. tell	D. conquer
5. A.easy	B. difficult	C. complex	D. important
6. A.before	B. after	C. during	D. about
7. A. ran out of	B. went away	C. broke into	D. crowded into
8. A. reluctant	B. free	C. embarrassed	D. bigger
9. A. still	B. no longer	C. continuously	D. mostly
10. A. confident	B. frightened	C. clear	D. successful
11. A. raised	B. stretched	C. grabbed	D. caught
12. A.quickly	B. purposely	C. restlessly	D. quietly
13. A. noisy	B. calm	C. thirsty	D. silent
14. A. predicted	B. expected	C.guessed	D. saw
15. A. impress	B. look	C. depend	D. tell
16. A. if	B. unless	C. even though	D. when
17. A. studying	B. practice	C. engineering	D. preparing
18. A. small	B. plentiful	C. hard	D. common
19. A. pass	B. lose	C. continue	D. attend
20. A. stopped	B. begun	C. finished	D. succeeded

Task 3: Have an overview of the "reading forest".

It was the last day of final examination in a large Eastern university. On the steps of one building, a group of engineering seniors students waited for it together, talking about the exam due to begin in a few minutes. On their faces was confidence. This was their last exam — then they would find the jobs. Some talked of jobs they already had; others of jobs they would get. With all this learning of four years of college, they felt ready and able to conquer the world. The coming exam, they knew, would be easy. The professor had said they could bring any books or notes they wanted. Asking only that they did not talk to each other during the test.

Happily they crowded into the classroom. The professor passed out the papers. And smiles began bigger as the students found there were only five questions. Three hours passed. Then the professor began to collect the papers. The students no longer looked confident. On their faces was a frightened expression. No one spoke as papers in hand, the professor faced the class.

He looked the worried faces before him, then asked: "How many completed all five questions?" Not a hand was raised.

"How many answered four?" Still no hands.

"Three? Two?" The students moved restlessly in their seats.

"One, then? Certainly somebody finished one."

But the class kept silent. The professor put down the papers. "That is exactly what I expected," he said. "I just want to impress upon you that, even though you have completed four years of engineering, there are still many things about the subject you don't know. These questions you could not answer are very common in everyday practice." Then, smiling, he added: "You will all pass this course, but remember — even though you are now college graduates, your education has just begun."

The years have made the name of this professor unclear, but not the lesson he taught.

Words, phrases and difficult sentences to understand (Translate them into Chinese).

1. restlessly ____________________

2. conquer____________________

3. crowd into ____________________

4. With all this learning of four years of college, they felt ready and able to conquer the world.

____

5. I just want to impress upon you that, even though you have completed four years of engineering, there are still many things about the subject you don't know.

____

Task 4: Cultivate your cultural awareness.

College is the best time of your life. Admittedly, there is a lot of knowledge in universities. When you are a freshman, you will bring in some; when you are a senior, you don't take away much. Even though your academic performance may be excellent, what do you really gain? As we all know, the university brings out all abilities, including incapability. Obviously, the chief value in going to college is study. The things taught in college are not exactly education, but the means of learning. Luckily, these are the preparations for life.

Lesson 2 Mother's Encouragement

Task 1: Step into the "reading forest".

Directions: Try to fill in the following blanks according to your imagination.

My parents divorced when I was 5, making my mother a single parent. We had __1__ money, but my mom gave me a lot of love. Each night, she sat me on her lap and spoke the words that would __2__ my life, "Kemmons, you are certain to be a great man and you can do anything in life if you work hard enough to get it."

At fourteen, I was __3__ by a car and the doctors said I would never __4__ again. Every day, my mother spoke to me in her __5__, loving voice, telling me that no matter what those __6__ said, I could walk again if I __7__ to do it badly enough. She drove that message so __8__ into my heart that I finally believed her. A year later, I __9__ to school — walking on my own!

When the Great Depression（大萧条）occurred，my mom lost her job. Then I left school to __10__ the family. At that moment, I was __11__ never to be poor again.

My real change occurred on a vacation I took with my wife and five kids in 1951. I was angry that the second-class hotel __12__ an extra $ 2 for each child. That was too __13__ for the average American family. I decided to open a motel（汽车旅馆）for families that would never charge extra for children. There were plenty of __14__ at that time.

Not surprisingly, my mother was one of my strongest __15__. We experienced a lot of __16__. But with my mother's words deeply __17__ in my soul, I never doubted we would succeed. Fifteen years later, we had the __18__ hotel system in the world — Holiday Inn. In 1979, my company had 1,759 inns in more than fifty countries with an __19__ of $1 billion a year.

You may not have started out life in the best situation. But if you can find a task in life worth working for and __20__ yourself, nothing can stop you.

Questions:

1. What did the mother do when the author was a child?

____

2. What is the clue of the passage?

____

Task 2: Appreciate "trees" in the "reading forest".

Directions: there will be four choices after each question, chose the best one for each of them according to the passage.

My parents divorced when I was 5, making my mother a single parent. We had little money, but my mom gave me a lot of love. Each night, she sat me on her lap and spoke the words that would change my life,"Kemmons, you are certain to be a great man and you can do anything in life if you work hard enough to get it."

At fourteen, I was hit by a car and the doctors said I would never walk again. Every day, my mother spoke to me in her gentle, loving voice, telling me that no matter what those doctors said, I could walk again if I wanted to do it badly enough. She drove that message so deep into my heart that I finally believed her. A year later, I returned to school — walking on my own!

When the Great Depression occurred, my mom lost her job. Then I left school to support the family. At that moment,I was determined never to be poor again.

My real change occurred on a vacation I took with my wife and five kids in 1951. I was angry that the second-class hotel charged an extra $ 2 for each child. That was too expensive for the average American family. I decided to open a motel for families that would never charge extra for children. There were plenty of doubters at that time.

Not surprisingly, my mother was one of my strongest supporters. We experienced a lot of challenges. But with my mother's words deeply rooted in my soul, I never doubted we would succeed. Fifteen years later, we had the largest hotel system in the world — Holiday Inn. In 1979, my company had 1,759 inns in more than fifty countries with an income of $1 billion a year.

You may not have started out life in the best situation. But if you can find a task in life worth working for and believe in yourself, nothing can stop you.

1. What did the mother usually do when Kemmons was a child?

A. She told stories about a great man.

B. She helped him work hard.

C. She spoke the words that would change my life.

D. She gave me a lot of love.

2. Why did the author decide to open a motel himself?

A. His mother asked him to.

B. It was the best way of making a living at that time.

C. He wanted to save money .

D. The extra of the hotel charge was too expensive for the average American family.

3. According to the passage, how to best describe the writer's mother?

A. hard working and warmhearted.

B. supportive and strong-willed.

C. thoughtful and sensitive.

D. strict and considerate.

4. What can be inferred from the passage?

A. The author's motel wouldn't charge extra money for the children.

B. The doctor told a lie to the writer's family.

C. The author didn't pay for the extra charge.

D. The author succeeded immediately he made the decision.

Task 3: Have an overview of the "reading forest".

My parents divorced when I was 5, making my mother a single parent. We had little money, but my mom gave me a lot of love. Each night, she sat me on her lap and spoke the words that would change my life, "Kemmons, you are certain to be a great man and you can do anything in life if you work hard enough to get it."

At fourteen, I was hit by a car and the doctors said I would never walk again. Every day, my mother spoke to me in her gentle, loving voice, telling me that no matter what those doctors said, I could walk again if I wanted to do it badly enough. She drove that message so deep into my heart that I finally believed her. A year later, I returned to school — walking on my own!

When the Great Depression occurred, my mom lost her job. Then I left school to support the family. At that moment, I was determined never to be poor again.

My real change occurred on a vacation I took with my wife and five kids in 1951. I was angry that the second-class hotel charged an extra $ 2 for each child. That was too expensive for the average American family. I decided to open a motel for families that would never charge extra for children. There were plenty of doubters at that time.

Not surprisingly, my mother was one of my strongest supporters. We experienced a lot of challenges. But with my mother's words deeply rooted in my soul, I never doubted we would succeed. Fifteen years later, we had the largest hotel system in the world-Holiday Inn. In 1979, my company had 1,759 inns in more than fifty countries with an income of $1 billion a year.

You may not have started out life in the best situation. But if you can find a task in life worth working for and believe in yourself, nothing can stop you.

Words, phrases and difficult sentences to understand (Translate them into Chinese).

1. divorce ________________
2. the Great Depression ________________
3. motel ________________
4. sit me on her lap ________________
5. drive...deep into my heart ________________
6. You are certain to be a great man and you can do anything in life if you work hard enough to get it.

____

7. But if you can find a task in life worth working for and believe in yourself, nothing can stop you.

____

Task 4: Cultivate your cultural awareness.

Mother's encouragement, mother's care, mother's support...mother's love can surround you all the time. When you are far away from your family and feel lonely, when you stand at a crossing in your life, when you encounter difficulties, when you face challenges, when you decide to make the most important decision, when you achieve your goal or realize your dream...mother is always standing by you. Mother's love is the greatest love in the world; mother's love is the safest love. No matter where you are , whether you are happy or upset, rich or poor, you deserve mother's love.

Lesson 3　First Aid

Task 1: Step into the "reading forest".

Directions: Try to fill in the following blanks according to your imagination.

When your pet has an emergency, first aid is not a substitute for veterinary（兽医的）treatment. However, before you are able to get your pet to a __1__, knowing some __2__ first aid can help.

Bite Wounds

Approach the pet carefully to avoid getting __3__. Wear a mask for the animal and then check the wound. Clean the __4__ with large amounts of saline（盐水）. If these are not __5__, then regular water may be used. __6__ large open wounds to keep them clean.

Bleeding

Apply firm, direct __7__ over the bleeding area until the bleeding stops. Hold the pressure for at least 10 minutes. Avoid bandages that cut off circulation.

Breathing Stops

Check to see if the animal is choking（窒息）on a __8__ object. If an animal is not breathing, place it on a __9__ surface with its left side up. Check for a __10__. If you __11__ a heartbeat but not breathing, close the animal's mouth and breathe directly into its nose-not the mouth-until the chest __12__. Repeat 12 to 15 times per minute.

Burns

Wash the burn __13__ with large amounts of cool, __14__ water. Apply an ice pack for 15–20 minutes. Do not place an ice pack __15__ on the skin. Wrap the pack in a light towel or other cover. If the animal has large quantities of dry chemicals on its skin, brush them off. Water may activate some dry chemicals.

Fractures（骨折）

__16__ include pain, inability to use a limb. Wear a mask for the pet and look for __17__ . If you can control bleeding without causing more __18__, then do so. Watch for signs of shock. Don't try to set the __19__ by pulling the limb. Transport the pet to the veterinarian immediately, __20__ the injured part as best as you can.

Questions:

1. What does the passage mainly talk about?

____

2. What's the structure of the passage?

____

Task 2: Appreciate "trees" in the "reading forest".

Directions: there will be four choices after each question, chose the best one for each of them according to the passage.

When your pet has an emergency, first aid is not a substitute for veterinary treatment. However, before you are able to get your pet to a veterinarian, knowing some basic first aid can help.

Bite Wounds

Approach the pet carefully to avoid getting bitten. Wear a mask for the animal and then check the wound. Clean the wound with large amounts of saline. If these are not available, then regular water may be used. Wrap large open wounds to keep them clean.

Bleeding

Apply firm, direct pressure over the bleeding area until the bleeding stops. Hold the pressure for at least 10 minutes. Avoid bandages that cut off circulation.

Breathing Stops

Check to see if the animal is choking on a foreign object. If an animal is not breathing, place it on a firm surface with its left side up. Check for a heartbeat. If you hear a heartbeat but not breathing, close the animal's mouth and breathe directly into its nose-not the mouth-until the chest expands. Repeat 12 to 15 times per minute.

Burns

Wash the burn immediately with large amounts of cool, running water. Apply an ice pack for 15–20 minutes. Do not place an ice pack directly on the skin. Wrap the pack in a light towel or other cover. If the animal has large quantities of dry chemicals on its skin, brush them off. Water may activate some dry chemicals.

Fractures

Symptoms include pain, inability to use a limb. Wear a mask for the pet and look for bleeding. If you can control bleeding without causing more injury, then do so. Watch for signs of shock. Don't try to set the fractures by pulling the limb. Transport the pet to the veterinarian immediately, supporting the injured part as best as you can.

1. What should you do if your dog pet get injured before you are able to get your pet to a veterinarian?

A. Ask your doctor friends for help.

B. Call UCC (urgent) care center.

C. Do first aid before veterinary treatment.

D. Drive it quickly to the pets' hospital.

2. If your pet stops breathing, what might we do? Put the following steps in right order.

a. close its mouth　　b. place on a firm surface

c. check for a heartbeat　　d. breathe directly into its nose

A. a-b-c-d　　B. b-c-a-d

C. b-a-c-d　　D. a-d-c-b

3. Which of the following steps are useful when your pet get burned?

A. Wash the burn immediately with large amounts of saline.

B. Apply an ice pack directly on the burned skin for 15–20 minutes.

C. Wrap the burn skin in a light towel or other cover.

D. Brush the dry chemicals on the skin off instead of water.

4. Where does this passage probably come from?

A. A science report.　　B. A travel guide.

C. An advertisement. D. A text book.

Task 3: Have an overview of the "reading forest".

When your pet has an emergency, first aid is not a substitute for veterinary treatment. However, before you are able to get your pet to a veterinarian, knowing some basic first aid can help.

Bite Wounds

Approach the pet carefully to avoid getting bitten. Wear a mask for the animal and then check the wound. Clean the wound with large amounts of saline. If these are not available, then regular water may be used. Wrap large open wounds to keep them clean.

Bleeding

Apply firm, direct pressure over the bleeding area until the bleeding stops. Hold the pressure for at least 10 minutes. Avoid bandages that cut off circulation.

Breathing Stops

Check to see if the animal is choking on a foreign object. If an animal is not breathing, place it on a firm surface with its left side up. Check for a heartbeat. If you hear a heartbeat but not breathing, close the animal's mouth and breathe directly into its nose-not the mouth-until the chest expands. Repeat 12 to 15 times per minute.

Burns

Wash the burn immediately with large amounts of cool, running water. Apply an ice pack for 15–20 minutes. Do not place an ice pack directly on the skin. Wrap the pack in a light towel or other cover. If the animal has large quantities of dry chemicals on its skin, brush them off. Water may activate some dry chemicals.

Fractures

Symptoms include pain, inability to use a limb. Wear a mask for the pet and look for bleeding. If you can control bleeding without causing more injury, then do so. Watch for signs of shock. Don't try to set the fractures by pulling the limb. Transport the pet to the veterinarian immediately, supporting the injured part as best as you can.

Words, phrases and difficult sentences to understand (Translate them into Chinese).

1. substitute ____________________ 2. veterinary ____________________

3. veterinarian ____________________ 4. foreign object ____________________

5. apply ____________________ 6. symptoms ____________________

7. inability ____________________ 8. limb ____________________

9. fracture ____________________ 10. circulation ____________________

11. When your pet has an emergency, first aid is not a substitute for veterinary treatment.

____

Task 4: Cultivate your cultural awareness.

In traditional Chinese culture, about pets, we consider more practical value than their spiritual value about pets. However, more and more people are keeping pets to raise their spirit with the influence of western culture and the development of economy. It has been reported that many people are bitten or injured by pets, with some bitten in hospital or even to death, so it's of great importance and necessary to learn some basic measures to make sure of first aid safety.

Lesson 4 Volunteering

Task 1: Step into the "reading forest".

Directions: Try to fill in the following blanks according to your imagination.

Volunteering

Just like the animals we shelter, people are very special to us. The Animal Shelter of Sacramento County has 300 active __1__ and is always eager to add more. If you have a few hours each week and a love for dogs and cats, we at the __2__ welcome your __3__.

Youth Volunteers

Children 10 years of age or older are __4__ to take part in some of our programs as youth volunteers when __5__ by an adult. The adult can be a __6__, or guardian 18 years of age or older. Volunteering is __7__ for a number of reasons. Youth volunteers learn __8__ as they serve the community. Volunteers are rewarded with the love for our __9__ animals. Volunteers learn about the __10__ of dogs and cats and how to care for those needs.

Youth Volunteer Qualifications

A youth volunteer must:

care deeply about animals and their happiness

complete an __11__ form

be at least 10 years of age and accompanied by an adult

attend a training program

Youth Volunteer Opportunities

Youth volunteers may fill the position of dog nuzzler, cat snuggler, or kennel aides, provided there are __12__. Please call our volunteer information hotline at 1-800-290-

5992 to hear a recording of the positions currently __13__ at the present time.

Dog Nuzzlers

Dogs need to __14__ with human and exercise to stay healthy and feel comfortable around people. Dog nuzzlers must be __15__ about dogs and able to deal with medium-sized to large-sized dogs. Youth volunteer dog nuzzlers must be able to work at least two hours between 9 am and 5 pm on either Saturdays or Sundays.

Cat Snugglers

Look after our cats, giving them lots of __16__. Cat snugglers must be knowledgeable about cats and their __17__ Youth volunteer cat snugglers must be able to work at least two hours between 9 am and 5 pm on either Saturdays or Sundays.

Kennel Aides

__18__ food and water for the animals at the shelter is a __19__ job. Kennel aides assist the Animal Shelter staff in __20__ the animals in our care. Kennel aides must be able to work at least two hours between 9 am and 5 pm on either Saturdays or Sundays.

Questions:

1. What does the passage mainly talk about?

____

2. What's the structure of the passage?

____

Task 2: Appreciate "trees" in the "reading forest".

Directions: Fill in each blank with the sentence that best fits the context. Two more choices are provided.

Volunteering

Just like the animals we shelter, people are very special to us. The Animal Shelter of Sacramento County has 300 active volunteers and is always eager to add more. __1__.

Youth Volunteers

Children 10 years of age or older are allowed to take part in some of our programs as youth volunteers when accompanied by an adult. The adult can be a parent, or guardian 18 years of age or older. Volunteering is rewarding for a number of reasons.

Youth volunteers learn responsibility as they serve the community. __2__. Volunteers learn about the needs of dogs and cats and how to care for those needs.

__3__

A youth volunteer must:

·care deeply about animals and their happiness

·complete an application form

·be at least 10 years of age and accompanied by an adult

·attend a training program

Youth Volunteer Opportunities

Youth volunteers may fill the position of dog nuzzler, cat snuggler, or kennel aides, provided there are openings. Please call our volunteer information hotline at 1-800-290-5992 to hear a recording of the positions currently available at the present time.

Dog Nuzzlers

Dogs need to communicate with human and exercise to stay healthy and feel comfortable around people. __4__. Youth volunteer dog nuzzlers must be able to work at least two hours between 9 am and 5 pm on either Saturdays or Sundays.

Cat Snugglers

Look after our cats, giving them lots of attention. Cat snugglers must be knowledgeable about cats and their needs. Youth volunteer cat snugglers must be able to work at least two hours between 9 am and 5 pm on either Saturdays or Sundays.

Kennel Aides

__5__. Kennel aides assist the Animal Shelter staff in feeding the animals in our care. Kennel aides must be able to work at least two hours between 9 am and 5 pm on either Saturdays or Sundays.

A. They must have a love of dogs

B. Youth Volunteer Qualifications

C. Youth Volunteer personal information

D. Providing food and water for the animals is a demanding job

E. Volunteers are rewarded with the love for our sheltered animals

F. Dog nuzzlers must be knowledgeable about dogs and able to deal with medium-sized to large-sized dogs

G. If you have a few hours each week and a love for dogs and cats, we at the shelter welcome your participation

Task 3: Have an overview of the "reading forest".

Volunteering

Just like the animals we shelter, people are very special to us. The Animal Shelter of Sacramento County has 300 active volunteers and is always eager to add more. If you have a few hours each week and a love for dogs and cats, we at the shelter welcome your participation.

Youth Volunteers

Children 10 years of age or older are allowed to take part in some of our programs as youth volunteers when accompanied by an adult. The adult can be a parent, or guardian 18 years of age or older. Volunteering is rewarding for a number of reasons. Youth volunteers learn responsibility as they serve the community. Volunteers are rewarded with the love for our sheltered animals. Volunteers learn about the needs of dogs and cats and how to care for those needs.

Youth Volunteer Qualifications

A youth volunteer must:

care deeply about animals and their happiness

complete an application form

be at least 10 years of age and accompanied by an adult

attend a training program

Youth Volunteer Opportunities

Youth volunteers may fill the position of dog nuzzler, cat snuggler, or kennel aides, provided there are openings. Please call our volunteer information hotline at 1-800-290-5992 to hear a recording of the positions currently available at the present time.

Dog Nuzzlers

Dogs need to communicate with human and exercise to stay healthy and feel comfortable around people. Dog nuzzlers must be knowledgeable about dogs and able to deal with medium-sized to large-sized dogs. Youth volunteer dog nuzzlers must be able to work at least two hours between 9 am and 5 pm on either Saturdays or Sundays.

Cat Snugglers

Look after our cats, giving them lots of attention. Cat snugglers must be knowledgeable about cats and their needs. Youth volunteer cat snugglers must be able to work at least two hours between 9 am and 5 pm on either Saturdays or Sundays.

Kennel Aides

Providing food and water for the animals at the shelter is a demanding job. Kennel aides assist the Animal Shelter staff in feeding the animals in our care. Kennel aides must be able to work at least two hours between 9 am and 5 pm on either Saturdays or Sundays.

Words, phrases and difficult sentences to understand(Translate them into Chinese).

1. shelter ____________________ 2. be accompanied by ____________

3. available ____________________ 4. nuzzle ____________________

5. snuggler ____________________ 6. kennel aides ________________

7. demanding ____________________

8. Children 10 years of age or older are allowed to take part in some of our programs as youth volunteers when accompanied by an adult.

____

Task 4: Cultivate your cultural awareness.

In different cultural and social backgrounds, people have their own different understanding of volunteer. However, we have a lot in common about voluntary spirit and voluntary service, which means we can volunteer from the bottom of heart, delicately and without any pay. Meanwhile, doing voluntary jobs helps facilitate the development of society. In recent years, international communication becomes more frequent, and voluntary culture has become the symbol of a country. Since last century, our country has sent many international volunteers to developing countries, which means our country has become more and more influential around the world. To keep this, we need to do more to offer more help to the needed.

参 考 答 案

Unit 1

Lesson 1

Task 1

1. a　2. reflecting　3. newly　4. the most expensive　5.as　6. has received
7. its　8. foundation　9. was put on　10. focuses

Questions:

1. *The Battle at Lake Changjin.*
2. *The Pioneer.*
3. They are all war films.

Task 2

1. a　2. reflecting　3. newly　4. the most expensive　5.as　6. has received
7. its　8. foundation　9. was put on　10. focuses

Task 3

1. 以……为背景　2. 以……为中心　3. 抗美援朝战争　4. 钢铁意志和伟大灵魂
5. 在他们与敌人斗智斗勇完成秘密任务的过程中彰显了智慧。　6. 上映
7. 为它的崛起奠定了基础　8. 聚焦　9. 贯穿他的整个人生
10. 展现了他作为共产党人在奋斗中的无私精神

Lesson 2

Task 1

1. played　2. joyful　3. beat　4. threw　5. uniformed　6. killed
7. devastated　8. homeless　9. tragedy　10. had managed　11. devoting
12. build　13. message　14. commit　15. was worth

Questions:

1. The passage tells a story of a special wedding given to a 24-year-old paramedic

who sacrificed her life in massive explosion that happened in her country Lebanon.

2. Part 1 (Para.1-2): The special wedding was held.

   Part 2 (Para.3): The massive explosion took place.

   Part 3 (Para.4-5): Sarah's story touched the Lebanese and became a message that there are people who commit to the nation.

Task 2

1—5 CDABB 6—10 ACABD 11—15 BDBAA 16—20 BCDBA

Task 3

1. 婚礼 2. 乐队 3. 节奏 4. 大规模爆炸 5. 让某人无家可归
6. 独一无二的 7. 悲剧 8. 扩散，涌起 9. 准新娘 10. 吸引，捕获
11. 意志坚定的 12. 中等的 13. 设法做到 14. 投身于……中
15. 致力于……中 16. 牺牲

Lesson 3

Task 1

Students' own answers.

Questions:

1. The popularity of bicycles.
2. The words related to time, such as in the late 1980s and early 1990s, in only 25 years. And the word "However".
3. The comparison between the popularity in the past and nowadays.
4. Objective.

Task 2

1—5 CEDGB

Task 3

1. 曲折前行 2. 容纳 3. 便宜的，负担得起的 4. 有意义的
5. 普通却有用的 6. 便利的 7. 结束 8. 可用性
9. 成为……的牺牲品，深受……之害
10. 一个小小的错误都会让你成为车水马龙的牺牲品。

Lesson 4

Task 1

Students' own answers.

Questions:

1. Laziness

2. To prove that mind wandering can a source of creativity.

3. The total score and total structure.

Task 2

1—5 BCADD 6—10 ACDBA 11—15 BBCAD 16—20 CADBC

Task 3

1. 游手好闲 2. 组成，构成 3. 视为，看成 4. 引起，唤醒

5. 出席者，在场者 6. 漫游，游荡 7. 棘手的，狡猾的 8. 轮流，反过来

9. 增长，推动 10. 假设，认为

11. 如果这些活动在周末进行，如打字、接听老板电话、打开任何形式的电子文件，那么这些会引起同情的活动也是工作。

12. 2021年出版的《研究者》杂志发现，与工作相关的棘手的问题会在专业人士中激发更多的白日梦，而且还发现这些白日梦反过来又能激发创造力。

Unit 2

Lesson 1

Task 1

略

Questions:

1. We can find this article in a magazine or on the newspaper.

2. Some books.

3. Paperback, hardback, E-book.

Task 2

1—3 ACC

Task 3

1. 柔软的 2. 神秘，秘密 3. 选举 4. 连接 5. 困惑的，动乱不安的

6. 精装书　7. 充满激情　8. 在……中间　9. 在……预期中
10. 处于危险中
11. 为了迎接2020年大选，这本书描述了唐纳德·特朗普的日常生活，从他在20世纪80年代与民众的关系到他在白宫的头两年陷入的困境。

Lesson 2

I. Task 1

1. breaking　2. older　3. explains　4. risk　5. places　6. definitely　7. process
8. received　9. positive　10. identified　11. shocking　12. worsened
13. aches　14. barely　15. lack　16. force　17. recovery　18. urging
19. take　20. impacts

Questions:

1. It is about a person's experience of COVID–19.
2. COVID–19, sore throat, cough...
3. Time order.

Task 2

1—5 DCBBC　6—10 AACAD　11—15 BDCAC　16—20 ADCAC

Task 3

1. 传播　2. 并发症　3. 过程　4. 辨认　5. 相当，非常　6. 暴力的
7. 上升到……　8. 丧失味觉和嗅觉　9. 非常干净的饮食　10. 增加……的风险
11. 到星期天，他的喉咙痛已经大大恶化，不停地剧烈咳嗽，体温飙升到39.5℃。
12. 因为他的家人患有基础疾病，他听说可能会增加病毒并发症或死亡的风险，所以他第二天打电话给他的医生。

Lesson 3

Task 1

1. Here are some tips for how to be a good friend through listening well.
2. Be curious about what your friend is saying, not saying, and where the conversation might lead.
3. Listen more than you talk.
4. A good friend listens first, leads with empathy, and waits to be. invited in.

5. We often have a biased view of how good or bad we are at something.

Questions:

1. It's mainly about "how to be a qualified friend" .

2. Friends, listen, curious, feedback.

3. A good friend can't be selfish, and he or she must be a good listener.

Task 2

1—5 DGAFE

Task 3

1. 真诚的，真正的　2. 挑战　3. 联系　4. 聚光灯　5. 抵抗　6. 同情

7. 注意　8. 对……有偏见　9. 走出你的定式思维　10. 给……留空间

11. 注意你周围的人是否正在和你失去联系，或者他们是否喜欢被听到。

Lesson 4

Task 1

略

Questions:

1. It's an instruction.

2. It's about an invention called "Water Wand".

3. City, water, sources, engineer, solution...

Task 2

1—4 DBCD

Task 3

1. 污染　2. 遥远的　3. 同事　4. 机械的　5. 包含　6. 潜在地

7. 一个更高级的版本　8. 对于……的需求　9. 一个环境工程师

10. ……的高版本

11. 我认为这可能是一个很好的诊断工具，因为它成本低，金属回收率高，并且优于重金属测试。

12. 它由一个塑料手柄组成，尖端是由聚合物制成的机械附件，其中包含吸引重金属离子的吸收性材料做成的小包装。

Unit 3

Lesson 1

Task 1

1. to speak 2. are 3. accidentally 4. a 5. national 6. presents 7. when 8. wishing 9. on 10. adaptation

Questions:

1. To arouse attention to women.

2. Its director has a different culture background.

3. The Joy Luck Club

Task 2

1. to speak 2. are 3. accidentally 4. a 5. national 6. presents 7. when 8. wishing 9. on 10. adaptation

Task 3

1. 忽略 2. 现代社会 3. 极具感染力的 4. 激发某人做某事 5. 偶然地 6. 风靡一时的事物 7. 票房 8. 世界杯 9. 主演 10. 大名鼎鼎的 11. 标志性的 12. 充当，担任 13. 辉煌的 14. 以……为基础 15. 分歧 16. 冲突，碰撞 17. 农村的 18. 改编

19. 这部由中国喜剧演员贾玲执导的感人喜剧，讲述了一个女人穿越时空意外遇见（年轻时的）母亲的故事。今年大受观众欢迎，领跑内地春节档票房。

Lesson 2

Task 1

1. grew 2. combination 3. Finally 4. sign 5. replaced 6. purposes 7. unexpected 8. reserved 9. poor 10. widened 11. mistaking 12. concerned 13. threw 14. as if 15. loving 16. happily 17. ranged 18. thinned 19. deserves 20. warm

Questions:

1. Warmth came from the heart.

2. He wanted to contact the native.

3. He admired the unique features of the place and was treated well by the native.

4. They could contrast sharply.

Task 2

1—5 CBDAA 6—10 BDCDC 11—15 CBABB 16—20 CACDC

Task 3

1. 毫不怀疑 2. 想象出 3. 斜移 4. 表明自己 5. 投来嫉妒的目光 6. 纵身投入
7. 从飞机上我可以看到格陵兰岛的东海岸只有一片广阔无垠冰雪，没有人类居住的迹象。
8. 交流的主题从格陵兰岛不寻常的天气，延展到他们对巨大冰盖变薄和外界对新发现的矿产资源投以羡慕的目光所感受到的变化的担忧。
9. 在格陵兰岛，在被带进这个格陵兰人的家之前，我发现自己几乎被空虚、浩瀚和寂静所征服。

Lesson 3

Task 1

1. making 2. contains 3. without 4. collect 5. strips 6. cost-effective
7. up 8. saves 9. electricity 10. cities 11. trying 12. paths 13. project
14. solves 15. developed 16. provide 17. work 18. approaches
19. ideal 20. night

Questions:

1. The passage introduces a newly-developed cost-effective fabric and how it can be used to help save energy.
2. It works simply by being put up in the place you want.
3. It can save energy and protect the environment.

Task 2

1—4 DACD

Task 3

1. 创新的 2. 遮光，避光 3. 条纹，灯带
4. 开创性的 5. 动力材料 6. 靠近
7. 因为这种织物还能用在餐厅或宾馆的户外座位区，Green公司已经设计了用这种织物编织的太阳伞，它能够在白天的时候遮阴，晚上的时候照明。

Lesson 4

Task 1

1. tips 2. basics 3. strategies 4. investing 5. healthier 6. ignore
7. achieve 8. elevators/lifts 9. schedule 10. goal

Questions:

1. They are unacceptable.
2. I can always do a bit more walking when in a meeting, when going to and from work, and by taking the stairs instead of elevators.

Task 2

1—4 CBAC

Task 3

1. 优先考虑的事 2. 投资 3. 增加 4. 战略 5. 相当多的 6. 忽略
7. 心理的 8. 认为……理所当然 9. 有意义
10. 但是如果你想增加效果，使用被专家测试并证实过的方法才有意义。
11. 你不想仅仅因为自己太懒惰而长时间坐在桌子旁工作而使自己的心理健康受到影响。

Unit 4

Lesson 1

Task 1

1. highest 2. activities 3. into 4. traditional 5. fixed 6. an 7. with
8. However 9. known 10. held

Questions:

1. It mainly introduces different aspects of Macao.
2. Exposition.
3. Bungee jump.

Task 2

1—3 ADC

Task 3

1. 备受推崇的，广受欢迎的 2. 大胆的，勇敢的 3. 浸入的，专注的

4. 行政的　5. 适应的　6. 景点　7. 被保存用于　8. 主题赌场
9. 持续地　10. 拿掉，取下
11. 它们当中的很多作为文化遗产、旅游景点或博物馆被保存下来。
12. 澳门大赛车圆形广场是世界上唯一一个用于机车竞赛的街头广场。

Lesson 2

Task 1

1. strolling　2. noticed　3. dancing　4. tide　5. ignored　6. waste　7. replied
8. matters　9. in　10. difference

Questions:

1. The topic of this passage is that the smallest thing can make a difference, like throwing starfishes into the sea..
2. Words: throw; starfishes;make a difference;stroll...
3. No,I don’t think so,I think everything is composed of the smallest thing in our life, thus we can make a difference to the world.....

Task 2

1. what　2. picking　3. which　4. by　5. your　6. lying　7. replied
8. matters　9. in　10. difference

Task 3

1. 闲逛；漫步　2. 究竟，到底　3. 冲上岸　4. 海星　5. 忽略这些标记
6. 有作用，有影响
7. 先生，你看太阳很快就要出来了，潮水到时就会退去。尽管我和妹妹不可能把所有的海星扔回海里，但是我们干的这件事对那些被扔回去的海星是很重要的。

Lesson 3

Task 1

略

Questions:

1. The passage talks about a story where the author wants to help a poor man who is truly a thief getting around different cities to steal things.
2. giving help to others; we can never about judge a book; fragrance in hand

3. a poor man; the author wants to help him(the reception& the bread); the policemen (the truth); conclusion (seeing the truth).

Task 2

1—5 BACBC　6—10 DBAAD　11—15 BCABD　16—20 ADBDC

Task 3

1. 疲惫和无聊　2. 褪色的裤子　3. 不时地，常常

4. 雨天的暮色变得更暗了。我感到焦虑不安。

5. 送人玫瑰，手有余香。

Lesson 4

Task 1

Questions:

1. The people who have a much more severe response to these noises.

2. It means "a hatred of sound".

3. Tinnitus retraining therapy, which helps people tolerate noises, may aid sufferers, while cognitive behavioural therapy and counselling could also help people manage the condition.

4. Avoiding places with lots of noises, like restaurants, or moving away when they feel like lashing out at someone due to their breathing.

Task 2

1. are irritating　2. or　3. as　4. that/which　5. at　6. so　7. be suffering

8. literally　9. existence　10. compared

Task 3

1. 这些噪声，对许多人来说仅仅是一种不便，可以分散我们对手头工作的注意力。

2. 然而，我们中有些人对这些噪声的反应要强烈得多。

Unit 5

Lesson 1

Task 1

略

Task 2

1—5 FCGAD

Task 3

1. 有经验的　2. 反抗　3. 选择　4. 实惠　5. 野营地　6. 客户评论

7. 在外吃饭　8. 地方风味　9. 找到　10. 娱乐活动

11. 探索你的目的地　12. 折扣　13. 廉价旅行　14. 极好的

15. 你自己做饭不仅可以省钱，还可以利用逛农贸市场的机会，寻找和享用当地的美味。

Lesson 2

Task 1

略

Task 2

1—5 DDBAC　6—10 BACAD　11—15 BADBA　16—20 DBACC

Task 3

1. 褪色的　2. 胆小的　3. 忽略　4. 挫败的　5. 立一座雕像　6. 呼喊

7. 到底　8. 建筑　9. 去掉，去除　10. 建立

11. 这对夫妇离开后就以他们的名字建立了一个大学。他们用这座大学来纪念那个哈佛大学不再关心的他们的儿子。

Lesson 3

Task 1

略

Task 2

1—4 DCDC

Task 3

1. 收获季节　2. 由……组成　3. 季节性的　4. 传统的做法

5. 戏法　6. 制造商　7. 感激的　8. 替代品

9. 一直到20世纪50年代，这种做法才在美国流行起来。

10. 在经济大萧条和"二战"过后，农村开始变得繁荣。人们开始追求快乐，邻里之间也更加熟悉。

11. 制造商把糖果做成适合入口的大小，然后装在袋子里面作为万圣节食品销售。

Lesson 4

Task 1

略

Task 2

1—4 BCBC

Task 3

1. 被认为是　2. 气候变化　3. 从……中去掉　4. 只要　5. 释放　6. 促进
7. 寿命　8. 交易　9. 分析　10. 排放

11. 这样可以有效地将二氧化碳从大气中除去，使树木成为对抗气候变化的重要组成部分。

12. 通过测量树木年轮的宽度，我们可以判断树木的生长速度，而计算树木年轮可以提供树木年龄的信息，并得以推断树木的最大寿命。

Unit 6

Lesson 1

Task 1

略

Questions:

1. How to help one of his best friends with depression.
2. Depression is a medical condition and is in no way a sign of weakness.
3. Encourage him to keep up with the treatment, to create an open safe environment and take care of himself as well.

Task 2

1—5 DCDCA　6—10 DADAB　11—15 BBADB

Task 3

1. 承认　2. 向某人求助　3. 依附于　4. 以做某事为羞耻　5. 医学问题
6. 软弱的象征　7. 令人难以承受的　8. 追求　9. 敦促做某事　10. 保持支持

11. 很多时候，人们认为承认自己有抑郁症会给自己贴上一个污名，并以寻求帮助为耻。

12. 尽管你很担心你的朋友，并迫切地想帮助他好起来是一件令人钦佩的事，但是抑郁症需要来自专业人士的治疗。

Lesson 2

Task 1

略

Questions:

1. “I” adopted a child that meant to be ours.
2. onesie; outfit
3. Narrative.

Task 2

1—5 ACCAB　6—10 BDDAC　11—15 BADDC　16—20 BBACD

Task 3

1. 怀孕　2. 医疗挑战　3. 更别说怀孕了　4. 使……从……上分心　5. 渴望联系
6. 依偎，位于　7. 扬起眉毛　8. 尊敬的，可敬的　9. 示意，召唤

Lesson 3

Task 1

略

Questions:

1. Cyber violence against women.
2. comments, the Internet, offensive
3. Argumentation.

Task 2

1—4 ABAD

Task 3

1. 欺负　2. 复仇　3. 粗鲁的评论　4. 多产的　5. 基础
6. 因为艾米丽，我们的女儿有机会获得更多像她们一样的科学家的知识。

Lesson 4

Task 1

略

Questions:

1. It introduces a pen that could be used in space.
2. It implies that China's technology is constantly developing.
3. China Produces a Pen Usable in Space.

Task 2

1. construction 2. closely 3. caught 4. which 5. nor 6. a 7. droplets
8. puncturing 9. valuable 10. was sent

Task 3

1. 发射 2. 放开，松开 3. 先锋，开拓者 4. 承受，经受住 5. 震动
6. 零重力 7. 由……组成 8. 黏性 9. 危险的，不安全的 10. 刺穿
11. 普通钢笔的结构既不能经受住火箭发射时航天器舱室所经历的冲击和振动，也不能在零重力环境下正常书写。
12. 钢笔内的墨水也是由高黏度的液体组成的，从而使书写的内容能够紧密地黏在表面，而不是像（普通的）液滴一样飞出去产生危险。

Unit 7

Lesson 1

Task 1

略

Questions:

1. It is about the author's dealing with the trouble in the work through a carpenter's method, realizing not to bring the trouble to the family, and everyone should have their own trouble tree to hang the troubles, in order not to affect the family.
2. Carpenter; a rough first day; underwent an amusing transformation.
3. A rough first day, an amusing transformation, hang up troubles;pick troubles up.

Task 2

1—5 BCABD 6—10 ADBDD 11—15 BBCCA 16—20 CCDAD

Task 3

1. 木匠 2. 使修复 3. 艰难的一天 4. 爆胎 5. 放弃 6. 一言不发地
7. 经历有趣的转变 8. 晒黑的脸 9. 环，圈 10. 难以掩饰，难以克制
11. 一到家，他就邀请我见他家人。
12. 当我们走到前门时，他在一棵小树前停了一会儿，用手抚摸着树枝。

Lesson 2

Task 1

略

Questions:

1. The influence of climate change on the Great Barrier Reef.
2. The Great Barrier Reef is turning white because of warmer temperature.
3. Scientists are searching for reefs that can act as shelters and raising heat resistant corals.

Task 2

1. have attacked 2. parts 3. but 4. causing 5. from 6. consequence
7. a 8. which 9. naturally 10. to die

Task 3

1. 持续不断的 2. 平均的 3. 驱逐 4. 减少 5. 预测 6. 严重的 7. 结果
8. 从……中恢复 9. 大量的 10. 很可能会……
11. 尽管秋季通常意味着较冷的环境，但近几周来，海洋温度过高，高达平均7华氏度，袭击了珊瑚礁。

Lesson 3

Task 1

略

Questions:

1. How to love our food better and grow respect for the world behind what we eat.
2. Open.

3. Open.

Task 2

1—5 BACFE

Task 3

1. 活下来　2. 获得；获取　3. 重要　4. 腐烂　5. 过多的　6. 剩饭菜

7. 赞誉；认可　8. 市场　9. 是……一部分　10. 代表

11. 当我们了解了全部，就很容易领会食物对于我们的意义和食物的珍贵。

Lesson 4

Task 1

略

Questions:

1. Social media and life.

2. Open.(The first sentence of each paragraph)

3. Open.

Task 2

1—5 BCADC　6—10 BABCA　11—15 DBDBA　16—20 DCBCA

Task 3

1. 没听说过　2. 互动　3. 负面的　4. 衡量　5. 误导　6. 沮丧的

7. 对比　8. 流行　9. 网络欺凌　10. 从……中分离

Unit 8

Lesson 1

Task 1

1. seen　2. a　3. able　4. promises　5. most　6. images　7. and　8. with

9. children's　10. completely

Questions:

1. The Immersive Van Gogh Exhibit.

2. To advertise the Immersive Van Gogh Exhibit.

3. On the Internet.

4. People interested in the immersive art.

Task 2

1—3 AAB

Task 3

1. 沉浸式 2. 技术的 3. 表明 4. 投影 5. 出名的作品 6. 使人入迷的
7. 突出，强调 8. 独特的 9. 贴心的纪念品 10. 风情景观

11. 沉浸式艺术不仅仅是在巨大空间中表现视频和音频的技术方法。

12. 沉浸式这个词表明了一种深刻的意图，通过图像和声音相结合的方式，让观众能够体验到一种不同的艺术方式。

13. 正如它的名字一样，这次展览将文森特·梵·高的标志性画作变成了移动的、充满墙壁的投影。

14. 你将体验到前所未有的艺术，沉浸在引人入胜的动态图像中，这些图像突出了笔触、细节和色彩，真正照亮了天才的心灵。

Lesson 2

Task 1

1. sweeping 2. rise 3. staying 4. wondered 5. happy 6. delivering
7. hungry 8. bad 9. pass 10. choice 11. best 12. fear 13. giving
14. helper 15. come

Questions:

1. The passage mainly talks about how the author lifts spirits when faced with the COVID-19 epidemic.

2. Spring; the COVID-19 epidemic; weight; crisis; however; lifted...off; smile; helpers; have no doubt; kinder; more loving; become a helper; happy.

3. The first paragraph is about the background of the story. The second paragraph mainly talks about the story. The third paragraph shows what the author has realized.

Task 2

1—5 BCABD 6—10 BACDA 11—15 CDBCD 16—20 BADCA

Task 3

1. 猛烈吹过，席卷，横扫 2. 使……消散 3. 滞留，停留（尤指不好的环境中）
4. 激发 5. 加强，巩固，使坚强；变强 6. 解放，释放，使摆脱令人不快之事
7. 然而，就是在那一刻，我目之所及让我心里的沉重烟消云散，且让我重

拾了微笑，开心不已。

Lesson 3

Task 1

1. that 2. a 3. their 4. reducing 5. individuals 6. of 7. physical
8. is found 9. compared 10. used

Questions:

1. Celebrated and used for various purposes, art is vital to human life and part of what makes us human.
2. General–Specific–General

Task 2

1. generates 2. When 3. a 4. their 5. reducing 6. individuals 7. of
8. physical 9. is found 10. used

Task 3

1. 微不足道的，无足轻重的 2. 产生，引起 3. 贯穿 4. 交迭，混合，融合
5. 为纪念…… 6. 常去，常到（某处） 7. 与艺术的关系更密切
8. 参与 9. 有对……的偏好 10. 更有希望；更有可能
11. 从事戏剧的人文学能力更强，而其他练习音乐的人在数学和语言方面表现出更高的技能。
12. 没有艺术的生活将是无聊和死气沉沉的，因为艺术是我们人类的一部分。

Lesson 4

Task 1

1. consumes 2. nation 3. cheaper 4. problems 5. natural 6. resources
7. poor 8. reduce 9. increasing 10. recommends

Questions:

1. Concerned.
2. Fast fashion; cheap labour; problems; environmental cost; poor working conditions; improvements; recommend, etc.
3. Para. 1 : A report about fast fashion in the UK ;
   Para. 2 : A general introduction to the fast fashion industry;
   Para. 3–4 : The problems caused by the fast fashion industry;

Para. 5–6 : The recommendations to reduce clothes watse.

Task 2

1—4 BDCC

Task 3

1. 总计为，等同于　2. 受害者，牺牲品　3. 流行的　4. 生产，制造
5. 碳足迹　6. 不足的　7. 长寿，持久耐用　8. 持久耐用的
9. 其次，快时尚行业面临着将最新流行商品快速上架的压力，这可能导致工人被剥削，被迫在恶劣的工作环境下劳动。
10. 环境审计委员会（EAC）向英国政府提出了18项改进建议，包括提高购买税、为回收中心提供资金、在学校开设更多的缝纫课以及倡导勤俭节约的态度。

Unit 9

Lesson 1

Task 1

略

Questions:

1. His mother's love for crime fiction and his reading experience.
2. Alan Turing is a historic person written in Neal's book.
3. To share Graham Moore's favorite books with readers.

Task 2

1. learning　2. of　3. taught　4. shared　5.seriously　6. surprising　7. how
8. styles　9. yourselves　10. latest

Task 3

Words

1. 畅销的　2. 轮流来读　3. 完完整整读完　4. 认真严肃对待科学
5. 利用，凭借　6. 让其他的人也参与讨论这本书　7. 解决
8. 他的新书《死亡之夜》现在发行了。
9. 它不仅点燃了我对犯罪小说的兴趣，更重要的是它让我知道阅读是一种可以共享的体验。
10. 我也了解到一个作者是如何将一个古人生动地展现在当代读者面前。

Lesson 2

Task 1

略

Questions:

1. The passage mainly talks about the return of a goose. When the author was seven, he brought a little goose home. One day the little guy named Peeper flew off. But amazingly, Peeper returned 20 years later.
2. The passage is developed in the order of time.

Task 2

1—5 BCCDA 6—10 ACDDB 11—15 BACAD 16—20 BBADC

Task 3

1. 看见 2. 坚持 3. 认领 4. 常规 5. 轻软的 6. 变老的

7. 认为 8. 反复地 9. 随意的 10. 回应

11. 差不多一年过去了，我们习惯了轻柔拥抱和陪伴的生活。

12. 两个星期以来，这只鹅一次又一次地回来，我终于明白这不是一只普通的鹅。

Lesson 3

Task 1

略

Questions:

1. Washing hands with soap can be better in protecting you from virus during the coronavirus outbreak.
2. 略
3. Deduction and summary.

Task 2

1—5 DCAFB

Task 3

1. 褶皱 2. 刺入，粘贴 3. 崩溃，倒塌 4. 风景，地形 5. 洗手液

6. 下落 7. 阻止某人做某事 8. 成为……的牺牲品；被……欺骗

9. 整体效果就像从房子里移除所有的钉子和砂浆，然后就像经历一场地震

的袭击一样。

Lesson 4

Task 1

1. far from 2. condition 3. tend 4. negative 5. fear 6. discomfort
7. ranging 8. experience 9. racing 10. numbers 11. held back
12. related to 13. assume 14. math 15. disadvantaged 16. manage
17. exploring 18. fail 19. overcome 20. motivate

Questions:

1. The passage is about what is math anxiety and how to treat math anxiey correctly.
2. math anxiety; emotional reaction; physical symptoms; manage your stress; motivate
3. (1) Recognize the symptoms correctly and treat math anxiety wisely.
   (2) Spend a few minutes exploring those feelings before the exam begins.
   (3) Use the nervous energy to help motivate yourself.

Task 2

1—5 DCBAA 6—10 CBBDB 11—15 DCACA 16—20 CBADD

Task 3

1. 远非 2. 核心的 3.（因害怕、兴奋而）急速跳动，快速转动
4. 抑制，阻挡 5. 认为 6. 激励，激发，成为……的动机
7. 在普通生活中，很多人面对数学问题时，会经历不同程度的不适，包括从轻微的紧张到强烈的紧张。
8.《卫报》称，他们然后可能会尽量去避免每一个与数字有关的情境，意味着他们会被抑制去追寻与数学学科相关的职业，如科学、技术和工程师。

Unit 10

Lesson 1

Task 1

1. founded 2. suitable 3. experienced 4. ability 5. violence
6. exercises 7. improved 8. benefits 9. ongoing 10. give up

Questions:

1. It is an advertisement. The karate club wants to attract readers to join it and introduces some good benefits of karate.
2. It is based on a lot of respect, self-discipline, self-control and non-violence.
3. It exercises the entire body. It can improve our strength, coordination, flexibility and agility of both sides of the body. What's more, it also helps concentration and produces the mental calm and assurance that come from knowing we can defend ourselves.

Task 2

1—3 BDA

Task 3

1. 适合　2. 获得　3. 自信　4. 自律　5. 自控　6. 非暴力　7. 礼节，规矩
8. 礼貌，礼仪　9. 协调性　10. 敏捷
11. 我们学习基本的礼节、礼仪和容忍，在任何时候都要有礼貌和为他人着想。
12. 训练需要持续的投入和勤奋的锻炼。

Lesson 2

Task 1

1. companionship　2. reservation　3. learned　4. thrilled　5. worried　6. Flora
7. walked　8. breath　9. soon　10. In that moment　11. continued
12. leg　13. constantly　14. suggested　15. fine　16. respected　17. caring
18. delight　19.need　20. water

Questions:

1. Steven loved his dog Molly and his cat Flora. I also loved my dogs Tilly and Chance. Steven and I started dating, and I found he treated animals well and carefully. Once Tilly had an operation,Steven suggested his house. Steven and I formed a good team caring for Tilly. The three dogs and the cat got on well with each other. One year later Steven proposed to me and I agreed.
2. Treat dogs; companion; thrilled; pour; offer; fall for; worry; suggested; form; pack; housemates; delight; propose; bring together
3. The first part(para.1) introduces the topic"You can tell a lot about a man by how he treats his dogs". The second part(para.2-para.4) mainly tells us the

process of the date between Steven and I. The third part (para.5) concludes a man treating animals well is a man worth marrying.

Task 2

1—5 CADDB　6—10 ABACD　11—15 ADBCC　16—20 BBACD

Task 3

1. 陪伴　2. 孤独　3. 保留　4. 约会　5. 兴奋的　6. 攻击　7. 歇口气

8. 跪下　9. 求婚　10. 喜欢/爱上　11. 想到未来

12. 三只狗打成一片，融为一体，但也尊重猫，从不侵犯弗罗拉的生存空间。动物们相处融洽，史蒂芬和我也成了好盟友，一起照顾Tilly。我们是友好的一家人。

Lesson 3

Task 1

1. situated　2. around　3. other　4. ranging　5. faced　6. in　7. terms

8. are forbidden　9. convenience　10. sign

Questions:

1. It is situated on the right bank of the Seine，centre of Paris.

2. Structural problems with the building.

3. It is necessary to sign in to the official website of Louvre Museum to buy tickets.

Task 2

1—5 ABCDD　6—10 CBABC

Task 3

1. 位于　2. 范围从……到……　3. 关于　4. 被禁止　5. 鉴于

Lesson 4

Task 1

1. As　2. collects　3. nature　4. Moreover　5. Unfortunately　6. useless

7. remove　8. unload　9. carry　10. lighter

Questions:

1. Forgiving our past mistakes can relieve us from guilty and anger.

2. Complex emotional beings; guilty and anger; remove; forgiving.

3. Yes, I do. Because forgiving can help us throw away the emotional burden and

further make us feel relieved.

Task 2

1—4 DACB

Task 3

1. 复杂性　2. 本质上　3. 处理　4. 找到出路　5. 内疚　6. 解决
7. 卸下包袱　8. 轻松的，愉快的
9. 事实上，我们应该处理并释放我们的情感，这样才能把它们从我们自身消除。我们不能只是希望它们消失。
10. 从你开始原谅的那一刻起，你会感觉轻松了许多，多年的沉重包袱也神奇地不见了。

Unit 11

Lesson 1

Task 1

1. gifted　2. wait　3. easily　4. poured　5. Thankfully　6. see　7. painful
8. practice　9. quietness　10. reflect upon　11. Most　12. ordinary
13. apologized　14. birds　15. routine　16. Besides　17. inner city
18. warmest　19. continue　20. feeds

Questions:

1. Because she was always in rush.
2. She learned to appreciate the truth of quietness.

Task 2

1—5 BDADD　6—10 BCCDA　11—15 BCDCA　16—20 BACDC

Task 3

1. 无瑕的　2. 倾倒　3. 幸好　4. 洒　5. 常规操作　6. 提醒某人某事　7. 回顾
8. 平常的　9. 道歉　10. 常规　11. 内地城市　12. 休闲地　13. 节奏　14. 安静
15. 我迫不及待地准备使用它，期待着明日煮咖啡那一刻，因为我知道这个壶不会像以前的那些壶那样易碎。
16. 似乎我们周围的世界也放慢了步伐，使我们反而能跟上。

Lesson 2

Task 1

1. However 2. appearance 3. salesman 4. combined 5. prize 6. fairness 7. taking turns 8. desirable 9. available 10. whenever 11. wandered 12. labor 13. up 14. profitably 15. gave 16. as 17. blinked 18. embarrassment 19. parked 20. merely

Questions:

1. Because that guaranteed every one had a fair chance to meet customers.
2. To imply the buyer was really a rich man, since Lincoln Continental convertible was quite an expensive car.

Task 2

1—5 DCABA 6—10 CBDCA 11—15 ACBDC 16—20 ADBDA

Task 3

1. 外貌 2. 说得过去的薪水 3. 周薪 4. 结合 5. 底薪 6. 额外提成 7. 公平 8. 称心如意的 9. 热情 10. 皱的 11. 鄙陋的 12. 体力活 13. 一瞥 14. 有利可图的 15. 走近 16. 存货 17. 眨眼 18. 支票簿 19. 尴尬
20. 在那个令人难忘的下午，音乐店的玻璃门敞开，溜溜达达地走进来一位男士，戴着皱巴巴的帽子，穿着脏兮兮的衣服，脚上套着土里土气的鞋子。这副尊容，与爱乐人士离题万里，倒像是一位苦哈哈的劳力工。

Lesson 3

Task 1

1. They stare off into space and wander by themselves.
2. Without wandering minds, we wouldn't have relatively, Coke or Post-it notes.
3. Having interesting things to think about also helps.
4. It involves slow, steady breathing for self-control that helps people stay calm and attentive.
5. Therefore, it's a good idea to keep a notebook or voice recorder nearby when you're in the daydream zone.

Questions:

1. It mainly talks about the benefits of daydreaming and how to come up with

brilliant daydreams.

2. Bad reputation; but ... greatest ideas and achievements; brilliant daydreams; feeling safe and relaxed; involved in another task; mindfulness; moved slowly away.

Task 2

1—5 BCAEG

Task 3

1. 名声　2. 未意识到　3. 笨拙的　4. 忽略　5. 对……负责　6. 成就

7. 相关地　8. 发明　9. 创造性的　10. 专注　11. 全神贯注　12. 稳定的

13. ……当你在幻想时，尝试一边幻想一边做其他事情——最好是一些简单的事情，如洗澡、散布甚至是无意义地涂画。

Lesson 4

Task 1

1. How could you start to forgive?
2. To make your anger die away, try a simple stress-management technique.
3. If you wait for people to apologize, you could be waiting an awfully long time.
4. Try to see things from your offender's angle.
5. For some people, forgiving themselves is the biggest challenge.

Questions:

1. Because it is beneficial to people's physical and mental health.
2. There are 5 ways introduced in this passage. They are: (1) Calm yourself. (2) Don't wait for an apology. (3)Learn to look for the love, beauty and kindness around you. (4)Try to see things from your offender's angle. (5) forgive yourself.

Task 2

1—5 BFGDE

Task 3

1. 美德　2. 有益的　3. 身心健康　4. 场景　5. 道歉　6. 角度

7. 无意　8. 挑战　9. 抢夺

10. 记住：原谅并非指你一定要和那些伤了你的心的人继续做朋友。

Unit 12

Lesson 1

Task 1

1. confidence 2. exam 3. ready 4. conquer 5. easy 6. during 7. crowded 8. bigger 9. no longer 10. frightened 11. raised 12. restlessly 13. silent 14. expected 15. impress 16. even though 17. engineering 18. common 19. pass 20. begun

Questions:

1. A life lesson was taught by the author's professor through the last exam.
2. Students changing expressions before, during and after the exam.

Task 2

1—5 BACDA 6—10 CDDBB 11—15 ACDBA 16—20 CCDAB

Task 3

1. 不安地，慌张地 2. 征服 3. 涌入
4. 因为有了大学四年的学习，他们感觉自己已经准备好并且也能够征服这个世界了。
5. 我想让你们记住的是：虽然你们已经完成了四年的土木工程的学习，但你们仍然有很多不知道的东西。

Lesson 2

Task 1

1. little 2. change 3. hit 4. walk 5. gentle 6. doctors 7. wanted 8. deep 9. returned 10. support 11. determined 12. changed 13. expensive 14. doubters 15. supporters 16. challenges 17. rooted 18. largest 19. income 20. believe in

Questions:

1. She gave him a lot of love and spoke encouraging words that would change his life.
2. Big events that had changed the author's life.

Task 2

1—4 CDBA

Task 3

1. 离婚　2. 大萧条　3. 汽车旅馆

4. 让我坐在她腿上　5. 使……深入我的内心

6. 如果你足够努力，你一定能成为一名伟人，做好生活中的任何事情。

7. 但是如果你能在生活中找到你能为之奋斗的任务并且相信自己，那么没有什么能阻止你。

Lesson 3

Task 1

1. veterinarian　2. basic　3. bitten　4. wound　5. available　6. Wrap

7. pressure　8. foreign　9. firm　10. heartbeak　11. hear　12. expands

13. immediately　14. running　15. directly　16. Symptoms　17. bleeding

18. injury　19. fractures　20. supporting

Questions:

1. Some basic first aid is introduced to help your pets in emergency.

2. Deduction.

Task 2

1—4 CBDA

Task 3

1. 替代物，代替者　2. 兽医的　3. 兽医　4. 外来物，异物　5. 敷，涂

6. 症状　7. 无能力　8. 肢体　9. 骨折　10.（血液）循环，畅通

11. 当你的宠物处于紧急情况时，急救不能作为兽医治疗的替代。

Lesson 4

Task 1

1. volunteers　2. shelter　3. participation　4. allowed　5. accompanied

6. parent　7. rewarding　8. responsibility　9. sheltered　10. needs　11. application

12. openings　13. available　14. communicate　15. knowledgeable　16. attention

17. needs　18. Providing　19. demanding　20. feeding

Questions:

1. Youth volunteering of the Animal Shelter of Sacramento County.

2. Deduction.

Task 2

1—5 GEBFD

Task 3

1. 庇护，庇护处　2. 随……而来，陪同，伴随　3. 可用的，可获得的，有空的　4. 管理，看护　5. 管理员，看护者　6. 养殖场助手　7. 要求高的，苛刻的　8. 在有成年人陪同的10岁或者10岁以上的孩子可以参加我们其中的一些项目。